India Briefing, 1993

India Briefing, 1993

edited by
Philip Oldenburg

Published in cooperation with
The Asia Society

Deborah Field Washburn,
Series Editor

Westview Press
Boulder • San Francisco • Oxford

Published in 1993 in the United States of America by Westview Press, Inc., 5500 Central Avenue, Boulder, Colorado 80301-2877, and in the United Kingdom by Westview Press, 36 Lonsdale Road, Summertown, Oxford OX2 7EW

Library of Congress ISSN: 0894-5136
ISBN 0-8133-8772-8

Printed and bound in the United States of America

The paper used in this publication meets the requirements of the American National Standard for Permanence of Paper for Printed Library Materials Z39.48-1984.

10 9 8 7 6 5 4 3 2 1

Contents

Preface

India Briefing, 1993 is the seventh in a series of annual reviews of major events, issues, and trends in Indian affairs. Previous volumes have reported on devastating droughts followed by economic recovery, separatist challenges followed by harsh central response, domestic protests and governmental collapse followed by orderly democratic transition. A common theme has been India's resilience in the face of turmoil and tragedy. This year's volume demonstrates that India is under greater stress than ever before.

At the close of 1992, the secular foundations of the Indian state were shaken by a cataclysmic event, the storming and destruction by Hindu extremists of the Babri mosque in Ayodhya, a town in Uttar Pradesh. The culmination of eight years of agitation for the "liberation" of the site and the construction there of a Hindu temple, this act of violence brought to a head the ideological (secular versus Hindu nationalist) and communal (Hindu versus Muslim) tensions that have continued to wrench India since partition in 1948. It also weakened the government of P. V. Narasimha Rao and may have hastened the decline of the ruling Congress Party. In the lead chapter of *India Briefing, 1993,* Ashutosh Varshney puts the eruption in Ayodhya into long-term perspective, showing its connection to the ongoing question of Indian national identity.

Other chapters in the volume deal with India's foreign policy and its economic reforms, which were disrupted but not derailed by the events at Ayodhya. Paul Kreisberg points to a positive thrust in India's relations with the outside world, despite the situation in troubled Kashmir and its deleterious effect on India-Pakistan relations. Particularly noteworthy are increased cooperation between India and China on a range of issues, including border negotiations, and Indian efforts to improve economic relations with the countries of East and Southeast Asia, the European Community, and the United States. The success of India's foreign policy depends on its domestic political stability and a continuation of economic liberalization.

Jay Dehejia takes up the subject of the economic reforms, arguing that though the pace of reform has been slow, the momentum is increasing, with a positive effect on the economy. Neither the Bombay stock market scandal of 1992 nor the riots and bombings of early 1993 have stanched the "trickle" of foreign investment into India, and Dehejia believes that as trade liberalization and other reforms take hold, investment will increase. By February 1993 India had lowered its inflation rate to 6.9 percent from a high point of 17 percent in August 1991 and reduced its budget deficit to 5 percent of GDP. As a result of these promising signs, donor countries have pledged a record $7.2 billion in aid.

The ultimate goal of economic reform is to eradicate poverty and produce a better quality of life for India's 885 million people. In his discussion of the Indian Constitution, Granville Austin demonstrates that the rule of law in India has worked to improve the lot of minorities and underprivileged social groups, up to a point. (The rights of religious minorities are constitutionally protected, but this has led to complications. Though the failure of the legal system to prevent the destruction of the Babri mosque is, in Austin's view, an "extreme example," it points to the basic incompatibility between religious and civil law.) Civil liberties, the Fundamental Rights granted by the Indian Constitution, need to be protected and access to the judicial system improved. These causes are increasingly being taken up by nongovernmental social action groups.

Democracy is exercised not only in the courts but at the grass roots. Smitu Kothari chronicles the growth of citizen-based groups fighting for social and economic justice. He presents as an illustrative case the controversy over the Sardar Sarovar dam on the Narmada River—a struggle that pits state and central government efforts at large-scale economic development against the subsistence economies of local indigenous groups. Like other chapters in this volume, Kothari's discussion addresses "major domestic and global questions of governance and responsibility."

As do previous volumes, *India Briefing, 1993* includes a chapter on culture, this year's topic being cinema and television. Pradip Krishen gives an illuminating account of the roots of contemporary popular culture in the theatrical traditions of the 19th and early 20th centuries. He goes on to discuss state-controlled television; here too, the emphasis is on the challenges that confront the government of India as it walks a fine line between subscribing to democratic values and maintaining its authority.

Every year our authors and editors express the fervent hope—or, in some cases, the conviction—that India will once again transcend the year's crises and turbulence. The events of late 1992 and early 1993 constitute a critical test of India's extraordinary resilience. India is grappling with unprecedented change in all aspects of its national life. *India Briefing, 1993* aims to increase readers' understanding of this vibrant evolutionary process.

The India Briefing series is prepared by the Contemporary Affairs Department of The Asia Society and copublished with Westview Press. The Society's Center for India-U.S. Education, with major funding from the Hinduja Foundation, sponsors the series to further its goal of supporting public education on India. We wish to thank the Hinduja Foundation for its generosity.

Thanks are also due to editor Philip Oldenburg and his superb team of authors, and to Susan McEachern and her dedicated staff at Westview Press. At The Asia Society, Senior Editor Deborah Field Washburn oversaw the project from start to finish. She was assisted by Sayu Bhojwani, who played a significant role in editing the chapters, in addition to managing communications with authors. Shyama Venkateswar compiled the chronology, bringing to it her substantial knowledge of India. Patricia Farr copyedited the manuscript with skill and sensitivity. Maria Tham made numerous helpful suggestions, and Lisa Park proofread and assisted in the final stages of editorial production. This volume is the result of the best efforts of all these individuals.

Marshall M. Bouton
Executive Vice President
The Asia Society

June 1993

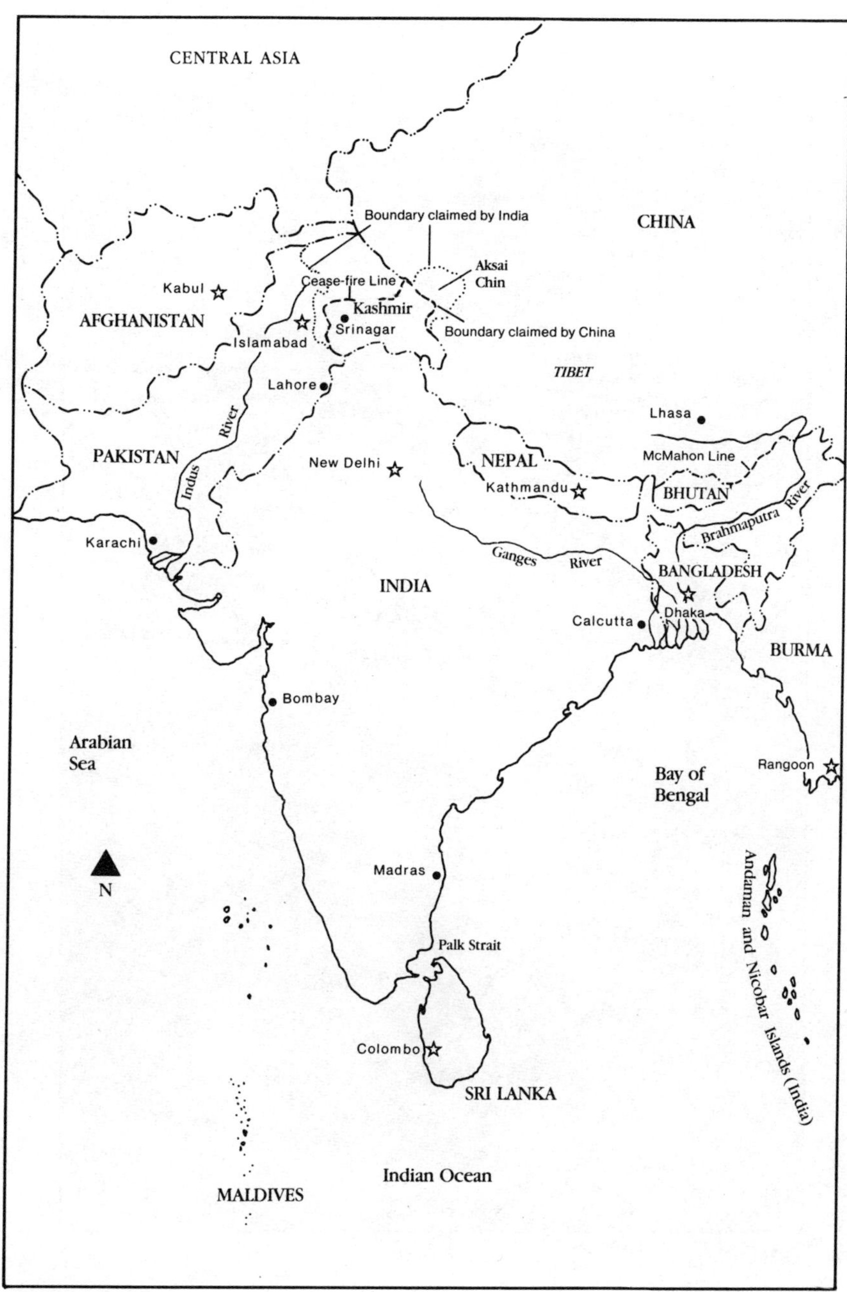

CENTRAL ASIA
CHINA
Boundary claimed by India
Aksai
Chin
Cease-fire Line
Kabul
Kashmir
AFGHANISTAN
Srinagar
Boundary claimed by China
Islamabad
TIBET
Lahore
Lhasa
Indus River
PAKISTAN
McMahon Line
New Delhi
NEPAL
Kathmandu
BHUTAN
Brahmaputra River
Karachi
Ganges River
BANGLADESH
INDIA
Dhaka
Calcutta
BURMA
Bombay
Arabian
Sea
Rangoon
Bay of
Bengal
N
Madras
Andaman and Nicobar Islands (India)
Palk Strait
Colombo
SRI LANKA
Indian Ocean
MALDIVES

South Asia

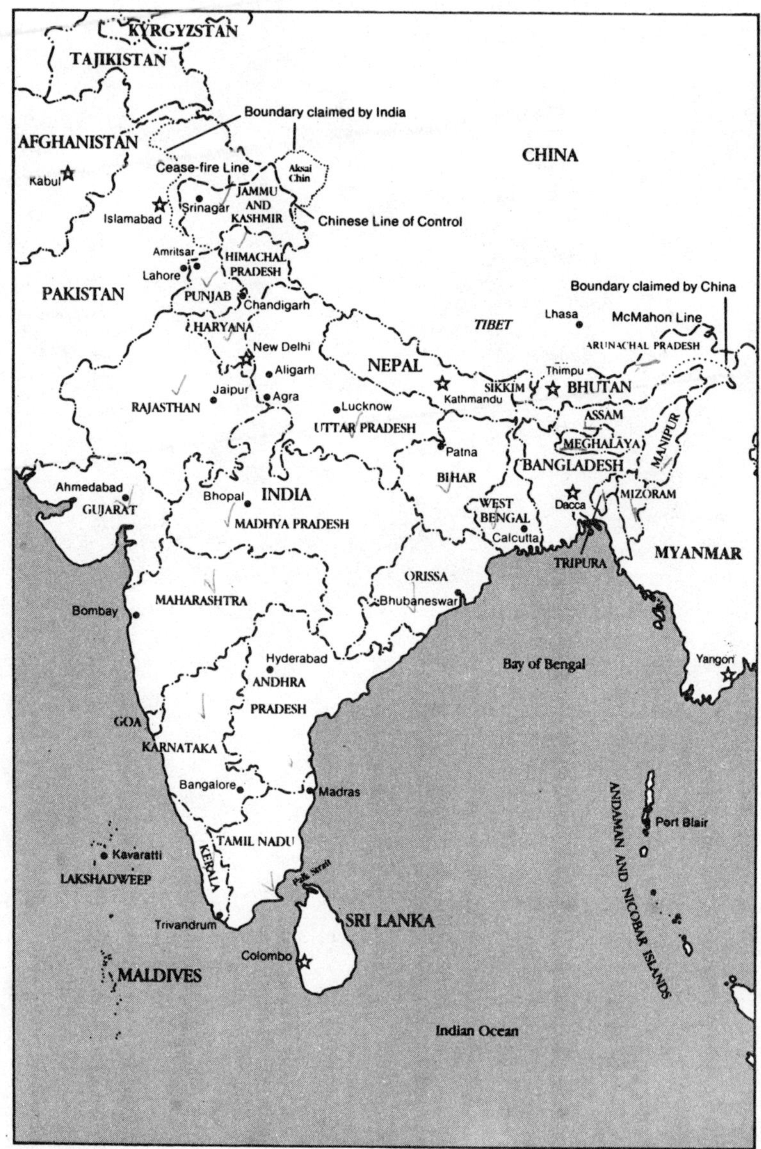

KYRGYZSTAN
TAJIKISTAN
AFGHANISTAN
Kabul
Boundary claimed by India
CHINA
Cease-fire Line
Aksai Chin
JAMMU AND KASHMIR
Srinagar
Islamabad
Chinese Line of Control
Amritsar
Lahore
HIMACHAL PRADESH
PAKISTAN
PUNJAB
Chandigarh
HARYANA
Boundary claimed by China
Lhasa
TIBET
McMahon Line
ARUNACHAL PRADESH
New Delhi
Aligarh
NEPAL
Thimpu
SIKKIM
BHUTAN
Kathmandu
Jaipur
Agra
RAJASTHAN
Lucknow
UTTAR PRADESH
ASSAM
MEGHALAYA
MANIPUR
Patna
BANGLADESH
Ahmedabad
Bhopal
INDIA
BIHAR
GUJARAT
Dacca
MIZORAM
MADHYA PRADESH
WEST BENGAL
Calcutta
TRIPURA
MYANMAR
ORISSA
MAHARASHTRA
Bhubaneswar
Bombay
Hyderabad
Bay of Bengal
Yangon
ANDHRA PRADESH
GOA
KARNATAKA
Bangalore
Madras
ANDAMAN AND NICOBAR ISLANDS
Port Blair
TAMIL NADU
Kavaratti
KERALA
LAKSHADWEEP
Palk Strait
Trivandrum
SRI LANKA
Colombo
MALDIVES
Indian Ocean

India

Introduction

Philip Oldenburg

On December 7, 1992, the pile of rubble of the Babri mosque in Ayodhya, and the makeshift temple to the god Ram-as-child placed in its midst, represented to many a profound change in the political and social landscape of India. The razing of the mosque the day before by a frenzied mob of Hindu holy men and young men committed to *Hindutva* (Hindu nationalism) seemed to symbolize an eruption of forces welling up from deep within the polity.

Yet had 1992 ended a month early, "before Ayodhya," it would have been called a year of slow but substantial progress on economic and political fronts. Some months later, despite several weeks of rioting and political uncertainty, India seemed to have regained its stability, paradoxically best seen in the reaction to the terrible bomb explosions in Bombay in March 1993, which did not provoke riots, but rather allowed Bombay residents to demonstrate their dedication to a civil society and a vigorous economy and polity. Perhaps the events at Ayodhya are better seen—less threateningly—as part of a political process deeply constrained by decades of democracy and a flexible and resilient net of social relationships among the myriad religious and other communities of India.

Analysts differ in evaluating the meaning of the turbulence that seems ever-present in India. Some see evidence of crisis-producing fault lines in the underlying economic and social structure of the country; others find the evidence for those deep divisions unpersuasive. At the same time, there are competing assessments of the role and strength of the Indian state. Some see the state as weakened to the point that it can no longer handle the seething social and economic forces of the country; others suggest that the limits of state capacity are yet to be tested and that recent events underline its continuing strength.

Do those forces arise from cleavages within the economy, in the interplay of classes? Is the basic problem the decay of a previously institutionalized state? Or should we turn to explanations derived from the emergence of new social groups? The chapters in this volume do not directly address these questions, but they can help us to understand how effective the state has been, and what the forces are that explain the seemingly triumphant emergence of Hindu nationalism.

Jay Dehejia presents a portrait of the Indian economy emerging from deep crisis, making, comparatively smoothly, the massive policy and ideological shift implied by the abandonment of the "Nehruvian" model of a quasi-command economy—as he puts it, a "shift from a subsidy culture to an investment culture." Since this change is clearly the product of state policy and has not been much altered by class forces or even vested interests, we can postulate that either the state has more than enough strength to deal with massive economic conflict, or that the economy is not deeply fissured and thus even a fairly weak state can formulate and implement policy change.

Dehejia presents a discussion of how the economic reforms put in place by the government of P. V. Narasimha Rao and his impressive team of financial policymakers, led by Manmohan Singh, are progressing. The number of obstacles surmounted and crises weathered is impressive. The stock market scandal and likely tightening up of control over stock trading, once the investigations by high-powered commissions of administration and parliament are completed, have not significantly altered the increasing importance of private investment in the economy. That the mammoth bomb blast that killed 50 people in the Bombay Stock Exchange on March 12, 1993, only disrupted trading for 48 hours is perhaps symbolic. The bumper spring 1993 harvest gives hope that the agricultural sector will underpin economic advance in the coming year. Despite the difficulties Dehejia notes—in the liberalization of trade, with public-sector enterprises, and in developing an industrial "exit" policy—his ringing assertion that "India has the potential to become another 'Asian Tiger' " cannot be dismissed.

Those who predicted that India's failure to implement sweeping land reforms, coupled with the advantages the "green revolution" allegedly gave to richer farmers, would produce unmanageable agrarian tensions (the revolution would turn inevitably "red," in views very popular in the late 1960s) have been proven wrong. "Small" to "middle" farmers—those who mainly work their own land, tiny holding though it may be, and produce enough to get by, or even live decently, with hope of a better life for their children—have been the main beneficiaries of change in the countryside. Landless workers, artisans, and "marginal" farmers have not done so well, but the increased infrastructural development that has permitted a wider labor market to emerge has cushioned their lack of progress. Workers can migrate not only for seasonal work but also daily to towns and cities that were "too far away" only a decade ago. There are only a few instances of major unrest or highly charged social tension in rural areas; almost the entire countryside remains free of communal riots, and even cases of clashes between landed and lower castes are, all things considered, few and far between. Those who populate the slums of places like Bombay, of course, are ready recruits to an underclass in which criminals flourish and communal violence can be easily provoked, as in Bombay in January 1993.

The pace of urbanization and industrialization has not, however, overwhelmed the social structure, even as slums have grown and various rootless groups—from migrants from the poorest part of the country to the educated unemployed—have made their presence felt. The class of entrepreneurs has proved to be open to all kinds of new entrants, from all parts of the country, and the class alliances some scholars posit have not emerged as coherent forces either to challenge the state or to enforce the continued immiseration of urban and rural workers. The standard of living of the poorest of the poor has not improved, but that category itself has shrunk, and enough people escape from it that others see the system as sufficiently open for a fortunate few to "make it."

The vested interests that were supposed to be powerful enough to derail the economic reforms have only, it would seem, been able to slow down their extension into certain areas. The state has successfully managed this initial phase of the transition, in significant part because virtually all segments of the political spectrum have either supported it or not been able to mount any strenuous opposition. The major industrial action of the past year, indeed, was undertaken to enhance the free market: the strike by long-distance truckers against the system of *octroi* (taxes on goods collected at the municipal limits), which has spawned corruption and wastage of time and effort ever since its introduction almost 150 years ago.

Forces that threaten India's stability are thus unlikely to have emerged from the deep structure of the economy. Another possible source of destabilization is the deep structure of the political system itself; the institutions of the state and the democratic regime are allegedly coming apart, especially at the grass roots. Corruption, in this perspective, is not simply an annoying or even occasionally shocking fact of life associated with particular individuals, as in Italy or the United States, but a well-advanced cancer eating at the vitals of the polity. The linkage of politicians and criminals is not a simple matter of protection for the latter, traded for "useful" electoral help every now and then, but an increasing merger of criminal and political enterprises and personnel.

The Indian state, like all others in the modern world system, has to deal not only with challenges to its domestic foundations but also with threats and opportunities presented in the international arena. These two faces of the state are linked: domestic strength can allow a country to pursue its international goals more vigorously; international links (security guarantees, cozy aid and market arrangements, and so forth) can back up the state's domestic initiatives. Conversely, the inability of the state to raise resources for development or basic government functions, or to control adequately domestic political forces, makes it vulnerable to other countries on which it depends for credit and aid; a country unable to manage its foreign affairs well is likely to suffer domestic political consequences as well.

The most important domestic foundations of the Indian state are its constitutional and legal order, analyzed by Granville Austin in his chapter. He explores the deep historical roots of both constitutional development and the system of laws and shows how the goals of securing the unity and integrity of the country, of putting in place a strong democracy, and of providing social justice (especially for the poor bottom half of the society) are linked. He argues that India has indeed made substantial strides in the direction of those goals. But the path will not be easy, as Austin points out: "as the bottom cries 'upward' and those above cry 'back,' there will be turmoil and some violence as elements within society test both the goals and the institutions of the constitution." Legal institutions with which the poor and powerless interact, at the district level particularly, are tainted by the fact and reputation of corruption, as Austin notes. Whether "justice" is something the ordinary citizen can hope to receive at the hands of police, lower-level judiciary, and the administration acting as regulator of society and economy remains in question.

The state's domestic strength has been sorely tried ever since independence by separatist nationalist movements and, at times, revolutionary armed revolts. The People's War Group continues to be active in its strongholds, the tribal areas cut through by the borders of Andhra Pradesh, Maharashtra, Madhya Pradesh, and Orissa, but the situation is certainly not out of control. In Punjab and Assam, as Ashutosh Varshney notes, the state seems to have gained an upper hand, bringing severe problems at least very close to resolution. The same cannot be said of Kashmir, which is of course linked to the other aspect of the Indian state, that having to do with foreign relations.

The Indian state's capacity to act in the global economic and political arena has not to date been undermined. As Paul Kreisberg argues, India is a country "succeeding in broadening the canvas of its economic, political, and security relationships, working through major changes in the priorities attached to relations with various countries in previous years, and trying to mesh these changes with complex domestic political and economic challenges." As in domestic policy, preserving India's unity and integrity was of high priority in India's foreign policy; Kreisberg notes that the importance that priority gave to India-Pakistan relations has been a constant feature of India's international relations. The shift in emphasis toward foreign economic relations, however, represents a significant new departure. Kreisberg also underlines the danger that communal tensions and a more militant domestic politics pose to a steady course of improved relations with neighbors and others; the "internal threats" to the Indian state not only challenge it directly but raise questions about India's credibility as a country with aspirations to be a major power.

The chapters on the economy, the legal framework, and foreign policy all point to an Indian state with continuing capacity to formulate and implement effective policy, albeit with weak spots. They also point to the rise of the Hindu nationalist forces led by the Bharatiya Janata Party (BJP) and symbolized by the demolition of the Babri mosque, as possibly calling into question the state's future strength in all three arenas. Indeed, as the author of an article in the *Economist* puts it: "The Hindu upsurge is a cause for real concern. But what it feeds on is something still more worrying, the decay of the state. . . . Hindu militancy is a symptom of the state's dangerous sickness, not the sickness itself."[1] Ashutosh Varshney's chapter on politics understandably devotes itself to assessing the meaning of Ayodhya in all its dimensions.

Varshney argues that with the demolition of the Babri mosque, "Indian politics have been transformed." He points to the ideological challenge the BJP and its "family" poses, as well as the political realignment that becomes possible: from an anti-Congress to an anti-BJP axis. The significance of the change goes well beyond the politics-as-usual questions of alliances and economic-issue politics, or even the more violent Punjab and Kashmir separatist movements and the Cauvery River waters dispute that Varshney discusses. Rather, "Today, the relationship between Hinduism and the Indian nation is a central, if not the only, question in Indian politics." Varshney analyzes the effort to define India's national identity on geographical, cultural, and religious dimensions, again focusing on the Hindu nationalist discourse now captured by the Rashtriya Swayamsevak Sangh, Vishwa Hindu Parishad, and BJP. Varshney denies that the triumph of the right wing of the BJP is a foregone conclusion that means "the end of

[1] "The Hindu Upsurge," *Economist*, February 6, 1993, p. 23.

India as a civilization (and perhaps also the breakup of its territory)." There are still responses within "routine" politics that can meet the BJP challenge.

Others fear the social fabric itself is tearing. The signs are horrific—communal rioting and the decline of "civility" inherent not just in increasing violence, but in untamed corruption and the criminalization of politics, among other signs of "political decay." In this view, the majoritarian nationalism of the BJP simply represents the political manifestation of the naked confrontation of groups cut adrift from their economic and social moorings. On the one hand, there is the swelling middle class that no longer accepts the orthodox religion of the older generation but seeks a more "modern" alternative, defining itself against the "pseudo-secularists" and those who would mobilize "backward classes" (a majority of the country) to claim a larger share of good jobs in government. At the other end of the social scale, there are the poor and oppressed, driven from the land into cities where jobs and housing are inadequate for the demand; they are ready material for mobilization by fanatics such as those of the Shiv Sena in Bombay, who point to "the other," the Muslim workers who compete with other oppressed groups for housing and jobs, as the cause of their inability to find a new economic and social place. And some Muslims in turn prepare themselves for armed confrontation with their tormentors and the Indian state.

Two of the chapters in this volume suggest that the picture is not so clear. Pradip Krishen, in his chapter titled "Cinema and Television," analyzes a central feature of the "public culture" of the country that bridges the class and the urban-rural divides. More important, he describes the historical roots of subjects and styles of the present-day mass media, and shows how the cinema "has remained remarkably consistent in its attention to the threats to traditional values." The transformation in this segment of the public culture brought on by the spread of television, and now the onset of television broadcasting taken out of government control by the spread of satellite-broadcast CNN and Star TV (from Hong Kong), is sure to affect profoundly the middle class that is television's prime audience.

Smitu Kothari's discussion of social movements and "action groups" moves us to the grassroots level, focusing largely on groups that mobilize struggles against the Indian state or provide support for those oppressed by exploitative social, economic, and political relationships. The India he reveals is not one of despair and defeat—although that is there in considerable measure—but of devotion and imagination and bravery, as men and women of all classes and conditions come together in voluntary groups to set out alternate visions of development, community, and political power. The richness of historical experience and the sheer variety of groups in terms of their goals and strategies suggest that we must weigh their influence, especially since they operate in the trenches of the battle against social dislocation and confrontation. As Kothari points out, "It is true that given the vastness of India and the centrality of party politics, these groups and movements occupy a small proportion of the country's political space. . . . There is little doubt, however, that [social action] movements . . . have an impact that has been and will remain significant." Together—though they are infrequently formally linked—they provide an alternate vision of democracy and governance that is invaluable.

Events of the first months of 1993—from the successfully conducted Punjab village *panchayat* elections to the lack of rioting in the wake of the Bombay bombings of March, from the smooth passage of the budget to the resumption of normal country-to-country relations (for example, the twice-postponed SAARC meeting was finally held in April)—indicate that the "Hindu upsurge" has been followed by a pulling back from confrontation. No one suggests that this means the beginning of the ultimate resolution of India's political, economic, and social problems, but there is reason to believe that those in power in the country, held accountable by literally hundreds of millions of citizens who want to live in peace, can make the wise choices in the near and far term that will move India closer to a benign transformation.

June 1993

1
Battling the Past, Forging a Future? Ayodhya and Beyond

Ashutosh Varshney*

> I remember that when *Midnight's Children* was first published in 1981, the most common Indian criticism of it was that it was too pessimistic about the future. It's a sad truth that nobody finds the novel's ending pessimistic any more, because what has happened in India since 1981 is so much darker than I had imagined. . . . But India regularly confounds its critics by its resilience, its survival in spite of everything. I don't believe in the Balkanization of India. . . . It's my guess that the old functioning anarchy will . . . keep on functioning. . . . But don't ask me how.
>
> —Salman Rushdie, *Imaginary Homelands*

Politics can be abstract and distant. There are moments in a country's life, however, when politics are experienced emotionally—as anxiety, as fear. Consider the implications of the questions on India's current political agenda. Can the nation build a future without debating its past? Must the nation's identity be defined before it can make progress, or is mere pragmatism enough? Abstract though these questions are, they have an unmistakable immediacy. "How is the nation to be defined?" becomes "Who are we?" In a multiethnic, multireligious society, "Must a nation be defined in terms of a religion?" becomes "Will my religion or ethnicity be excluded from the definition, and what then will happen to my rights as a citizen?" These questions are about both identity and interests. Once they become the subject matter of politics, they engage the deeper coherence, the "inner being," of a nation. Emotions get tangled, political mobilization takes place, and violence erupts. Times such as these can be called "transformative moments" in a country's life.

* Comments by Robert Frykenberg, K. Jairaj, Atul Kohli, John Mansfield, Uday Mehta, Pratap Mehta, Philip Oldenburg, and Vibha Pinglé improved parts of this chapter. Abha Dawesar provided excellent research assistance. The responsibility for the content is entirely mine.

Regardless of where one stands on the intellectual and political spectrum, one cannot deny that 1992 was a transformative year in Indian politics. What was attacked in Ayodhya on December 6 was not simply a mosque, but a widely accepted way of conducting politics. India's political and ideological discourse has altered dramatically. A weak political force since its birth seven decades ago, Hindu nationalism has finally put its defining question on India's political agenda: *What is the relationship between Hinduism and the nation's identity?* Hindu nationalists believe that the term "Hindu" is not simply religious: it also depicts the national or cultural life of India. Locating figures and concepts in Hinduism that could also be national symbols and ideas, and convincing the nation of this correspondence, has been their overarching quest for decades. Until now, even though they themselves did not doubt that link, the Hindu nationalists were unable to shape the political agenda. With the demolition of the Babri mosque in Ayodhya, they have achieved that goal. Today, the relationship between Hinduism and the Indian nation is a central, if not the only, question in Indian politics.

How, then, will India as a nation be defined in the coming years? On the answer may well depend the de facto, if not the de jure, definition of citizenship. Numbering 110 million, constituting 12 percent of the population, and scattered over most of India, Muslims are India's largest minority. As an ideology, Hindu nationalism seeks a reevaluation of their relationship with India and of how the polity should treat them.

Because the implications of the Babri mosque's demolition are profound, an assessment of recent Indian politics is bound to be dominated by Hindu nationalism and Hindu-Muslim relations. There was, however, more to Indian politics in 1992 than Ayodhya and Hindu nationalism. This chapter, thus, is divided into a narrative and an analytic part. In the narrative, two kinds of politics—transformative and routine—are discussed. The analytic part focuses on Hindu nationalism and asks the larger questions: How do Hindu nationalists view India as a nation and why? Why, after failing for decades, have the Hindu nationalists become such a political force? The conclusion speculates on the political trends in the 1990s.

What Happened and How

Transformative Politics: Ayodhya

On December 6, 1992, defying a Supreme Court ruling, a large crowd mobilized by Hindu nationalists demolished the Babri mosque.

The mosque was located in Ayodhya, a small town in the northern state of Uttar Pradesh (U.P.). The Hindu nationalist claim is that the mosque was built on a site where a temple celebrating the birth of Lord Ram had existed before 1528. The mosque was, according to Hindu nationalists, built by Babur, a king of Turko-Mongol heritage whose Indian conquests laid the foundations of the Mughal Empire. The Mughal period lasted from 1526 through roughly 1757, when the British took control of Bengal (and the Mughal rule in Delhi progressively unraveled). To announce his conquest of India, say the Hindu nationalists, Babur demolished the preexisting Ram temple and erected a mosque.

Associated with the great epic *Ramayana,* Ram is among the most popular gods in the Hindu pantheon, especially in the North and West of India. Where (and whether) Ram was actually born, and whether a temple existed where the mosque stood, are matters of dispute for historians.[1] In popular Hindu perception, however, Ayodhya has long been viewed as Ram's birthplace. Moreover, whether or not "scientific history" or archaeology can establish the existence of a Ram temple where the mosque stood, local perceptions examined by anthropologists leave no doubt about it.[2] The gap between belief and evidence has, finally, led to the argument by some historians that the "oral history" or "popular tradition" of the town supports the existence of the temple, though "documentary history" does not.[3]

Complicating matters for the average viewer, the architecture of the disputed structure was, literally, a monument of ambiguity.[4] The pillars of the mosque had Hindu-Buddhist iconography. Just outside the mosque, several idols associated with the story of Ram (concerning his mother and wife) existed and had been used for worship for decades. Surrounded by tens of temples, each depicting some aspect of the tale of Ram, the mosque appeared to be a lone Islamic structure placed in a veritable sea of Hindu religiosity. According to the local folklore, several struggles to "liberate" the birthplace had been launched over the last four centuries, the most significant of which in

[1] Romila Thapar, "A Historical Perspective on the Story of Ram," and K. N. Panikkar, "A Historical Overview," in *Anatomy of a Confrontation,* ed. S. Gopal (Delhi: Penguin, 1991).

[2] For details, see Peter van der Veer, *Gods on Earth* (Delhi: Oxford University Press, 1989), and "Gods Must Be Liberated: A Hindu Liberation Movement in Ayodhya," *Modern Asian Studies,* Vol. 21, no. 2, 1987, pp. 283–303.

[3] Harbans Mukhia, *Perspectives of Medieval History* (Delhi: Vikas Publications, 1993), chapter titled "The Ram Janmabhumi-Babri Masjid Dispute: Evidence of Medieval Sources."

[4] Based on a personal visit to Ayodhya, January 1991.

modern times was the placement of an image of Ram in the middle of the Babri mosque, presumably the place where Ram was born, by some Hindu believers in 1948.[5] Afraid of riots, the courts padlocked the mosque. It remained padlocked until 1986, when it was reopened for Hindu worship by a district court. The reopening of what was now a "temple-mosque" site emboldened Hindu nationalists. It reinforced their resolve to get rid of the "mosque" in the "temple-mosque" structure.

Reconstructing the Politics of the Ayodhya Dispute. The politics of Ayodhya cannot be understood if differences between the organizational and ideological factions within Hindu nationalism are ignored. Organizationally speaking, Hindu nationalism has two aspects: electoral and nonelectoral. The distinction has blurred of late, for both kinds of organizations have worked together in recent mobilizations. Nonetheless, the distinction is important. Electoral organizations of Hindu nationalism have been, and may in the future be, caught between maintaining ideological purity and building coalitions if they wish to come to power. And if already in power, they may also be torn between ideological purity and the necessity of maintaining order. Committed to "cultural rejuvenation," the nonelectoral organizations are not under such compulsions, making them less willing to compromise their positions. The Bharatiya Janata Party (BJP) represents the ideology of Hindu nationalism in electoral politics today, replacing its predecessor, the Jana Sangh, which fought elections until the 1970s. Another Hindu nationalist party, the Shiv Sena, is based in Maharashtra, and of late has collaborated with the BJP. The Shiv Sena is the most right-wing party of India. Its power is primarily confined to Bombay, though it has made efforts to establish itself in rural Maharashtra. Its leader, Bal Thackeray, openly admires Hitler.[6] The three principal nonelectoral organizations are the Rashtriya Swayamsevak Sangh (RSS; National Volunteer Corps), the Vishwa Hindu Parishad (VHP; World Hindu Council), and the Bajrang Dal, the youth wing of the VHP. The RSS has been in existence since 1925; the VHP, since 1964 (but it became nationally and internationally visible in the 1980s); and the Bajrang Dal, committed to a militant defense of Hinduism, since

---

5 For a summary, see Shekhar Gupta, "The Gathering Storm," *India Briefing, 1990*, ed. Marshall M. Bouton and Philip Oldenburg (Boulder: Westview Press, 1990). Writing with remarkable insight, Gupta anticipated some of the post-1990 developments, including the current dilemmas of Hindu nationalists. See also van der Veer, "Gods Must Be Liberated."

6 Interview, *Time* (International edition), January 25, 1993. For revealing insights on Bal Thackeray's politics, see the comments by George Fernandes, a senior politician of India, in *George Fernandes Speaks* (Delhi: Ajanta Publications, 1991), pp. 278–89.

the late 1980s. Leaving aside the Shiv Sena, the remaining organizations are clubbed together as the *Sangh parivar* (the RSS family).

How did the politics of these organizations affect the Ayodhya movement? Two distinctions are necessary: the first is between the VHP and the BJP, and the second, between the right wing of the BJP, led by Murli Manohar Joshi, president from 1991–93, and its moderate, center-right faction, led by Atal Behari Vajpayee. A nonelectoral body, the VHP has been committed to the rebuilding of the temple on the disputed site regardless of its legal or political ramifications. As a political party, the BJP is constrained by electoral dynamics. There have been, and are, divisions within the party over the extent to which the VHP agenda should be supported. Both factions of the BJP are committed to a reshaping of Indian politics and have viewed the Ayodhya dispute as a way to put Hindu nationalism on India's political agenda. But serious differences over the means have existed.[7] The center-right has been emphasizing dialogue and debate with the Muslim and secular communities on a common civil code, state grants to minority cultural and educational institutions, and the special status of Kashmir (making it equal to all other states). The right wing does not wish to limit itself to dialogue and would not shy away from more aggressive politics. For the right wing, the ends would essentially justify the means. L. K. Advani, the BJP's most popular leader, has been straddling the two factions, not siding clearly with either.

In 1984 the VHP called for a movement to "liberate" the "birthplace" of Ram and rebuild a temple where the mosque stood. This meant that the mosque would either have to be moved or demolished. The moving of the mosque depended on a political compromise between the VHP and Muslim leadership. Thus began the virtually endless series of meetings between the Muslim leadership, organized as the Babri Masjid Action Committees (BMAC), and the VHP.

In 1986 when the government of India decided to overturn the Supreme Court decision, passing a law to make all Muslim women subject to the *shari'a* on marriage and divorce, the BJP began supporting the VHP movement for Ayodhya. In the 1989 elections, the BJP campaigned on this issue. Winning 86 seats, it emerged as the third largest party in the Lok Sabha (the lower house of central parliament). In

[7] Atal Behari Vajpayee, interview, *Dharmyuga* (Bombay), January 16–31, 1991. Among the most senior leaders in the BJP and its past president (1981–86), Vajpayee was also minister for external affairs in the Janata government (1977–79). See also "Stoking Factionalist Fires," *India Today*, October 15, 1992, and "Hindu Divided Family," *India Today*, November 30, 1991. All citations from *India Today* are from the international edition.

TABLE 1
Jana Sangh/Bharatiya Janata Party in National Elections (1952–91)

Election Year	% of National Vote	Seats in the Lok Sabha		
		Won	*Contested*	*Total*
1952	3.1	3	93	489
1957	5.9	4	132	494
1962	6.4	14	196	494
1967	9.4	35	250	515
1971	7.4	22	157	518
1984*	7.4	2	224	515
1989	11.4	85	226	529
1991	20.2	119	460	511

Source: David Butler, Ashok Lahiri, and Prannoy Roy, *India Decides: Elections 1952–91* (New Delhi: Living Media India Limited, 1991), and News Services Division, All India Radio, *Lok Sabha Poll: An A.I.R. Analysis* (New Delhi: Government of India, 1991).

*The Jana Sangh merged with the Janata coalition in 1977 and 1980, making it impossible to derive good estimates of its popular vote.

1990 the BJP led a mobilization to build the temple. The mobilization brought down the V. P. Singh government.[8] In the 1991 midterm elections, it emerged as the second largest party in parliament and won control of four state assemblies, forming governments in Uttar Pradesh, Madhya Pradesh, Rajasthan, and Himachal Pradesh. Ayodhya was clearly paying off politically. Electoral support for the BJP grew to an unprecedented degree. (See Table 1.)

However, the fact that the BJP came to power in Uttar Pradesh, the state where the contested site was located, created a dilemma. As an opposition party aiming to widen its political base and win power, the BJP had a vested interest in mass mobilization. As a party of government, however, it also had to maintain law and order. The political imperative of governance and the maintenance of law and order required a lowering of the rhetoric.[9] The BJP could not lead yet another mobilization to build the temple and also expect to preserve law and order, a necessary function of the government.

[8] This development, of course, had a context, rooted as it was in the Mandal politics of the Janata Dal. For the background, see Philip Oldenburg, "Politics: How Threatening a Crisis?," *India Briefing, 1991* (Boulder: Westview Press, 1991), and Walter Andersen, "Lowering the Level of Tension," *India Briefing, 1992* (Boulder: Westview Press, 1992).

[9] Interview with Kalyan Singh, chief minister, Uttar Pradesh, *Indian Express*, June 28, 1991.

Matching this pragmatic push toward constitutionality was the mounting chorus of the VHP and the right wing of the party. The VHP cadres were galvanized into action by the promise of a Ram temple, and wanted the promise to be kept, whether or not the promise violated the law and regardless of what it entailed for a state government committed to protecting the law.[10] The BJP might have led the Ram temple mobilization, but the VHP cadres were the mainstay of the mobilization. Without them, it is questionable whether the BJP, which won a mere two seats in the 1984 parliamentary elections, would have acquired such political strength.

Something thus had to be done to resolve the contradiction between keeping VHP support and not violating the law. Anticipating trouble and looking for a crisis-management strategy, the BJP government, through an ordinance in October 1991, acquired 2.77 acres of land *outside the Babri mosque.* The calculation was that the VHP could start constructing the temple on this plot, without tearing down the mosque for the time being. The VHP, after all, had planned a spectacular Ram temple; the disputed "mosque-temple" (that is, the Babri mosque) could remain in the center, but the periphery of the Ram temple could be built on the land outside the mosque. The construction could continue on the periphery until the dispute over the "mosque-temple" site was legally or politically settled, then presumably the activists would move inward.

The government acquisition of land, however, was challenged by the Muslim Waqf Board in the U.P. High Court. The court ruled that while the U.P. government could legally acquire the land, it could not allow construction of a temple on the 2.77 acres outside the mosque until all sides of the case had been heard.

The VHP did not wish to be chained down by legal stipulations, but a brazen defiance was not easy. There were two VHP-led *kar sewa*s (mobilizations for building the temple) in 1992—one in July, and a second, fateful one in December. The July mobilization led to some construction activity, but because of the Supreme Court ruling, which the U.P. government had to follow, the mosque could not be touched. Not getting full support from the state BJP government, the VHP ultimately had to look for a face-saving solution. An assurance from Prime Minister P. V. Narasimha Rao that his government would work toward a negotiated settlement between the VHP and the Muslim leaders of the Babri Masjid Action Committees offered such a solution. Because such negotiations in the past had not led to a political

---

[10] "Temple Trauma," *India Today*, September 15, 1991; "The Politics of Opportunism," *India Today*, August 15, 1992.

solution, the VHP insisted on a deadline, a point finally accepted by New Delhi. December 6 was announced as the next day of *kar sewa,* which thereby became the deadline for a negotiated solution. Prime Minister Rao got roughly four months of breathing space, but no settlement was reached between the VHP and the BMAC.

In response to a government suggestion, however, the BMAC made a concession. "Muslims will give up their claim on Babri Masjid," it said, "if the court accepts that it was built after demolishing a temple in 1528." The VHP argued that "the birthplace of Ram is a matter of faith and it cannot be determined in a court of law," an argument supported by the right wing of the BJP.[11] The moderates of the party kept quiet.

The BJP government in Uttar Pradesh was now caught in a bind. It did not want to antagonize the VHP, a sister organization, but it could not violate the court ruling either. Having already postponed *kar sewa* for temple construction several times due to legal difficulties, the VHP for its part was not prepared to accept further delays. In the past, it had brought volunteers to Ayodhya only to tell them to go back until a legally appropriate time arrived. Worrying increasingly about the disaffection of its cadres, the VHP stuck to December 6 as the date of *kar sewa.* Meanwhile, the U.P. High Court stated that December 11 was the earliest it could give a decision on whether the VHP could start building a temple on the 2.77 acres outside the mosque.

Since the VHP was not willing to wait for a court decision (because "it was a matter of faith") although the Muslim leaders had agreed to wait, the BJP government in Uttar Pradesh had to think of a compromise. Unable legally to defy the courts, the U.P. government promised that it would protect the mosque and also not allow construction of a temple until the court gave its verdict on December 11. However, it requested that the VHP be allowed to do a "symbolic *kar sewa*"—that is, a performance of devotional rituals and singing of hymns. The Supreme Court accepted the "symbolic" solution.

In the event, with nearly 300,000 cadres and volunteers mobilized for *kar sewa,* the mosque was demolished. The *kar sevak*s (volunteers) also constructed a makeshift Ram temple at "Ram's birthplace." Expressing regret that it was unable to maintain law and order, the BJP government in Uttar Pradesh resigned. Using constitutional powers, New Delhi dismissed the state government and the state assembly. Accepting the resignation would have meant keeping alive the state legislature, where the BJP had a majority. The following day, accept-

[11] *India Today,* December 15, 1992, p. 29.

ing moral responsibility, L. K. Advani apologized to the nation and resigned as the leader of the opposition in parliament. The moderate right of the BJP expressed regret, too, as did the RSS. The VHP, Bajrang Dal, and the Shiv Sena in Bombay expressed no remorse.[12]

Widespread rioting, perhaps the worst since India's partition in 1947, followed, claiming some 1,700 lives during a week of rioting in December. In retaliation, several temples were pulled down in Pakistan, Bangladesh, and England, presumably by incensed Muslims. The government of India banned a number of "nonpolitical" but "communal" organizations—the RSS, VHP, and Bajrang Dal as well as Muslim organizations of a similar description. A little later, seven leaders of the BJP, VHP, and Bajrang Dal were arrested, including Advani and Joshi. New Delhi dismissed the remaining three BJP state governments of Madhya Pradesh, Rajasthan, and Himachal Pradesh. Since a large number of ministers in these state cabinets were also members of the banned RSS, the BJP state governments, New Delhi argued, could not effectively implement the outlawing of the RSS. Advani and Joshi were later released by the court on the grounds that they were not *legally* culpable for what happened. They were at most *politically* culpable.

Another week of rioting hit Bombay in January, and the cruelty witnessed was shocking. Reports indicate that the Shiv Sena, which incidentally is not part of the *Sangh parivar*, conducted pogroms against the Muslims and that for all practical purposes, the police did not intervene.[13] Hundreds of Muslims died. The savagery came as a shock to the country and, most of all, to Bombay residents. Generally viewed as the premier city of India, whose cosmopolitanism was said to be impervious to communal madness, Bombay was not immune to the general rot. Another city, Surat (Gujarat), long considered a haven of communal harmony, defied its historical character and witnessed scenes of chilling brutality.[14]

While the violence following the demolition of the mosque shook India and was widely reported, a fairly large number of exceptions were underreported. To put the violence in perspective, the state of Bihar, otherwise known to be the most ungovernable in India, did not have a single riot. While the city of Bombay burned, the adjacent

---

[12] Bal Thackeray, the leader of Shiv Sena, said he was proud of the destruction. See *Times of India*, December 7, 1992.

[13] "Savagery in Bombay," *India Today*, January 31, 1993; and an excellent though macabre piece of reportage by Edward Gargan, "Trust is Torn: Police Role in Bombay Riots," *New York Times*, February 4, 1993.

[14] See Asghar Ali Engineer, "Bastion of Communal Amity Crumbles," *Economic and Political Weekly*, February 13, 1993.

town of Bhiwandi, with a horrible record of rioting in the 1980s, did not. In the state of Uttar Pradesh, several towns with a recent history of rioting—Meerut, Aligarh, and Varanasi—were quiet. Living up to their more peaceful history, Awadh and eastern Uttar Pradesh were also free of violence. An interesting paradox marks Awadh, a culturally distinct region in the heart of Uttar Pradesh. Ayodhya is located in Awadh, and though a whole movement was built on Ayodhya, the town of Ayodhya did not have local violence nor did the areas surrounding Awadh have rioting. The violence in Ayodhya was perpetrated by the activists who came from outside to demolish the mosque. Finally, the villages where most Indians still live remained peaceful.

All of this is not to understate the ferocity of the violence or the significance of the demolition of the mosque. But it is worth keeping in mind that communal violence is not new to Indian politics. Its eruption, along with repulsive brutality in pockets of the country, continues to coexist with the absence of violence in other areas. What was distinctive about the events after December 6 was not the violence itself, but the reason for that violence. The masses have never before been politically mobilized in India to destroy a mosque. The ideological and political implications of Ayodhya are thus enormous: an important symbol of India's governing principles was violated.

The violation of a key political principle in which a political party was involved means that serious political battles lie ahead. It does not imply that an escalation down the path of fratricide is inevitable. The impression in December that the entire country was coming apart was overdrawn. India is still not a Bosnia, nor is it likely to become one, unless the right wing captures power or is close to capturing power. As will be argued later, that scenario is far from inevitable.

Politics over Law? The demolition of the mosque raises two immediate issues: Could the Rao government have saved the mosque? Was the BJP leadership involved in a conspiracy?

Once the U.P. government had stated that it would obey the Supreme Court and not allow a full-scale *kar sewa*, the Rao government was caught in a dilemma. If it was not willing to accept the assurance of the state government that the *kar sewa* would only be a symbolic one, it could dismiss the U.P. government; and if it did accept the assurance, which the Supreme Court had already done, it could not then deploy large numbers of the central armed forces near the site without the state government's permission. Undeterred by the courts, which they had decided to defy anyway, the VHP cadres were being mobilized in large numbers. Given how much planning it takes to tear down the large domes of a mosque, it is unlikely that the central intelligence did not provide reports to Prime Minister Rao about the intentions of the volunteers.[15] Rao claimed otherwise in an interview with *India Today*. He argued that he had no option but to trust the assurances of a duly elected state government, both to the central government and to the Supreme Court. There are, however, indications that the *kar sevaks* had prepared for the demolition ahead of time.

It would seem that the prime minister's decision to stick to the constitution had an underlying political rationale. It was a marriage of politics and constitutionality. The experience of 1990 was perhaps at the back of Rao's mind. In 1990 Prime Minister V. P. Singh and the U.P. government had decided to block the entry of volunteers into Ayodhya by force. The ensuing bloodshed helped the Hindu nationalists electorally, bringing the BJP to power in Uttar Pradesh. The prime minister was *not* prepared to use force, spill blood, and make the Hindu nationalists into martyrs even before the law was violated. Instead, he decided to gamble on the BJP government's delivering its promise, saying that "the Center cannot be planning a military coup against a state government." Decisive action, if any, would be taken only after the "crime" was committed.

Some suggest that the BJP leadership was involved in a conspiracy and that it engaged in "doublespeak."[16] Against this, the leaders of the BJP and RSS simply argue that they take pride in being the most disciplined organizations in India. However, in Ayodhya, more than 300,000 volunteers, *including a large number of non-RSS cadres*, had gathered around the congested site. Emotions ran high, and the BJP and RSS, their leaders say, lost control of the crowds. The on-site reports suggest that this may be true.[17]

However, it seems unlikely that the BJP leaders did not anticipate crowd fury. Atal Behari Vajpayee, a moderate leader of the BJP, testified in an interview that the possibility of crowd fury was discussed at the level of leadership.[18] It would seem therefore that, like the gov-

---

[15] *India Today*, December 31, 1992, pp. 36–37. See also interview with Narasimha Rao, *India Today*, January 15, 1993.

[16] Rao, in the interview cited above, makes this claim, which paradoxically suggests an even bigger failure of intelligence. Several English-language periodicals have also made this charge, especially *India Today*, December 31, 1992, pp. 32–37.

[17] "11:55 a.m. H. V. Sheshadri, RSS General Secretary, appeals to the defiant *kar sevaks* in at least four or five different languages to stop the demolition and destruction. No one listens to him. His voice is barely audible over the chants of the crowd. Neither are the subsequent appeals issued by Advani and Singhal. The leaders have become the led." Dilip Awasthi, "A Nation's Shame," *India Today*, December 31, 1992, pp. 23–24.

[18] *India Abroad*, December 18, 1992.

ernment in New Delhi, the BJP leadership (and the BJP government of Uttar Pradesh) also took a political decision about the law. The law would not be broken if the crowds did not violate it, but if they did, the BJP government would not interfere, and the state government would simply resign for failing to deliver its promise to the Supreme Court. In an article written while he was temporarily in jail, L. K. Advani points out that the affidavit given by the U.P. chief minister to the Supreme Court had an "addendum: that he would not use force against the *kar sevaks*."[19] "I shudder to think," says Advani, "what would have happened that day at Ayodhya if firing had taken place. . . . There would have been a holocaust not only in Ayodhya but also in the whole country."[20]

The two observations—that the right-wing cadres of the VHP had planned the demolition and that the BJP had decided not to use force even if it was required to implement the law—indicate that the VHP and Bajrang Dal (and possibly the right wing of the BJP) staged a *political coup on the entire political and legal system*. For this coup to happen, the BJP leadership as a whole did not have to be involved in a conspiracy. Because of the specter of a possible bloodbath, no political actor involved was prepared to defend the law. *The right wing simply used this fear as an opportunity and accomplished its ends.* Vigorously though he denies it, Advani could not "dismount the tiger" he had ridden for the last three years.[21] In the past, leaders like Nehru and Gandhi are known to have thrown themselves amidst rioting crowds to impose peace.[22] Advani, however, was not prepared to do this.

The State of the Insurgencies: Transformative Politics in Punjab?

From the viewpoint of New Delhi, the weakening of militancy in Punjab was the big political news of the year, though crowded out by Ayodhya. One should, of course, not speak too soon, but by early 1993 there were firm indications that the political process had returned to Punjab. A series of calculated political risks, combined with some unprecedented successes in anti-terrorist operations, produced this outcome. Between 1986 (when the elected state government was dismissed by New Delhi on charges of inability to stop terrorism) and 1992, militancy had continued virtually unabated.

[19] *Indian Express*, December 28, 1992.

[20] Ibid., December 27, 1992.

[21] Ibid.

[22] This part of the history of the national movement is well known. The post-1947 generation of Indians was reminded of it by K. S. Duggal, "The Frenzied Fringe," *Indian Express*, January 4, 1993.

In February 1992 New Delhi took the risk of holding elections in Punjab. The turnout was an all-time low of 20 percent, as against 65 percent in 1985 when state assembly elections were last held.[23] All factions of the Akali Dal (except for one led by Amarinder Singh) boycotted the elections. The militants also called for a boycott, threatening retaliation if the people voted. Their call was more successful in the villages and districts on the India-Pakistan border than in the towns and interior districts. On the whole, the threat, reflected in low turnouts, was successful enough to make observers question the electoral verdict in favor of the Congress Party.[24] Still, a Punjabi government, even if it had a thin electoral legitimacy, was better than direct rule of the state from New Delhi. After the elections, the state government, not the central government, had to take on the militants. K. P. S. Gill, a somewhat controversial figure but also an established veteran of anti-insurgency operations in the Northeast, was reappointed as the state's police chief. Gill received determined political support from the newly elected state government, which after all had campaigned on an anti-militancy platform. His police force penetrated the militant outfits, and by the end of the summer, a large number of top militants had been captured or killed.

Progress on the military front was paralleled by signs of a reemerging political process. In the September 1992 municipal elections, the turnout was more than 70 percent, despite the boycott call given by the militants and by most Akali Dal factions. Buoyed by the outcome, the state government announced elections for the village *panchayats* (village governing councils) in January 1993. The turnout was between 75 and 80 percent, in contrast to 15 percent in March 1992. The militants had clearly lost control over popular sentiments.

Assam and Kashmir have been sites of the two other recent insurgencies. In early 1992 the United Liberation Front of Assam (ULFA) militants reached a political compromise with the state government. In April, however, on grounds that the militants had failed to keep their promise to give up violence, the army, assisted by the paramilitary forces, resumed its operations. As the year unfolded, it seemed that the ULFA militants had spent themselves and the militancy had been crushed.

Perhaps the only major event in a year of stalemate in Kashmir took place in February and March 1992, when the Jammu and Kashmir Liberation Front (JKLF), a militant organization committed to the

[23] For details, see Gurharpal Singh, "The Punjab Elections 1992: Breakthrough or Breakdown?," *Asian Survey*, November 1992.

[24] *India Today*, March 15, 1992.

independence of Kashmir and headquartered in Pakistan-occupied Kashmir, mobilized its supporters to cross the India-Pakistan border in Kashmir. The ostensible aim was to "liberate" Kashmir. The government of Pakistan did not allow the crossing of the border and used force to roll back the march. The government action made it clear that Pakistan was not willing to risk a war with India over Kashmir and that it was not going to let the independence-minded JKLF steal a march on militant groups like the Hizb-ul-Mujahidin, which is committed to Kashmir's integration with Pakistan.

Routine Politics

Ayodhya and the insurgencies notwithstanding, politics as usual continued in good measure. There were the customary factional fights, splits, and mergers in party politics. As a result of factional infighting within the state Congress units, chief ministers were changed in the southern states of Andhra Pradesh and Karnataka. In October, Vijaya Bhaskar Reddy replaced Janardan Reddy in Andhra Pradesh. In November, M. Veerappa Moily succeeded S. Bangarappa in Karnataka. In Gujarat, Chimanbhai Patel, chief minister of the state and, until recently, leader of a faction of the Janata Dal, merged his faction with the Congress Party. The merger was, among other things, aimed at dealing with the BJP, which had won an unprecedented 51 percent of the state vote in the 1991 parliamentary elections. Had there been state assembly elections alongside the parliamentary ones, the BJP would in all probability have won power in the state.

In the Lok Sabha there were two major splits. Twenty members of parliament (MPs) led by Ajit Singh, former industry minister, left the Janata Dal, whose leader, V. P. Singh, had long had differences with Ajit Singh. Earlier in the year, eight MPs of the Telugu Desam, an Andhra-based regional party, became a breakaway group in the Lok Sabha. During most of the year, the Congress had between 245 and 251 MPs in the Lok Sabha, whereas a minimum of 273 is required to have a majority (assuming that the full house is voting). Since both breakaway groups supported the Congress Party, they bolstered the longevity and parliamentary fortunes of the Rao government.

Two other political developments were more than routine but considerably less than transformative. Organizational elections in the Congress Party were held for the first time after having been suspended by Indira Gandhi in 1973. Political scientists have repeatedly argued that the suspension of internal elections has inflicted untold damage on the organizational health of the Congress Party.[25] When the elections were announced, Prime Minister Rao was hailed for re-democratizing a huge but unhealthy machine. However, as faction leaders opposed to Rao emerged with big victories in the Congress Working Committee (CWC), the highest body of the party, Rao asked some of them to resign. The ostensible ground was that there was not enough representation of the Scheduled Castes, Scheduled Tribes, and women in the CWC. The press concluded that Prime Minister Rao wanted a more supportive CWC. The elections were an improvement over the existing practices of the party, but after the postelection changes, earlier hopes were substantially dampened.

The river water dispute between two southern states, Karnataka and Tamil Nadu, was another surprising development. North-South tensions, especially over the issue of language, have been part of the popular perception in the North and East. However, since the linguistic reorganization of southern states in the 1950s, intra-South political violence has not been part of the popular imagination. Defying this perception, Karnataka and Tamil Nadu rioted over the distribution of irrigation waters of the Cauvery River. The Cauvery is the only major river of Tamil Nadu and provides the water for 85 percent of its canal-irrigated area.

The trouble began with the interim order of the Cauvery Water Disputes Tribunal, which directed Karnataka to limit irrigation in the Cauvery basin to 1.12 million acres and to release 205 billion cubic feet of water from its reservoir to Tamil Nadu.[26] The Karnataka government felt that the restriction to 1.12 million acres was barely sufficient for the farming needs of the Cauvery basin. Karnataka issued an ordinance overriding the interim award of the tribunal, but the Supreme Court struck down the ordinance, thereby embarrassing the state government.

Riots broke out in Karnataka, leading to the reverse migration of thousands of Tamils who had been living there. New Delhi had to intervene, partly because the Rao government, for its survival, depended on the support of the All-India Anna Dravida Munnetra Kazhagam (AIADMK), the regional party ruling Tamil Nadu.[27] Plentiful rainfall last year ensured that even after releasing 205 billion cubic feet of water, Karnataka had enough left for its irrigation needs. However,

---

[25] The most recent account is Atul Kohli, *Democracy and Discontent: India's Crisis of Governability* (New York: Cambridge University Press, 1991).

[26] For details, see *India Today*, December 15, 1991, January 31, 1992, and March 15, 1992.

[27] AIADMK has now left the Congress as a coalition partner. However, because of the support of the breakaway Telugu Desam and the Ajit Singh faction, the Congress can still put together a majority in the Lok Sabha.

droughts induced by inadequate rains may bring the crisis back in the future.

Analyzing the Ayodhya Movement

Religious Nationalism, Not Religious Fundamentalism

Holy structures have been desecrated in India before—innumerable times, as one would expect, in the medieval age, but also a few times in postindependence India. To give the most widely noted and shocking recent example, the Golden Temple, the holiest shrine of the Sikhs, was attacked in June 1984 by the Indian government on grounds that "armed criminals" had taken shelter there. Why, then, should the destruction of the Babri mosque in Ayodhya be viewed by everyone as a "watershed"?

Ayodhya concerns Hindu-Muslim tensions. If one looks at India's history, patterns of both coexistence and hostility have marked the Hindu-Muslim relationship. Over the last century, however, hostility and violence have on the whole tended to overpower intercommunal warmth. In 1947 India's partition and the resultant birth of Pakistan institutionalized the separation. Of the 100 million Muslims in the undivided India of 1947, 65 million acquired the citizenship of Pakistan. Thirty-five million Muslims stayed behind, becoming citizens of India—out of choice or because they were too poor to migrate. Partition was accompanied by 250,000 to 1 million deaths—no one knows exactly how many. Between 12 million and 15 million people migrated both ways across the border. It was a tragedy of cataclysmic proportions. Pushed to its limits, religion-based politics has the potential of bringing the pain of India's history back. To many Indians, it is an agonizing prospect.

Moreover, the demolition of the Babri mosque was preceded by a political movement. Mass mobilization is not new to India. The nation, after all, was born with a mass mobilization that lasted nearly three decades. Also, religious symbols were used by Mohandas K. Gandhi. At no point, however, were the masses mobilized, despite frequent use of religious symbols, to *destroy* a holy place. Thus, even though the Babri mosque in Ayodhya had not been used as a place of worship by the Muslims for several decades whereas the Golden Temple is the Vatican of the Sikhs, the potential consequences of Ayodhya are unparalleled. The symbolism of a decrepit mosque is historically charged.

The term "religious fundamentalism" has often been used to describe the kind of behavior seen in Ayodhya. *Sadhus* (Hindu holy men) and religious fanatics are indeed involved in the movement to rebuild the Ram temple, and many religious Hindus also support it as an act of faith. That, however, is only a fraction of the movement. Basically, the Ayodhya movement is an expression of religious *nationalism*, not religious *fundamentalism*. Both religious fundamentalists and religious nationalists may share an aversion for a certain kind of "secularist," and both may attack groups perceived as "recalcitrant." The similarities end there. Unlike Islamic fundamentalists, for whom sovereignty in an Islamic state would reside in Allah, who would swear by the *shari'a*, and who target "heretics" as enemies, the Ayodhya movement is neither a call for *Ramrajya* (the kingdom of Lord Ram) nor a plea for a return to traditional Hindu law. Moreover, the doctrinal diversity of Hinduism rules out the notion of heresy.

Another mainstream argument does not appear to be valid. A large number of commentators have argued that Ayodhya represents a turn in Hinduism toward what has been called the "Semitic" model—"one book, one God, one sacred city"—instead of its intrinsic pluralism on all of these dimensions.[28] While trying to organize the Hindus as never before, at no point have the leaders of the Ayodhya movement called for an abandonment of Hinduism's multiple gods in favor of Ram. In fact, the right wing continues to talk about the "liberation" of the birthplaces of two more Hindu gods: Krishna (in Mathura) and Shiva (in Varanasi).

The aim of Hindu nationalists is neither to "Semitize" Hinduism nor to enforce religious uniformity and orthodoxy. Rather, it is to create a political unity among the Hindus, divided otherwise by the various castes, languages, and doctrinal diversities. BJP leader L. K. Advani readily admits that he is not very religious.[29] Nor does the BJP as a party consist primarily of religious Hindus. The major tracts of Hindu nationalism clearly state, as Advani recently argued, that "Indian nationalism is rooted . . . in a Hindu ethos," known as "Hindutva."[30] Since the birth of their ideology, Hindu nationalists have made a distinction between Hindutva and Hinduism. According to them, the former term is cultural ("the ethos or culture of India"), the latter religious.[31]

In a curious irony, Hindu nationalists are closer to Muslim nationalists like Mohammed Ali Jinnah, the founder of Pakistan, than to Islamic fundamentalists like Maulana Maududi, the founder of Jamaat-i-

---

28 See, for example, Rajni Kothari, "The December 6 Watershed," *Hindustan Times*, December 27, 1992; Salman Khurshid, "How Does One Repair a Damaged Hinduism?," *Indian Express*, December 16, 1992; and Lloyd Rudolph and Susanne Rudolph, "Modern Hate," *The New Republic*, March 22, 1993.

29 Interview, *Newstrack*, January 1991.

30 L. K. Advani, "BJP is Unequivocally Committed to Secularism," *Indian Express*, December 27, 1992.

31 V. D. Savarkar, *Hindutva* (Bombay: Veer Savarkar Prakashan, 1989), 6th ed.

Islami. Hindu nationalists intensely dislike comparisons with the party that led the movement for Pakistan. The 1947 partition, according to them, was the most traumatic moment of 20th-century India. In truth, however, Jinnah's argument was similar, though it was made on behalf of Muslims. A modern man not known for religiosity, Jinnah argued that one did not have to be religious to appreciate the cultural differences between Islam and Hinduism. The cultural distinctiveness of Indian Islam, he stressed, constituted the rationale for a separate nation-state of Pakistan:

> Islam and Hinduism . . . are not religions in the strict sense of the word, but are in fact different and distinct social orders. . . . [T]hey belong to two different civilizations which are based mainly on conflicting ideas and conceptions. . . . They have different epics, [and] their heroes are different. . . . Very often, the hero of one is the foe of the other and likewise their victories and defeats overlap.[32]

Ayodhya thus is not merely a religious dispute. It is a political contestation over India's national identity. A secular view of national identity has ruled Indian politics so far. For secular nationalists, Indian culture is syncretistic and pluralistic, something to which all groups in India have made contributions. For Hindu nationalists, India's national identity and Hindutva are inseparable.

It is clear that the recent demolition of the Babri mosque has benefited Hindu nationalists in the short run.[33] Whether it will bring the Hindu nationalists to power or will necessarily strengthen them in the long run is by no means clear. In a house of 545 seats, the North and the West, where the BJP is powerful, have about 300 seats. If the BJP is unable to penetrate the South and the East, where it continues to be weak, it will have to win 90 percent of the northern and western seats. That is a tall order, especially because the northern state of Bihar has so far refused to join in the BJP momentum. To have a chance of coming to power, the BJP must penetrate the South[34] and/or the East. The distance between 170 seats, its highest in opinion surveys

[32] This is the famous Jinnah speech that formed the intellectual bedrock for Pakistan. It was given on March 23, 1940, in Lahore and has been reproduced in several documents. See *Some Recent Speeches and Writings of Mr. Jinnah*, ed. Jamil-ud-Din Ahmed (Lahore: Ashraf, 1952), Vol. I, p. 138.

[33] An opinion poll conducted in December 1992 indicates that if elections had been held then, the BJP would have secured 170 seats in parliament instead of its current 119, though it would still not hold as many seats as the Congress Party. Prannoy Roy, "A Nation Divided," *India Today*, January 15, 1993.

[34] Realizing this, the BJP is exploring an alliance with the AIADMK in Tamil Nadu.

so far, and 273 seats, the minimum required to form a government in New Delhi, is enormous. The BJP has a long way to go before it can capture power in New Delhi.

Nonetheless, that something as inconceivable as the mass demolition of a mosque could be undertaken and executed as a political project demonstrates the new mobilizing capacity of this ideology. The assassination of Mohandas K. Gandhi in 1948 was the last politically critical act of Hindu nationalism. That, however, was an insane act by an angry individual who was motivated by the ideology of Hindu nationalism, not a manifestation of its organized strength or an expression of its capacity to mobilize the masses.

Should the BJP come to power, Ayodhya and December 1992 will in retrospect be seen as the single most important political event of independent India. Whether the vivid political symbolism of a decrepit mosque will haunt India in the coming years or India's legendary resilience will prevail, only time will tell. It is often forgotten that politics, especially democratic politics, are considerably open-ended. Both decay and restoration are possible, and the best that analysts of politics can do is present scenarios. It is impossible to predict what will happen to India as a nation. All one can say with confidence is that Indian politics have been transformed ideologically and politically. "Congress versus anti-Congress" was the principal axis of Indian politics. "BJP versus the rest" has replaced that axis. The change of axis does not necessarily mean that the BJP will also rule India.

Still, the question needs to be asked: Why have the BJP and Hindu nationalism risen to such prominence? What accounts for the BJP's transformation from a party of the periphery to a party increasingly shaping India's political agenda? The reasons are both underlying and proximate. Competing strains in India's national identity constitute the base. The political circumstances of the 1980s supplied the proximate reasons, pushing the underlying ideological disputes to the fore.

Competing Strains in India's National Identity[35]

Since the rise of the Indian national movement, efforts to define India's national identity have wrestled with three competing themes—geographical, cultural, and religious. The first notion, emphasized for 2,500 years since the time of the Mahabharata, is that India has a "sacred geography."[36] The cultural notion is that ideas of *tolerance, plural-*

[35] This section relies heavily on my essay "Contested Meanings: Hindu Nationalism, India's National Identity and the Politics of Anxiety," *Daedalus*, Summer 1993.

[36] Diana Eck, "The Mythic Construction of the Land of India" (Paper presented at the South Asia Seminar, Center for International Affairs, Harvard University, March 16, 1990).

ism, and syncretism define Indian society. India is not only the birthplace of several religions—Hinduism, Buddhism, Jainism, and Sikhism—but it has also regularly received, accommodated, and absorbed "outsiders"—Parsis, Jews, and "Syrian" Christians (followers of St. Thomas, arriving as early as the 2nd century A.D., thus reaching India before Christians reached Europe). In the process, syncretistic forms of culture (and even syncretistic forms of religious worship) have emerged and become part of India. Urdu, a language combining Persian and Hindi and written in Arabic script, is a prototypical syncretistic language, developed under Muslim rule in medieval times. Apart from syncretism, the coming together and merging of cultures, pluralism and tolerance have also existed: different communities have found their niche in India and developed principles of interaction while keeping their identity intact. *Sarva Dharma Sambhava* (equal respect for all religions) is the best cultural expression of such pluralism. The third, religious notion is that India is originally the land of the Hindus and that it is the only land the Hindus can call their own. India has the Hindu holy places (Benares, Tirupati, Rameshwaram, Puri, Hardwar, Badrinath, Kedarnath, and now Ayodhya) and the holy rivers (Cauvery, Ganges, and Jamuna). Most of India is Hindu by religion—anywhere from 65 to 70 percent in the early 20th century and 82 percent today. A faith in Hinduism brings India's proverbial diversity together. India is thus viewed as a Hindu nation.[37]

These three elements have yielded two principal concepts of India's national identity—the secular nationalist and the Hindu nationalist. The former combines geography and culture; the latter, religion and geography. The best source for the secular nationalist construction is Jawaharlal Nehru's *The Discovery of India*. Syncretism, pluralism, and tolerance are the main themes of Nehru's recalling of India's history:

> Ancient India, like ancient China, was a world in itself, a culture and a civilization which gave shape to all things. Foreign influences poured in and often influenced that culture and were absorbed. Disruptive tendencies gave rise immediately to an attempt to find a synthesis. Some kind of a dream of unity has occupied the mind of India since the dawn of civilization. That unity was not conceived as something imposed from outside, a standardization . . . of beliefs. It was something deeper and, within its fold, the widest tolerance of belief and custom was practiced and every variety acknowledged and even encouraged.[38]

[37] M. S. Golwalkar, *We or Our Nationhood Defined* (Nagpur: Bharat Publications, 1939).

[38] Jawaharlal Nehru, *The Discovery of India* (Delhi: Oxford University Press, 1989), p. 62.

Nehru finds the unity in culture, not in religion. He has no conception of a "holy land." Ashoka, Kabir, Guru Nanak, Amir Khusro, Akbar, and Gandhi—all syncretistic or pluralistic figures, subscribing to a variety of Indian faiths—are the heroes of India's history, while Aurangzeb, the intolerant Mughal, "puts the clock back."[39]

Perhaps the best way to illustrate the difference between culture and religion is to cite Nehru's will. Nehru, after his death, wanted his ashes scattered in the Ganges, not because it was religiously sacred but because it was culturally appropriate:

> When I die, I should like my body to be cremated. . . . A small handful of [my] ashes should be thrown into the Ganga. . . . My desire to have a handful of my ashes thrown into the Ganga at Allahabad has no religious significance, so far as I am concerned. I have been attached to the Ganga and Jamuna rivers in Allahabad ever since my childhood and, as I have grown older, this attachment has grown. . . . The Ganga, especially, is the river of India, beloved of her people, round which are intertwined . . . her hopes and fears, her songs of triumph, her victories and her defeats. She has been a symbol of India's age-long culture and civilization, ever-changing, ever-flowing, and yet ever the same Ganga. . . . Ganga has been to me a symbol and a memory of the past of India, running into the present and flowing on to the great ocean of the future.[40]

To religious Hindus, the river Ganges is sacred. To Nehru, it was part of India's culture, and equally dear. Similarly, India's geography, to him, was sacred, not literally but metaphorically. The emotions and attachment generated by the geography can be equally intense for the religious and the secular-minded. To draw a parallel, one does not have to be a religious Jew to celebrate and love the land of Israel. Secular Jews may also do that.

That being said, multiple strains in a national identity have their own political implications. An excessive shift toward one of the strains produces a reaction. If secular nationalists violate the principle of pluralism—for example, by attacking federalism on the argument that too much federalism interferes with "national integrity"—they undermine a serious principle underlying the nation itself and begin to generate a reaction; such attacks do not tally with the concerned state's view of national identity, which has a place for regional identity as well. A man from Tamil Nadu is both a Tamilian and an In-

---

39 Ibid., p. 270.

40 "Will and Testament," in *Jawaharlal Nehru: An Anthology*, ed. S. Gopal (Delhi: Oxford University Press, 1980), pp. 647–48.

dian. Sometimes the reaction takes the form of separatist agitations. And these agitations, in turn, generate concern about territorial integrity. The centralizing "solution" thus worsens the disease. Something like this happened under Indira Gandhi when she repeatedly undermined federalism on grounds of "national integrity," only to generate separatism.

On the other hand, one can also go too far in protecting pluralism. For example, Kashmir was given a special status in the Indian Constitution. New Delhi was to be responsible only for foreign affairs, defense, communications, and currency; the state government would handle the rest. Other Indian states had fewer powers. The Kashmir arrangement, thus, had a ready potential to contradict the territorial principle, if Kashmiris claimed they were still unhappy. Nehru loved Kashmir and was instrumental in promoting its special status, but he himself had to deploy force to quell Sheikh Abdullah's vacillations between India and independence.

A second form of pluralism deemed excessive and therefore harmful for national integrity concerns "personal laws." Should the various religious groups in India be under a common civil code, or under their distinct religious laws? If secular nationalists claim that separate "personal laws" destroy national unity, they generate a reaction in the religious community whose personal laws are at issue. If, on the other hand, they promote personal laws on the argument that such concessions make minorities secure, they set off a reaction in the "majority" community that the state may have gone too far in minority appeasement, opening up fissiparous tendencies and undermining "national unity."[41]

From Religion Versus Culture to Religion as Culture

Pluralism in the secular view is embodied in laws (such as personal laws and protection of minority educational institutions) and in political institutions (such as federalism). Finding a blending of territory and cultural pluralism insufficient, the Hindu nationalists argue that emotions and loyalty make a nation, not politics, laws, and institutions. Laws, they say, can always be manipulated politically. What they consider a "proliferation" of "pro-minority laws" has not led to the building of a cohesive nation. A "salad bowl," according to them,

[41] Nanaji Deshmukh, *Rethinking Secularism* (Delhi: Suruchi Prakashan, 1989); H. V. Sheshadri, K. S. Sudarshan, K. Surya Narain Rao, and Balraj Madhok, *Why Hindu Rashtra* (Delhi: Suruchi Prakashan, 1990). Deshmukh and Sheshadri are important functionaries of the RSS.

does not produce cohesion; a "melting pot" does.[42] Rather than run away from Hinduism, which is the source of India's culture, one should explicitly ground politics in Hinduism, not in laws and institutions:

> The Hindu *Rashtra* [nation] is essentially cultural in content, whereas the so-called secular concept pertains to the state and is limited to the territorial and political aspects of the Nation. . . . [T]he mere territorial-cum-political concept divorced from its cultural essence can never be expected to impart any sanctity to the country's unity. The emotional binding of the people can be furnished only by culture and once that is snapped then there remains no logical argument against the demand by any part to separate itself from the country.[43]

In their conception of Hinduism, however, Hindu nationalists fluctuate between two meanings of Hinduism—Hinduism as a civilization or culture, and Hinduism as a religion. According to them, "Hindu is not the name of a religious faith like the Muslim and the Christian; it denotes the national life here."[44] In the same vein, Advani once argued that because the term "Hindu" described the nation, Muslims could be called Muslim Hindus; Sikhs, Sikh Hindus; and Christians, Christian Hindus.[45] Hindu nationalists are right in saying that the term "Hindu," in its original meaning, meant those who lived in Hindustan (the everyday term for India in much of the North). However, over the last few centuries, "Hindu" has become a religious term, and "Indian" has replaced "Hindu" for the civilizational/national meaning.[46]

The dispute is not simply semantic. The term "Hindu" is further specified by Hindu nationalists. According to V. D. Savarkar, the ideological father of Hindu nationalism, "A Hindu means a person who regards this land . . . from the Indus to the Seas as his fatherland (*pitribhumi*) as well as his holy land (*punyabhumi*)."[47] The defini-

---

[42] I borrow this way of distinguishing the models from Ashis Nandy. See Ashis Nandy, "The Ramjanmabhumi Movement and the Fear of Self," paper presented at the South Asia Seminar, Harvard University, April 1992.

[43] H. V. Sheshadri, "Hindu Rashtra: What and Why," *Hindu Vishwa*, Vol. 25, no. 12, Silver Jubilee Special Issue, 1989–90, p. 30. *Hindu Vishwa* is the journal of the Vishwa Hindu Parishad.

[44] Ibid.

[45] Interview, *Sunday* (Calcutta), July 22, 1990.

[46] Robert Frykenberg, "Constructions of Hinduism at the Nexus of History and Religion," *Journal of Interdisciplinary History*, Vol. 23, no. 3, Winter 1993.

[47] V. D. Savarkar, *Hindutva* (Bombay: Veer Savarkar Prakashan, 1989), 6th ed., title page and pp. 110–13. *Hindutva* is the classic text of Hindu nationalism.

tion is thus territorial (land between the Indus and the Seas), genealogical ("fatherland"), and religious ("holy land"). Hindus, Sikhs, Jains, and Buddhists can be part of this definition, for they meet all three criteria: all of these religions were born in India. Christians, Jews, Parsis, and Muslims can meet only two, for India is not their holy land.

Can the non-Hindu groups be part of India? Only by assimilation, say the Hindu nationalists. Of the groups whose holy land is not India, Parsis and Jews, they argue, are already assimilated, having become part of the nation's mainstream.[48] This leaves the Muslims and Christians. "They," wrote Savarkar, "cannot be recognized as Hindus. For though *Hindustan* (India) to them is the Fatherland as to any other Hindu, yet it is not to them a holy land too. Their holy land is far off in Arabia or Palestine. Their mythology and godmen, ideas and heroes are not the children of this soil. Consequently their names and their outlook smack of a foreign origin. Their love is divided."[49]

With the departure of the British, Christianity lost its political edge, for it was no longer associated with the rulers. Ultimately, Muslims became the principal adversary of the Hindu nationalists—partly because of their numbers, and partly because a Muslim homeland in the form of Pakistan after all did lead to India's partition in 1947. Muslims were 25 percent of pre-1947 India, and even after the formation of Pakistan they remained the largest minority, constituting about 12 percent of the country's population at this time. Hence the enormous attention given to the Muslims by Hindu nationalists.

The Hindu nationalist claim is not that Muslims ought to be excluded from the Indian nation, though that may be the position of the extremists. One has only to hear the tapes of the recent speeches made by Sadhvi Ritambhra, a prominent VHP activist, to realize how much hatred the right wing has for the Muslims. "Assimilation," however, is the generic Hindu nationalist argument. That is, to become part of the Indian nation, Muslims must admit the centrality of Hinduism to Indian civilization; accept key Hindu figures such as Ram as civilizational heroes, not disown them as mere religious figures of Hinduism; remorsefully acknowledge that Muslim rulers of India between 1000 A.D. and 1757 A.D. destroyed pillars of Hindu civilization, especially Hindu temples; not claim special privileges such as maintenance of religious personal laws; and not demand special state grants for their educational institutions. By means of *ekya* (assimila-

[48] Nanaji Deshmukh, *Rethinking Secularism;* also, L. K. Advani in several speeches and interviews in recent years.

[49] V. D. Savarkar, *Hindutva,* p. 113.

tion), they will prove their loyalty to the nation. Maintaining distinctiveness would simply mean that "their love," as Savarkar put it, "is divided."[50]

Because of the insistence on assimilation to an India that is, in turn, defined as the land of the Hindus, the intended distinction between culture and religion breaks down. Specifically, Hindu nationalists make no attempt to incorporate Muslim symbols in their conceptions of Indian culture and history. Akbar, the tolerant Muslim ruler of the Mughal period, does not figure in their list of Indian heroes. Instead, Aurangzeb, the intolerant one, represents the Muslim essence. The Hindu nationalist attitude toward the great Mughal monuments such as the Taj Mahal also remains unclear. Many have objections even to the Muslim names of North Indian cities: Aligarh, they say, should be called Harigarh; Allahabad, Prayag; and Lucknow, Lakshmanpur.[51]

The Hindu nationalist discourse on Islam is selective and ominous. In India, Islam developed two broad forms: syncretist and exclusivist. Syncretistic Islam integrated into the preexisting Indian culture, just as in Indonesia Muslims retained their pre-Islamic heritage of the Ramayana and Mahabharata. Exclusivist Islam can be a personal faith, or may also enter the political sphere, thus becoming an ideology, sometimes displaying what are known as fundamentalist qualities.[52] Syncretistic Islam has produced some of the pillars of Indian culture, music, poetry, and literature. It is unclear how one can conceptualize India's culture *today* if Muslim influences are completely excluded. Moreover, many Indian Muslims have fought wars against Pakistan. By generating an anti-Muslim discourse, the Hindu nationalists risk embittering 110 million Muslims permanently, including those who are syncretistic in their religiosity and culture, as well as those for whom Islam is a faith, a way to sustain troubled private lives, but not a political ideology. One may argue that the political and ideological battle of nationalists is against Islamic fundamentalism and Muslim separatism. How can it be against everybody professing faith in Islam? In the Hindu nationalist discourse, these distinctions easily blur; an anti-Muslim hysteria is its natural outcome.

To secular nationalists, the terms "religion" and "culture" are clearly separable, and syncretism and tolerance are properties of all religions and communities in India. Consider the non-Hindu "heroes" of Indian civilization according to Nehru: Ashoka, a Buddhist; Kabir,

---

[50] Ibid., p. 115.

[51] Interviews with Hindu nationalists, Lucknow, January 1992.

[52] Ashis Nandy has suggested the distinction between faith and ideology in "The Politics of Secularism," *Alternatives*, Fall 1989.

a syncretistic saint, Muslim by birth; Amir Khusro, a Muslim who pioneered Indian classical music; Nanak, the first Sikh Guru; Akbar, a Mughal ruler. A celebration of Indian culture thus does not require being a Hindu. In Hindutva, the cultural and religious meanings of Hinduism blend into each other, and the distinction so critical for the secular nationalist disappears.

To sum up, Hindu nationalism has two simultaneous impulses: building a united India, and "Hinduizing" the polity and nation. Muslims or other groups are not excluded from the definition of India, but inclusion is premised upon assimilation and acceptance of the *political and cultural* centrality of Hinduism. If assimilation is not acceptable to the minorities, Hindu nationalism becomes exclusionary, both in principle and in practice.

It should also now be clear why secular and Hindu nationalisms are ideological adversaries, and have remained so for decades. In an ingenious way, Gandhi sought to combine the two. He was a Hindu and a nationalist, not a Hindu nationalist. He argued that his tolerance stemmed directly from his religiosity. Being a Hindu and having respect for Muslim culture, he argued, could go together easily. The essence of his belief is symbolized in one of his famous prayers, *Ramdhun*: *Ishwar Allah Tere Naam, Sabko Sanmati de Bhagvan* (God and Allah are two names of the same entity; may God give wisdom to everyone). He frequently referred to his appreciation of Christianity, Buddhism, and Jainism. More important for politics, he never defined India as a Hindu nation. The nation could incorporate all religions, and being a Muslim in no way meant not being an Indian.

Gandhi, of course, could not dissuade Jinnah and the Muslim League from making Pakistan. The failure of Gandhi to prevent the partition of India sent two signals. To the secular nationalists, it highlighted the antinomy between religion and Indian nationalism. To the Hindu nationalists, it reinforced their belief in the complementarity of Hinduism and the Indian nation on the one hand, and the basic contradiction between Islam and Indian nationalism on the other. "The attitude of the Muslims," argue Hindu nationalists, "was the reason for India's partition, an attitude that the Muslims are different from the Indian nation."[53] Since Gandhi's death, therefore, Hindu and secular nationalists have been locked in a conflict for political power and for the ideological shaping of India. The first battle for political and

[53] Deen Dayal Upadhyay, *Akhand Bharat aur Muslim Samasya* (Undivided India and the Muslim Problem) (Noida: Jagriti Prakashan, 1992), p. 1. Also see M. S. Golwalkar, *Rashtra* (Nation) (Delhi: Suruchi Prakashan, 1982), especially the chapter entitled "Musalman aur Hindu Rashtra" (Muslims and the Hindu Nation).

ideological hegemony after independence was won by secular nationalism; the battle today is not so clearly in favor of secular nationalists.

Why should Ayodhya as an issue have come alive in the 1980s, even though it existed as a potential source of conflict earlier? The BJP was part of the Janata coalition that ruled India between 1977 and 1979. L. K. Advani, who finally led the Ayodhya movement, was a cabinet minister in the Janata government. There was no talk of Ayodhya then. What was so distinctive about the circumstances of the 1980s?

This question cannot be fully answered at present. The rise of Hindu nationalism is obviously a complex phenomenon, calling for a multiple-level explanation. Until the social base of the BJP is properly researched, explanation in terms of social causes will be mainly speculative, though not incorrect for that reason. A political explanation can be given with greater confidence, partly because trends in the political realm are clearer than the linkages between social, cultural, or economic changes on the one hand and political developments on the other.

The Organizational Decay of the Congress Party

Once a powerful organization associated with the founding and building of a nation, the Congress Party has of late been a rusty, clay-footed colossus. Under Indira Gandhi (1966–84) and Rajiv Gandhi (1985–91), the decline of the Congress was precipitous. Electoral persistence coexisted with organizational emaciation. Nehru had used charisma to promote intraparty democracy, not to undermine it, strengthening the organization in the process. Indira Gandhi used her charisma to make the party utterly dependent on her, suspending intraparty democracy and elections, and weakening the organization as a result.

By the late 1980s, there was an organizational and ideological vacuum in Indian politics. Organizationally, the Congress was listless. Ideologically, it was not clear what it stood for. Though they professed secularism, its leaders were not afraid to use religion for political purposes, as Indira Gandhi did in Punjab. Though they professed socialism, some of its leaders were wholeheartedly willing to embrace the free market. The Congress was no longer a party but an undifferentiated, unanchored medley of individuals sustained by patronage. What was worse, most opposition parties followed the Congress lead. They did not have organizational elections either, nor for that matter did ideological cohesion exist.

There were two major exceptions to this institutional rot: the Communist Party of India–Marxist (CPM) and the BJP. The class-based mobilization of the CPM has some inherent limitations in India, making it hard for the CPM to extend popularity beyond isolated pockets. At the national level, the discipline of the BJP has emerged as the alternative to the Congress. If the available reports are correct, the demolition of the Babri mosque in Ayodhya was the party's first major failure in discipline.[54] Before that, in popular perception, the BJP came increasingly to be associated with a party that had discipline, probity, principles, and organization. The BJP was one of the few parties whose leaders voluntarily left office after their organizational terms expired. Having not been in government for long, it was not tainted with a lust for power or corruption.[55] Most politicians and parties looked hopelessly compromised by the end of the 1980s. It is to be seen whether these images of the BJP will survive the Ayodhya imbroglio.

Secularism and Muslim Politics

In India, secularism is not defined as a radical separation between the church and state.[56] The founders of the nation argued that in the Indian context, keeping the state equally distant from all religions was the best solution.

Unlike the clarity entailed in a radical church-state separation, secularism as equidistance is a nebulous concept. "Equal distance" can also be translated as "equal proximity." If it is alleged that the state is moving toward one particular religion, the state, to equalize the distance, can subsequently move toward other religions. Each such equalizing step may be aimed at soothing the religious communities. But the state gets more and more embroiled in religion. An unstable equilibrium results, breeding distrust all around. Under Nehru, equidistance was not turned into equiproximity. Under Rajiv Gandhi, the opposite happened.

The turning point was the Shah Bano case in 1986. Shah Bano, a Muslim woman, filed for maintenance after being divorced by her husband. The husband argued that maintenance was not permissible under Islamic law. Shah Bano sought protection under the country's civil law, not the Islamic personal code. The Supreme Court argued

[54] Interview, Atal Behari Vajpayee, *India Abroad*, December 18, 1992.

[55] Based on field interviews during the parliamentary elections of May–June 1991.

[56] For conceptual implications, see T. N. Madan, "Secularism in Its Place," *The Journal of Asian Studies*, November 1987, and his "Religion in India," *Daedalus*, Fall 1989.

that the country's civil law overrode any personal laws.[57] Faced with a Muslim furor, Rajiv Gandhi first supported the court. Then, to soothe Muslim feelings, he ordered his party to legislate a law that made the *shari'a* superior to the civil law in matters concerning maintenance of divorced Muslim women. A Hindu storm erupted. Then, the mosque-temple site in Ayodhya, closed for years, was opened to Hindu pilgrimage. A large demonstration of Muslims in Delhi followed, and riots broke out. Thus, ostensibly trying to equalize distance between religions, the government increasingly became trapped in religion.

The Shah Bano case gave Hindu nationalists a remarkable opportunity to press their claims on the disputed mosque-temple site. Hindu belief about the birthplace of Ram, argued Hindu nationalists, was enough for the construction of a Ram temple. Courts, they said, could not pronounce judgments on matters of faith. The government's response that civil laws had priority over religious faith (or religious laws) had become untenable. In the Shah Bano case, after all, the superiority of religious faith over civil law had already been affirmed by the government, and the Supreme Court had been overturned. The secular contention about the superiority of law over faith could not possibly apply to only one community.

After agitating for and getting a faith-based legislation, Muslim leaders also could not, without contradiction, claim the mosque on the basis of either a legal or a religious argument. The legal argument was that as a mosque, the building was their property and could not be destroyed. The religious argument was that a mosque was always a mosque even if it was not in use. By the time Advani led the mobilization to rebuild the Ram temple in 1990, these arguments were becoming part of the political process where a different logic operated.[58] Whatever the merits of the arguments, they had to be made acceptable to the masses.

---

[57] The Supreme Court also argued that even the *shari'a*, if read carefully, permitted maintenance. Muslims responded that a secular court had no business passing judgments on religious matters. Strictly speaking, the second argument was not required for the judgment. For the political controversy around the Shah Bano case, see Asghar Ali Engineer, *The Shah Bano Controversy* (Delhi: Ajanta Publishers, 1987). For the legal issues involved, see John Mansfield, "Personal Laws or a Uniform Civil Code?," in *Religion and Law in Independent India*, ed. Robert Baird (Delhi: Manohar Publications, 1993).

[58] John Mansfield, "Personal Laws," argues that legally speaking, both the secularists and Muslim leaders had a case. First of all, Indian courts since British times have mostly given precedence to religious laws on personal matters. The Supreme Court in the Shah Bano case broke the tradition by declaring the superiority of the civil code. Rajiv Gandhi merely restored an old practice. Secondly, the existing mosque, in legal terms, was also Muslim property, which called for protection. The legal verities, unfortunately, lost their meaning against the emerging political verities. Advani's political

It is in the political realm that the secular and Muslim leadership showed a remarkable lack of imagination and played into the hands of Hindu nationalists. So long as the issue was presented as a *mosque versus temple* issue, the dispute remained religious and could not generate a movement. Initially, the movement had been led by the VHP. When the BJP got involved, it presented the dispute as a *Ram versus Babur* issue. The mosque versus temple axis was religious. The Ram versus Babur axis acquired nationalistic overtones. Babur was unquestionably an alien conqueror, whereas Ram was not. Though several of Babur's descendants, especially Emperor Akbar, blended into India's culture, Babur himself remains an outsider in popular imagination. Contrariwise, though no Hindu god is uniformly popular all over India, Ram is one of the most popular gods in the pantheon. His popularity has made him both a religious and a cultural figure. The Ramayana is among the two most popular epics of India. An annual and hugely popular enactment of the tale of Ram (*Ramlila*), in which many Muslims have also traditionally participated, makes Ram part of everyday culture in much of India. One does not have to be religious to experience the Ramayana culturally.

The Muslim and secular leadership kept harping on the religious meaning of Ayodhya, refusing to encounter the second, nationalistic meaning.[59] Worse, the various mosque action committees (and the secular historians) initially argued that Ram was a mythological figure, for there was no historical proof for either Ram's existence or for his birthplace. This was a gratuitous argument. Core beliefs of many religions flourish without proof. How can one *prove* that Prophet Mohammed's hair was brought to a mosque in Srinagar as Muslims of Kashmir believe? Similarly, how can one prove that the enshrined tooth in Sri Lanka is Buddha's, or that Jesus was born to a virgin? Religious belief does not depend on rational evidence. If the *shari'a* was the word of God for which no proof was required, as the Muslim leaders had claimed in the Shah Bano controversy, how could proof be sought for a Hindu belief?

The problem was compounded by three more facts. First, the disputed mosque had not been used for several decades. Second, mosques are known to have been moved in the past, even in Muslim countries. Finally, while the Muslim leadership was conducting its

---

mobilization was indeed enormous, making legal intricacies largely irrelevant against the rising political tide.

[59] Javed Habib, a member of the BMAC, was among the few Muslim politicians to demonstrate a keen appreciation of this meaning. See Javed Habib, "Main Bhi Ram Ko Maryada Purushottam Manta Hun" (I also accept Ram as a symbol of moral excellence [in this culture]), *Dharmyuga*, January 16, 1991.

struggle to save the Babri mosque, some of the most visible leaders of the Muslim community, among them Shahabuddin and Imam Bukhari, chose a strategy that was symbolically disastrous. In 1987 they called for the boycott of India's Republic Day. In January 1991 some of them tried to develop an alliance with Sikh separatists bent upon undermining the nation. The aim, according to them, was to draw attention to their demands. The strategy did not go down well with a large number of secular Indians, let alone Hindu nationalists. Republic Day was a matter of pride for the entire nation, not simply for the Hindus. The fight was presumably with Hindu bigotry, not with India as a nation. Some of India's Muslim leaders did indeed reject the call for boycott. Unfortunately, prominent leaders like Imam Bukhari and Shahabuddin continued undeterred.

As I have argued, Indian Islam has taken syncretistic as well as separatist forms. Most Muslims are syncretistic in their culture, if not in their religious beliefs. Why Muslim leaders chose dangerous symbolic politics is an unresolved puzzle. A reaction against the existing Muslim leadership is emerging, and many Muslims have begun to make the argument that Muslim leadership in India has not taken good care of the Muslim community.[60]

What kind of Muslim leadership would best represent the interests of Muslims, and whether that leadership will emerge, is increasingly becoming a central question of Indian politics. In addition to Ayodhya, Muslim leadership was also an issue in the Jamia controversy that attracted a great deal of political and media attention in the summer of 1992. In an interview given to a magazine over Salman Rushdie's *Satanic Verses*, Professor Mushirul Hasan, pro-vice chancellor of Jamia Milia (a university founded in 1920 by Muslims committed to Indian nationalism), argued that even though *The Satanic Verses* was offensive to many Muslims, the government's ban on the book was not justified because Rushdie had a right to free speech. The interview touched off a student agitation on campus. On the charge that Hasan had defended the "apostate" Rushdie and thereby offended Muslim sentiments, the students demanded his resignation. A well-known scholar, Hasan refused to resign on the grounds that as an academic, he had the freedom to express his views.[61] As Hasan continued to defy the student pressure for resignation and the Hindu-Muslim situation worsened with developments in Ayodhya, the

[60] *India Today*, February 15, 1993. Also see Muslim critiques in *Saptahik Hindustan* (December 1992).

[61] For details, see Louise Fernandes, "Rhyme and Punishment," *Sunday*, April 12–18, 1992, and "Verses of Contention," *Sunday*, May 17–23, 1992.

students finally attacked Hasan in December, injuring him in the process.[62]

The Jamia controversy raised two important political issues. The first issue has to do with Muslim political leadership. University students in India have made many irrational demands in the past; irrationality therefore is not confined to Jamia students. It is perfectly conceivable that many students were genuinely hurt by Professor Hasan's remarks. The situation required delicate handling by the Muslim leaders if they got involved in the dispute, and they soon did. However, instead of defending Hasan's right to speak as an academic and as a citizen (a right guaranteed by the Indian Constitution) while at the same time trying to persuade students not to push religion into an academic matter, they supported the students' demand for Hasan's resignation even as students were turning unruly and issuing violent threats against Hasan. The conclusion seemed inescapable that the Muslim leadership was not ready to tolerate dissent even from a widely respected Muslim intellectual.

The second important issue raised by the Jamia controversy concerns the mounting anxiety of India's Muslim middle class. That a relatively harmless interview given by a respected member of the Muslim community led to such political furor indicates the level of anxiety being experienced by the Muslim middle class about its identity and the possible threats to it.[63] Sadly, even those Muslim scholars and intellectuals who identify with the Muslim community but wish to introduce debate and discussion on matters of importance to the community can be suspect and targets of attack. The context of mounting Muslim anxieties calls for an imaginative effort on the part of India's intellectuals and politicians. Muslim politicians will have to play a critical role in this process; supporting each act of defiance by members of the community, however politically or legally inappropriate, will simply add to those anxieties, not alleviate them. The challenge before the Muslim leadership is to inspire confidence not only in the Muslim community, but also in India at large. Symbols, language, and issues have to be identified that will allow both tasks to be undertaken simultaneously.

---

[62] *Times of India*, December 7, 1992.

[63] For an insightful analysis of the problems of Muslim identity, see Akeel Bilgrami, "What Is a Muslim? Fundamental Commitment and Cultural Identity," *Critical Inquiry*, Summer 1992.

Conclusion

Inevitably, what happens to India now depends on who rules and what the ruling ideology is going to be. At the national level, there are four possibilities. The first is a continuation of Congress rule, though with a changed, pro-market economic ideology (with or without a revived party organization). The second is the rise of the BJP to national power with the center-right in command. The third scenario is the rise of the BJP with the right wing in command. And the fourth is a non-Congress coalition, or a coalition of the Congress with other anti-BJP parties. If Hindu nationalism were to come to power at all, the second scenario could be its relatively peaceful face as it would probably entail an inclusive view of Hinduism. Whether the moderates can define BJP politics remains unclear. Much depends on where the most popular leaders of the BJP, still in the moderate right camp, go and how well they communicate with the base; how the Congress behaves; and whether Muslim politics will change at all.

The third scenario—the right wing in power—would mean the end of India as a civilization (and perhaps also the breakup of its territory). As Ayodhya has shown, the right wing is bigoted, communal, and exclusive. Hatred is the cornerstone of its politics. It would bring back the hatred associated with the 1947 partition, not the tolerance that created India as a nation. To believe that 110 million Muslims can be beaten into submission is to believe a lie, and a dangerous one.

Lacking ideological stalwarts at the moment—politicians willing or capable of mobilizing the masses—the Congress is almost certain to play the "economic card" in the short run. By unleashing more, and deeper, economic reforms, it will try to change the political agenda, thereby also seeking to lower the religious temperature in the country. In a legislative sense, the Congress government is not in trouble and can risk dramatic reform. Given the support of two smaller parties—the Janata Dal(A) and the breakaway Telugu Desam—it has a majority in the lower house.

It is not clear, however, that an economic shift in the country's political agenda, while welcome in itself, will be enough to combat the BJP. Faced with such a shift, the BJP's interest would obviously lie in returning to questions of national identity. Since the Congress is not the only major player in politics, it may not be able to control the agenda fully. There is perhaps no escape from the larger ideological issues.

Much, therefore, is at stake. Politics created a nation in the first half of the century. Politics will revive it, add to its troubles, or even unmake it. Syncretism, pluralism, and tolerance—defended as attributes of Indian culture as it has historically existed, not simply of Hinduism, and placed at the center of India's political discourse—remain India's best bet. The political party that can give a forceful and organized political expression to this cultural reading has the best chance of keeping India together. It is not clear which political party will mount an *ideological* challenge to the BJP on these lines.

2
Foreign Policy in 1992: Building Credibility

Paul Kreisberg

India's efforts to increase its relevance to the rest of the world were given new credibility in 1992 by the economic liberalization policies of Prime Minister P. V. Narasimha Rao's administration. The traditional tripod of Indian foreign policy over the preceding 40 years—national unity and integrity, nonalignment, and self-reliance—was not abandoned. But India's relations with the major industrial states, its links with Russia, its attitude toward the rest of Asia, and its relations with the old "nonaligned world" are in the process of undergoing major change. Indian president R. Venkataraman's speech opening the February 1992 parliament (Lok Sabha) session aptly summarized both the continuity and the change in Indian policy and articulated some important new themes.

The unity and territorial integrity of India was the president's first priority. This emphasis conveyed the continuing importance to India's foreign and domestic policies of India-Pakistan relations as well as of tensions elsewhere along India's borders. India's relations with its immediate neighbors during 1992 remained uneasy. Some progress was made on reducing prospects for accidental conflict with Pakistan, and both countries made it clear that they were determined to avert another war. But continuing violence in Kashmir, several dangerous incidents along the Kashmir line of control, and domestic political weakness in both countries prevented any progress on either the Kashmir issue or other outstanding bilateral disputes.

The second priority was geopolitical security, stability, and peace in the region. India achieved considerable success during 1992 in broadening its defense and political contacts and significantly enhancing its relations during the year with all the key countries whose policies could affect its security—the United States, Russia, China, Singapore, Malaysia, Israel, Japan, Iran, and the new Central Asian States (CAS).

The third priority was India's economic well-being. Including this in a discussion of India's foreign policy represents a major shift from earlier years. However, this theme has been progressively emerging in Indian foreign policy over the last six years. India's leaders now acknowledge openly that their foreign policy must increasingly focus on countries capable of contributing to the success of India's economic liberalization policies. "Self-reliance" has been replaced by a new stress upon the need for India to compete effectively in international markets, for Indian manufacturers and service industries to enhance their competitiveness within India by going "head-to-head" with foreign competition, and for India to provide an investment climate that can successfully woo foreign investment, credits, and technology from more developed trade and investment partners.

Despite domestic political and economic resistance to these objectives during the year, there was strong evidence that national policy had changed: steady progress in altering Indian laws and regulations to attract foreign investment, growing foreign interest in India as a new economic partner, and incipient—albeit slower than hoped for—progress in increasing Indian exports and raising the quality of Indian manufactures. Government approvals of foreign investment from the West and Asia rose six times in 1991 over 1990 and another six times in 1992 over 1991. In 1992 these amounted to just over US$1 billion, indicating vividly the sharp rise from a scarcely noticeable base only two years earlier.

The fourth and final priority—a brand new one—was to link India with a "resurgent Asia." India has given little attention to East and Southeast Asia in earlier decades other than as part of its long political rivalry with China and the broader nonaligned movement. In 1992 China, Malaysia, and South Korea were increasingly cited by Indian officials and scholars as models for India to follow, both in their specific policies and for their economic achievements. Indian policymakers groped for the best means of attracting the interest and attention of these Asian states, not always successfully, but consistently throughout the year.

Not singled out in the president's remarks was the collapse and disintegration of the Soviet Union, which dramatically affects India's foreign policy and its defense and economic priorities. India had been in the process of adjusting to the changes in the global environment that began in the late 1980s, but the breakup of the USSR in 1991 came as a particularly unwelcome shock.

India had depended on Moscow for 70 percent of its imported weapons and spare parts. These were now increasingly difficult to get, and Indian officials were forced in 1992 into complex and frequently unsuccessful negotiations with a half-dozen new states that had emerged from the former USSR. Serious logistical and readiness problems confronted the Indian armed forces throughout the year. These, understandably, were downplayed by government spokespersons but nonetheless were potentially critical for Indian security.

Moreover, the USSR had been India's second largest trading partner and a major source of oil. Trade with the former socialist bloc states dropped dramatically—by 64.4 percent.[1] This seriously and adversely affected India's overall trade performance in 1992.

A new strategic threat potentially appeared in the shape of linkages between Pakistan and the new Muslim-majority states of Central Asia, at least one of which, Kazakhstan, had stockpiles of nuclear weapons and missiles. Indian high-level exchanges with and new aid programs to several of the Central Asian States, as well as negotiations with Iran, were intended to build diplomatic and economic bridges to this area, avert the growth of a new Islamic alliance that might be directed against India, find new sources of oil as well as markets for Indian goods, and ensure that trade routes into Russia through the CAS remained open.

Finally, in his policy remarks early in 1992 President Venkataraman could not have anticipated the Hindu-Muslim riots that swept through numerous Indian cities at the end of the year, but these clearly were of fundamental importance to Indian foreign policy goals. The government knew there was danger of violence if a peaceful solution to the bitter and intensely emotional claims over a mosque standing on an allegedly sacred Hindu site in the northern state of Uttar Pradesh was not found. The violence, arson, and national shock in the face of about 1,700 deaths that occurred in December 1992 and early 1993 in northern and western India underscored two central points of uncertainty about the course of Indian policy in the coming years:

- Hindu nationalism is clearly rising, fueled by economic frustration among the urban lower-middle class and unemployed, political frustration at rampant political corruption and venality, and a yearning for a greater sense of Indian identity in broad sectors of Indian society. The Bharatiya Janata Party (BJP), the political party that most strongly symbolizes these demands and has been

[1] This figure is for April–December 1992, although Indian trade data are usually compiled on an April–March basis for each fiscal year. Source of figures: Indian Embassy, Washington, D.C.

growing most rapidly in the last three years, has a different policy agenda from the ruling Congress Party. This includes an emphasis on Indian military power, including an explicit nuclear weapons program, greater assertiveness in defending any challenge to Indian territorial or national interests by its neighbors, and greater suspicion of foreign investment despite overall support for domestic economic liberalization, all positions that could seriously derail India's efforts to improve its relations with its neighbors and with other countries.

- The current course of Indian economic development and reform could be undermined by deterioration in the domestic political and social environment. Western and Asian states could become more hesitant to commit themselves to investment and trade with India, vital cooperative relations with major international financial institutions could be undermined, and democratic institutions and human rights practices could be severely impaired, producing a series of confrontations with the United States and other Western states.

Despite this uncertainty, however, the overall picture of India's foreign relations in 1992 and early 1993 was of a nation that was succeeding in broadening the canvas of its economic, political, and security relationships, working through major changes in the priorities attached to relations with various countries in previous years, and trying to mesh these changes with complex domestic political and economic challenges. These elements have not always come together, and the most uncertain of all are the domestic political factors. Nevertheless, the direction in which the current Indian administration is striving to go is generally clear and, despite some setbacks, progress has been considerable.

The Subcontinent

Pakistan

India-Pakistan relations were aptly summed up by Prime Minister Rao in his Independence Day speech on August 15:

> Whenever the situation comes or an opportunity arises to take a step forward [with Pakistan], something happens somewhere which puts us right back to square one. Who is doing this, why it is being done, and how it is being done is anyone's guess but I understand we must continue this dialogue.[2]

[2] *Foreign Broadcast Information Service* (FBIS), NES-92-163, August 21, 1992, p. 31.

At the beginning of 1992, Rao met with Prime Minister Nawaz Sharif of Pakistan at the Davos Economic Conference in Switzerland. Sharif told reporters afterward that 1992 would be a year of reconciliation between the two countries. Rao said that each was trying to understand the other's opinions, problems, and difficulties so as to promote friendship and good relations. There were three further meetings between the two prime ministers—in Rio de Janeiro, Jakarta, and New York—and encouraging and positive comments were made after each, but by the end of the year relations had not improved measurably between the two countries.

The simplest and probably most accurate explanation is that domestic political challenges made it impossible for either prime minister to take initiatives that might lead to a fundamental change in the relationship. Both leaders had sharply divided political parties and confronted political opponents willing to torpedo any policy initiative in order to gain domestic political advantage. And both had to deal with mass constituencies conditioned for decades to believe and accept the worst of the neighboring state.

Kashmir. At the center of the dispute between India and Pakistan is Jammu and Kashmir, the huge Muslim-majority state whose Hindu ruler acceded to India rather than Pakistan in 1947. The subject of three wars between India and Pakistan, the Kashmir Valley, the smallest but most densely populated part of the state, has been in turmoil now for five years. More than 500,000 Indian military and paramilitary forces are believed to be involved in maintaining order against more than 100 militant groups (although only five or six of these represent major threats) who disagree among themselves over whether Jammu and Kashmir should become part of Pakistan, be independent, or have some other form of government but who share a common hostility to Indian rule. Most of the Kashmir Valley's Hindu population has been forced to take refuge in Jammu or elsewhere in India.

The international human rights community, together with increasing numbers of Indian human rights groups, has for several years focused attention on human rights violations in Jammu and Kashmir by both Indian security forces and Kashmiri militants. The evidence—or at least the burden of the accusation—has been far heavier against the security forces, who bear an added moral burden as forces of government.

One of the striking developments in 1992 was the growing sensitivity of the Indian government to such accusations. An official Human Rights Commission was established by the prime minister during the year, but for most of 1992 this had little effect on the willingness of authorities in Kashmir to acknowledge problems. Although a major general was dismissed and several soldiers sentenced to long prison terms for human rights violations during the year, the government was reluctant even to admit this or permit the information to be published. In December, however, following an alleged "police riot" in a Kashmir town north of the capital in which more than 100 persons were reported killed and hundreds of houses destroyed in retaliation for the death of two paramilitary soldiers, the government announced that a formal court inquiry would be convened to investigate the entire incident.

India argues that the insurrection has been stimulated and supplied from Pakistan. The origins of the uprising are complex but almost certainly have been internally driven by events in Kashmir itself and by callous manipulation over many years by New Delhi of politicians and politics in the state, not created by Pakistan. But Pakistan has certainly encouraged and helped supply the militants, or at least turned a blind eye to the training of guerrillas and the transfer of weapons by interested groups within Pakistan. The United States during 1992 began increasing pressure on Pakistan to halt the smuggling or transfer of arms to both Kashmiri and Punjabi militants, warning that continuation would risk Pakistan's being declared a "terrorist state" under U.S. law and being cut off from any military or economic trade.

Pakistan is convinced that India has been retaliating against it by stimulating anti-government attitudes in the Pakistani state of Sindh, which adjoins the Indian border with Rajasthan and Gujarat, and encouraging violence and criminal activity to the point that in mid-year the Pakistan army was sent in to restore order. India is determined that it must hold on to Jammu and Kashmir or be forced to acknowledge that its grand secular experiment has failed—an admission that would have potentially catastrophic consequences for national unity. The dilemma for both India and Pakistan is whether there is a middle ground on the Kashmir issue.

As both governments found themselves unable to agree even to begin official discussions about Kashmir (although there were repeated hints that this process was about to start), informal groups of Indians and Pakistanis, and Kashmiris as well, began to discuss what might be done. A poll of urban Indians in October 1992 found two-thirds supportive of negotiations between the two governments, with only 29 percent opposed.[3] What kind of concessions, if any, the two-thirds who favor negotiations would accept is uncertain, though they would probably be within the broad context of association with the Indian

[3] "Indian Elites Value U.S. Ties but Wary of U.S. Influence," *Opinion Research Memorandum* (USIA, Washington, D.C.), March 24, 1992, p. 17.

Union. Even if the public is more tolerant than politicians believe, there are no signs of the strong political leadership that would be required to achieve an acceptable solution.

If there was a shadow of hope, it lay in such murky areas as the use by Kashmiris of all affiliations of a single ambiguous word—"azadi"—to express their aspirations. Since "azadi" means self-governance, self-determination, independence, autonomy, and many similar abstractions, the question was whether some form of "azadi" that met Kashmiri, Indian, and Pakistani political needs might be found. There were hints on both sides of an interest in exploring this approach, but at the end of the year neither government was prepared to take the initiative.

The BJP not only has opposed any "concessions" on Kashmir but wants to reverse even those granted in the early 1950s, which in theory limited New Delhi's control to defense, communication, and money; it proposes to make Kashmir an ordinary state within the Indian Union, opening it to settlers from elsewhere in India and ensuring that in a limited period of time it would become a Hindu-majority state.

Given the other economic, political, social, and security priorities on the agenda of the government in New Delhi, compromise and concessions on Kashmir were not even dimly in view despite occasional comments by Rao after his meetings with Nawaz Sharif.

Military Tensions. As dialogue stagnated between India and Pakistan, a confrontation both sides agreed was pointless continued at the Siachen Glacier, 20,000 feet above sea level, in the far northeastern part of Kashmir close to the Tibetan border, where more soldiers regularly died of exposure and pneumonia than combat, and India was reportedly spending roughly $1 million a day to sustain its forces. Agreement to withdraw to lower altitudes and halt fighting had been reached in 1989, but neither side could agree on the points to which forces should withdraw and how to describe the "line of control" in the area. Both sides continued a battle of spies, with expulsion of agents from embassies on either side and charges of torture and beating. Although a modest understanding on treatment of civilian officials and diplomats was achieved, shortly before the end of the year Pakistan was bitterly protesting the alleged murder of two civilian Pakistani visitors to Punjab, while India insisted that the two had been caught red-handed working with Sikh militants and slain in a shootout.

Efforts to resolve long-standing arguments over the effect of water flow into Pakistani territory should India pursue certain engineering improvements on a reservoir in Kashmir, and over the point at which the Sir Creek flowed into the Arabian Sea and thereby determined Indian and Pakistani territorial waters, remain stalled. Appeals to increase trade, ease travel regulations, simplify acquisition of books and other publications, and expand cultural interchange, which had been agreed upon in earlier years, fell on deaf bureaucratic and political ears in both countries.

Nevertheless, both countries did make progress on confidence-building measures in the areas of both conventional and nuclear weapons. Senior political and military leaders on both sides publicly and repeatedly were quoted in the press as saying that war was "unthinkable." Agreements were concluded on several confidence-building measures relating to military deployments and exercises and the identification of nuclear sites in both countries. The exchange of views on current problems may have contributed to holding relations steadier than might otherwise have been the case after the destruction of the Babri mosque in December.

Moreover, during the year Pakistan took steps twice, and at considerable domestic political risk, to halt marches by thousands of Pakistani Kashmiris across the line of control into Indian-held Kashmir, which could have led to serious casualties and new cross-border tensions. Pakistan's defense minister was clearly serious when he stated in mid-August that there was "no possibility of armed conflict between Pakistan and India on the Kashmir dispute. . . . [B]oth desire to negotiate and decide issues by putting their cases [forward] rather than taking decisions by force. . . . The use of force will be no option."[4]

Japan and Germany have cautioned India and Pakistan that unless both reduce military expenditures, the two major aid donors to the subcontinent will reduce their assistance, although little was done in 1992 to follow through on these warnings. Other donors through international aid consortia may begin to add their own pressure. Pakistan alleges that Indian security expenditures on Jammu and Kashmir already virtually equal Pakistan's entire defense budget. It is hard to prove such broad allegations, but the drain on both nations' economies is clearly a serious burden on economic development and growth.

Hindu-Muslim Tensions. The political importance of Hindu-Muslim relations for the subcontinent was underscored by the fact that the salient "foreign policy" event of 1992 was actually a domestic incident, the destruction in December of the Babri mosque in Ayodhya, Uttar

[4] *FBIS*, NES-92-160, August 18, 1992, p. 50.

Pradesh.[5] Once the mosque was demolished, rioting and looting swept dozens of Indian cities throughout the country, causing some 1,700 deaths. Limited retaliatory violence against Hindus in neighboring Bangladesh and Pakistan erupted. Both governments moved swiftly to halt the violence but sharply condemned Indian failure to protect Muslims. After a two-week period of relative calm at the end of the year, new communal violence erupted in Bombay, India's most sophisticated and modern city and the nation's banking and financial center, in which more than 500 people were reportedly killed.

Local criminal gangs, corrupt landlords, and anti-Muslim political groups were all involved in the violence, and for a week, the police and other security forces seemed unwilling or unable to contain or halt the killing, looting, and arson. This was a particular source of concern to Indian and foreign business leaders, and symbolic demonstrations of power by the Indian army were used to ensure order in city after city.

The net effect was to cast a new pall over all forms of India-Pakistan dialogue, at least for the moment. The violence emphasized the extent to which political leaders on both sides are constrained by fanatical and violent forces that threaten to repudiate any moves toward reconciliation.

Burma, Nepal, and Bangladesh

India's relations with the smaller countries of South Asia were uneven during the year, but essentially positive. Burmese expulsions of Muslim tribals (Rohingyas) into Bangladesh beginning at the end of 1991 became troubling for India when Islamic "fundamentalist" militancy began to grow among the refugees, spurred, India believed, by propaganda and activists from the Middle East. In July India protested to Burma against military intrusions into India's tribal eastern state of Mizoram and intensified its own patrolling of the border. By September India was concerned over the onward movement into India of as many as 20,000 of the 200,000 Burmese refugees in Bangladesh. The issue began to fade late in the year as Burma and Bangladesh worked out arrangements for the return of refugees.

Official relations with Nepal were generally good. Both countries agreed on new cooperation over a hydroelectric dam project that had been pending for several years, but in Nepal, the issue remained deeply controversial politically and had not been approved by the Ne-

[5] For details on events leading up to the destruction of the mosque and further discussion of its political implications, see Chapter 1 in this volume.

palese parliament by spring 1993. An Indian decision to make Nepali a new "national" language was a gesture to the many persons of Nepali origin in northern India who for years had sought greater recognition and even autonomy. The Nepalis on their side were increasingly cooperative with Indian security efforts to counter cross-border movement by "terrorists" and "criminal elements," particularly those involved in supporting Sikh militants in the northern districts of Uttar Pradesh.

India-Bangladesh relations blew hot and cold during the year, but overall the relationship seemed better by year's end, except for the aftermath of Hindu-Muslim violence following the Babri mosque incident. On the "plus" side was resolution of a territorial dispute whose roots went back to partition. A tiny enclave of Bengalis within India was finally linked to Bangladesh by the transfer, under a perpetual lease, of a strip of land 176 meters long and 60 meters wide. The agreement was greeted as a major policy success in Bangladesh and by most Indians, but was sharply criticized by Indian nationalists as abandonment of rightful Indian land. Other major issues involving distribution and control over water resources and transit of Indian goods to other parts of India across Bangladesh territory remained on the agenda and were discussed amicably, but agreement seemed as distant as in the past.

On the more negative side were Indian plans to deport "illegal" migrants from Bangladesh back home. India insists that hundreds of thousands of illegal Bengali settlers have infiltrated Indian territory along the border for years. Bangladesh categorically denies this. India ultimately suspended deportation plans (only 132 refugees were reportedly in the initial batch), but the problem, which has high political resonance in both countries, is unlikely to disappear. In the short term India announced that it would limit its actions to accelerating the building of roads and fences all along the Bangladesh border (900 kilometers of which had already been fenced in the last few years) in an effort to reduce new illegal immigration. The issue is particularly sensitive for both the Communist Party of India–Marxist government in West Bengal and the Congress government in New Delhi. The illegal immigrants have aroused Hindu nationalist feelings in border districts of West Bengal that were largely responsible for increasing BJP votes in the 1992 elections in that state to 12 percent of the total compared to 1 percent three years earlier.

Nonalignment and Geopolitical Security

The "nonaligned" leg of Indian foreign policy was partially sustained by New Delhi but in a lower key than in any year since the early 1950s. This classic ideological theme in Indian foreign policy had been gradually diminishing, like Lewis Carroll's Cheshire cat, since the mid-1980s, and now little seemed to be left but its "smile."

Indian foreign secretary J. N. Dixit made this explicit in his description of India's new foreign policy in an August interview.[6] That policy, he said, was "realistic" and "practical" rather than focused on some "hypothetical norms of India's role and importance in world affairs." Nonalignment now meant only that "India shall retain freedom of taking decisions in tune with our own perceived interest," as distinct from the ideological flavor it had during the cold war.

Nevertheless, the Nonaligned Summit in Jakarta, September 1–6, 1992, provided an opportunity for Narasimha Rao to show the Cheshire cat "smile" and restate traditional Indian views about cooperation among developing countries against developed-country pressures, including on human rights, in nonpolemical terms. The concept of nonalignment still resonates for some Indian officials and for a still influential domestic political constituency that remains committed to the ideals of socialism, opposition to capitalist exploitation, and anti-colonialism. The basic theme of the 1992 summit, however, was cooperation, not confrontation, with the West, which fit India's new policy priorities, and indeed the priorities of most of the participating nations.

Russia, the Former USSR States, and Afghanistan

Russia. Money, trade, and resources were at the heart of India-Russia relations in 1992, and negotiations over these dominated bilateral exchanges until January 1993 when President Boris Yeltsin visited New Delhi on a twice-postponed trip. Russia was no longer a reliable supplier of weapons, a reliable source for petroleum products, or even a reliable partner in nuclear energy.

India's large debt in uncleared rupee balances for past Soviet trade and aid was not the most urgent problem in the relationship during the year, but it hung like an albatross around the necks of negotiators on a broad range of issues. The ruble had been falling like a stone on the open market (from rubles .57=US$1 at the beginning of 1992 to rubles 420=US$1 at the end of the year), and agreeing on prices for

[6] *India News* (Indian Embassy), Washington, D.C., August 16–31, 1992, pp. 3–4, Vol. 31, no. 16.

current transactions as well as for repayment of past debt was difficult.[7]

In a complex agreement signed during the Yeltsin trip, both sides compromised, expressing some dissatisfaction with the deal but accepting it as the best that could be reached. Total debt was denominated in rupees (Rs. 317 billion) with two-thirds to be paid off over 12 years at a January 1990 ruble/rupee rate of exchange (Rs. 19.9=1 ruble) and one-third over 45 years at a January 1992 rate (Rs. 32.57=1 ruble). The Indians calculated this would represent about a one-third total reduction in India's debt service each year.

Throughout 1992 Russian negotiators insisted that India pay in hard currency for most products Russia had agreed to provide, including petroleum shipments (Russia had originally committed itself to provide 4 million tons of oil and 1 million tons of other petroleum products), although exceptions were made for some military supplies. But the real problem was the inability of Russians to supply anything at all.

In January negotiators concluded a memorandum of understanding on the supply of military spare parts; in February both sides worked out the "deal" for India to pay for military and certain industrial equipment in rupees and for oil, wheat, and fertilizer in hard currency. But virtually nothing came through the pipeline. Another round of negotiations in May seemed to confirm arrangements for dollar clearing of trade and for maintaining continuity in defense supplies. By the middle of June, however, Indian military procurement specialists were desperately searching through Russia, the Ukraine, and Eastern Europe for military spares that Russia was not providing. By mid-October only 60,000 tons of the 5 million tons of POL products promised early in the year had arrived, and it was only at the end of November that a further 80,000–100,000 tons actually reached Indian ports.

Indian defense training and operational exercises were sharply cut back as a result of shortages of spares (70 percent of Indian military equipment was from the former USSR, and no more than 45 percent of any major defense system was produced in India). Air defense and radar equipment, helicopters, naval anti-ship surface-to-air missiles, self-propelled guns, and routine maintenance throughout the armed forces were seriously affected. Then–defense minister Sharad Pawar

[7] Exchange rates are drawn from the Hong Kong Dao Heng spot rates published each week in the *Far Eastern Economic Review*. These are different from the figures cited in the next paragraph in the India-Soviet debt agreement of January 1993, which significantly overstate the value of the ruble on the open market and thus the amount of Indian debt.

went personally to Moscow and Ukraine in September in a desperate effort to resolve the problem and concluded it would not be easily solved.

One option proposed by the Russians was to move entire defense manufacturing plants to India. This would not only meet India's defense needs but provide spares for weapon systems Russia was selling elsewhere in the region. During Russian president Boris Yeltsin's late January 1993 visit to New Delhi, agreement was reached to do just this as well as to continue a broad range of cooperation in technology transfers and training. How this was to be paid for was not made public during the visit. Nor were the details of arrangements for continuing barter trade between the two countries announced. The problem, however, had been as much over actually procuring equipment and parts as over the form of payment, and it remained uncertain how and whether this would be improved in 1993.

Nevertheless, India was sufficiently encouraged by the talks with Moscow that it lost no time in following through with a prime potential partner in Southeast Asia—Malaysia—which had been dickering for a year with Moscow on purchasing MIG-29s and other Soviet military aircraft equipment. For Malaysia a key consideration was whether it would be able to find a reliable source of spare parts. India and Malaysia agreed in early February 1993 to discuss arrangements for such supply and potentially for joint production as well. The defense ministers of both countries concluded a memorandum of understanding in Kuala Lumpur that would, the Malaysian minister said at the signing, "widen the scope of bilateral cooperation to include joint ventures, procurements, and logistical and maintenance support." His Indian partner added that the agreement would enable India and Malaysia to address "common security concerns" in the region.

India hoped to turn a serious defense spare-parts problem into a new opportunity for expanding economic and political relations with a key member of ASEAN, broadening its credibility as a security partner in the region, and strengthening its prospective competitive position in the regional "arms sales" market. Unfortunately, it was still unclear late in the spring of 1993 whether Malaysia would actually buy Russian aircraft or whether it was simply bargaining for U.S. planes, which it hoped to be able to buy at sharply reduced prices as a result of the new competitive environment in arms sales. Nevertheless, the increasing numbers of Soviet weapons being sold around the world presented an opportunity to a country like India that could offer a reliable selection of spare parts and maintenance assistance. This opportunity may have been behind the defense minister's hope to double Indian military exports from a modest $40 million in 1992 to $80 million in 1993.

In short, throughout 1992 Russia was a "problem" for India, affecting its defense and economic policies in many ways. And, despite the positive twist given to Yeltsin's visit to India, the trip did not go as well as it might have. A participant in the discussions observed on his return home that Russia would not provide two nuclear reactors for India because terms could not be agreed upon, and that any cooperation in the nuclear field was uncertain because of India's refusal to sign the Nonproliferation Treaty. A new (as yet unpublished) India-Russia cooperation treaty was concluded, but this was believed to be far blander than its 1970 counterpart (with its provision for close security cooperation).

The relationship with Russia has clearly changed, underscoring the importance of new relationships with the West and the rest of Asia. In this context it is not surprising that polls of public opinion among Indian college graduates showed a drop from a "good" or "very good" opinion of Russia or the USSR, from 88 percent in November 1990 to 56 percent in October 1992.[8]

The Central Asian States and Afghanistan. India's efforts begun in 1991 to build new relationships with the new Central Asian States of the former USSR continued, but with relatively modest success. India had little money to offer in direct economic aid, Indian investments were limited to a few enterprising hotel builders, and communication links with the CAS were difficult.

India agreed to broaden trade and agricultural cooperation with the Kyrgyz Republic and to provide training in foreign affairs, agriculture, banking, and management. By the end of 1992, however, it had not responded to a Kyrgyz offer to sell enriched uranium to India under International Atomic Energy Agency (IAEA) safeguards.

Similar agreements on broad economic cooperation were reached with Uzbekistan and the Turkmen Republic, and trade with Kazakhstan had already been put high on the agenda by an agreement at the end of 1991. A major problem for India, and for Pakistan as well in its parallel efforts to pursue relations with the area, was physical communication other than by air. India negotiated arrangements with Iran for the shipment of goods through the Persian Gulf up to the Black Sea and then on into Central Asia, and this complicated route began to operate by mid-1992. Nevertheless, prospects for substantially expanding trade in the medium term seemed small.

---

[8] "Indian Elites More Positive on U.S. Ties, but Negative on NPT," *Opinion Research Memorandum* (USIA, Washington, D.C.), December 15, 1992, p. 7.

Should Afghanistan become more stable and India-Pakistan relations improve, the vision shared by India and Pakistan of greatly expanded trade in energy and other products through new rail and road links, financed substantially by Iran, may become feasible. But these seem only faint, though enthusiastically touted, prospects until much later in the decade, at the earliest. India's diplomatic relations with the communist Afghan government throughout the Afghan war do not promise strong influence by New Delhi in the complicated Afghan politics of the postwar period.

Growing Ties with the United States

Momentum for improving India-U.S. relations began under Rajiv Gandhi during his first administration in the mid-1980s. India gradually moved out from under a long-held U.S. perception that it was a "collaborator" of the USSR. This trend continued and intensified under Narasimha Rao's Congress Party administration in 1992 and enabled both sides to weather several incidents that in earlier years might have led to extended periods of ill feeling and antagonism.

The earliest and politically one of the most delicate issues of the year revolved around a leak in early March of a Pentagon draft study that characterized Indian aspirations in the Indian Ocean as "hegemonistic" and implied that India was a potential U.S. adversary. Political reaction in New Delhi was predictably adverse but was swiftly eased by high-level U.S. assurance that the draft did not represent the position of the U.S. government. After visiting Washington the following month, then–defense minister Sharad Pawar further eased any residual resentment by describing the atmosphere of India-U.S. relations as "totally changed." Far from an atmosphere of suspicion between the two countries, he suggested, both the United States and India anticipated continued expansion of cooperation between their navies, armies, and air forces, as well as exchanges of high-level teams to military academies and participation in one another's military exercises.

This was consistent with the steady interflow of high-level military visits in 1992, during which the chiefs of the U.S. naval and army forces as well as the commanders of U.S. air, naval, and army forces in the Pacific visited New Delhi. In addition to the Indian defense minister, the Indian naval and air chiefs traveled to Washington, as had the Indian army chief of staff in 1991. These high-level exchanges were accompanied by a series of small but significant military-training and familiarization activities and observations by Indian military officers of several U.S. exercises in the Pacific, and reciprocal Indian invitations to the United States seem likely in the coming year.

There has been a long history of close U.S. monitoring of high-technology exports to India as a result of past India-Russia military cooperation, and this is still changing only very slowly despite urgings by officials in the U.S. State and Commerce departments. Indians have continued to see the United States as attempting to prevent their development of indigenous capabilities in high technology that has "dual" uses.

One example of this, which aroused great indignation in India in 1992, was the imposition in May of sanctions on India's space agency for an agreement with the Russians to procure a system for a rocket that, American officials argued, could be used on ballistic missiles. The Indians argued that the cryogenic engine parts involved had never been used in any military missile in the past and could not be; a number of American and European experts agreed with the Indians. The part, nevertheless, did fall within a banned category under the Missile Technology Control Regime, which the United States and most other developed countries have adopted as a means of preventing proliferation of missile technology, and there was strong U.S. bureaucratic resistance to making an exception for India. Journalists and members of parliament demanded the cancellation of the India-U.S. naval exercise scheduled for the same month, but the prime minister and defense minister stood firm and the incident faded relatively quickly from view. The joint exercise, the first since Indian independence, was held on schedule.

The Nuclear Issue. On another sensitive issue, U.S. senator Larry Pressler (R-SD) told Indian officials during a visit to New Delhi in January 1992 that he saw no reason to extend the reach of his amendment banning all aid to proliferating nuclear states to India, despite CIA director Robert Gates's warning to Congress that same month that India had nuclear weapons, or at least the capability to assemble these swiftly from growing stores of plutonium. The United States expressed "regret" later in the year that India was continuing to test its 1,500-km intermediate-range missile, and many in Washington were privately pleased that the June test did not appear to have been a success.

Indian and Pakistani nuclear and missile programs continue to pose a dilemma for Washington, not least in that treatment of Pakistan has consistently been far tougher than of India. Neither country is likely to succumb to U.S. pressure to abandon its programs completely, nor is there any evident way of ensuring that neither might secretly preserve some weapon capability even if each did agree to walk away from such programs.

The primary U.S. objectives have been principled opposition to nuclear proliferation in *any* country, concern that nuclearization of the subcontinent would increase the risk of the use of nuclear weapons should India and Pakistan again meet on the battlefield, and apprehension that the technology developed in India or Pakistan might be transferred to another country. There were hints both from the Bush administration during 1992 and from reports by influential "think tanks" in Washington that some compromise on these issues might be possible. One approach suggested in academic studies and nonofficial meetings was to obtain separate or joint formal commitments by India and Pakistan not to test nuclear weapons or devices, not to transfer weapons technology, and in some way to "cap" production of "weapons-grade" nuclear material. It was unclear whether these possibilities had yet begun to figure in official discussions.

Although a proposed five-power (or larger) meeting to discuss proliferation on the subcontinent was rejected by India, privately Indians and Pakistanis have begun talking about confidence-building measures, including both mutual and international assurances relating to nonuse, nontransfer, and capping of any nuclear-related weapons research and development. India and Pakistan exchanged lists of nuclear sites in both countries early in the year, completing an agreement reached in 1991, and while neither was convinced the other's list was complete, Indian, Pakistani, and U.S. officials saw the exchange and other discussions about reducing the threat of nuclear conflict as important steps forward.

The Economic Dialogue. The India-U.S. economic dialogue was mixed, but generally positive. Progress was made on several intellectual property questions, including the distribution of videos and films in India, but not on the more difficult issue of pharmaceutical patents. In April the United States suspended preferential tariffs for about $60 million in Indian drug exports to the U.S. There is strong and politically influential resistance from small Indian drug manufacturers to any changes in policy, although the actual number of products likely to be affected by greater protection for new drugs would be small. A potentially major case involving the production of AZT (a drug to combat AIDS) using new manufacturing techniques despite patents held on them by U.S. and British companies was developing at the end of the year.

U.S. corporate commitments to new investment in India continued to grow, rising from approximately $20 million in 1990, to $70 million in 1991, to $387 million in 1992. Most individual investments in 1992 were relatively small in U.S. corporate terms. The outgoing chairman of the U.S. Export-Import Bank, John Macomber, signaled the growing interest of U.S. companies in the Indian market at the end of the year, describing India as the most important new market for the United States in the 1990s. The key word in this observation may be "new." The statement did, however, seem to signify continuing U.S. business confidence that the Indian liberalization program would ultimately yield high benefits both to the Indian economy and for American business leaders astute and active enough to take advantage of the opportunities. A U.S. investment delegation to India in December 1992 returned feeling positive about long-term prospects in India despite the communal riots earlier that month, but U.S. business may continue to be cautious about making major commitments for some time.

The Middle East

India supported a U.N. Security Council resolution early in the year condemning Libyan state-supported terrorism, but refused to support a succeeding one that would have authorized the use of military force against Libya. This pattern characterized India's votes in the Security Council on a number of other issues during the year as well. An exception was Somalia, in which all sovereign authority appeared to have collapsed and India supported humanitarian intervention. At the end of 1992 it was considering sending a battalion of troops to support U.N. peacekeeping efforts there, but it had still made no decision by late spring 1993. India's positions reflected the new geopolitical pressures in the post–cold war world and India's search for acceptance by the United States and other permanent Security Council members. But they were also consistent with India's reluctance since independence to condone foreign intervention in the "internal affairs" of national states.

Israel. One striking signal of India's new pragmatic foreign policy was its December 1991 General Assembly vote to reject the "Zionism is Racism" resolution, which it had enthusiastically supported for over a decade. A second was its upgrading of relations with Israel to the ambassadorial level early in 1992. Foreign Secretary Dixit acknowledged that secret debate over the shift in policy had been intense for over two months and was a response to the changing situation in the Middle East.

Indian ambivalence toward the state of Israel has deep roots. Mohandas K. Gandhi, the spiritual leader of the Indian independence movement, had long opposed Zionism because he was opposed to defining nationhood by religious affiliation. Nehru shared this view, and although he recognized Israel as a state, he declined to permit any Israeli diplomatic mission in New Delhi, limiting the Israelis to a Consulate General in Bombay. This initial "principled" position was subsequently entangled with Indian relations with other Muslim states, particularly Abdul Gamal Nasser's Egypt in the 1960s, with the nonaligned movement, with efforts to balance Pakistan's influence in the Middle East, and with close coordination between Indian and Soviet policies in the Arab world, all of which exerted pressure on India to support the Palestine Liberation Organization and hold Israel at a distance.

In the changing international climate of the 1990s, as Dixit suggested, other practical policy considerations, including the participation of a number of Arab states in negotiations with Israel, the strong support of many of the Arab states for the United States in the Persian Gulf war (where India floundered, supporting neither the anti-Iraq entente nor Iraq), Indian interest in easing relations with the United States, and a general need for India to take a fresh look at its whole Middle Eastern strategy, took on new salience. Even China, which had long shared India's reluctance to "normalize" relations with Israel (although Israel had been the first Western state to recognize China), established relations with Israel in 1991, and the "cost" to India of following suit virtually disappeared.

Many Indian politicians had long sought a change in policy, arguing that India and Israel shared many interests. These included common concerns about a potential threat from "Islamic fundamentalism" in West and Central Asia, the potential ability of Israel to help India with dry-land and desert irrigation and farming, and Israeli skills in counterterrorism techniques and sophisticated military technology that India could expect to trade for or buy. Israelis and Jewish merchants in Amsterdam had also worked increasingly closely in the preceding decade with Indian businesspeople in the diamond-cutting trade, for which India had become the largest center in the world during the 1980s. An additional advantage India "discovered" early in 1993 was Israel's "free trade" agreement with the United States, which could give joint India-Israel manufactured products a clear advantage in U.S. markets. Both governments agreed to work to develop such opportunities.

India promptly sent an exceptionally skilled and effective diplomat as ambassador to Tel Aviv, and economic and security relations developed swiftly. Indian officials have been reluctant to talk much about security relations but acknowledge that discussions on counterterrorism may have occurred. Israeli sources made clear that active collaboration was indeed going on in this area (Kashmiri militants alleged—and India and Israel denied—that Israeli "tourists" in Kashmir were really intelligence specialists). By the end of 1992 both sides also acknowledged that they were discussing Indian acquisition of Israeli military technology, including unmanned aerial reconnaissance vehicles, as well as conducting joint research in desert agriculture techniques.

India's interest in a "seat at the table" in Middle East peace negotiations was welcomed by both Palestine Liberation Organization chairman Yasser Arafat and Israeli spokespeople, although no opportunity for this participation had occurred by early 1993.

Iran and the Arab States. India resumed efforts during 1992 to revive the close relations it has attempted to maintain with Iran since the 1960s. Iranian foreign minister Ali Akhbar Velayati was in New Delhi in May, Indian minister of state Eduardo Faleiro visited Iran in June, and Indian foreign secretary Dixit went to Iran in July. The reasons for the intense exchange of visits were unclear, although conclusion of a contract for 1.5 million tons of oil at the end of 1992 suggested one ongoing subject of discussion. During the last years of the Shah, India had exerted strong efforts to build India-Iran relations with a view to cooperating in maintaining security in the Indian Ocean. Conceivably such broad strategic issues are still in play, along with Indian interest in establishing links into Central Asia through Iran. Iranian prime minister Hasami Rafsanjani seemed to touch on several of these themes himself during Foreign Secretary Dixit's July visit when he identified improving India-Iran relations as an important factor for stability in the entire region, especially in Central Asia, and called for an expansion of cooperation in railways, energy, and trade.[9]

The energy side of proposed India-Iran cooperation, however, also included an Indian agreement to sell Iran a nuclear research reactor. Although Iran is a member of the IAEA and the reactor would have been under IAEA safeguards, the United States expressed strong reservations to India, arguing that it suspected Iran was engaged in a clandestine nuclear weapons program despite its IAEA commitments. The Indian offer was withdrawn, but, much to New Delhi's subsequent irritation, China then agreed to provide a similar reactor to Iran despite U.S. objections, which have become an important and abrasive element in China-U.S. relations.

In another gesture of its new sensitivity to Western concerns about sales of material with potential military use to certain Middle Eastern

[9] *FBIS*, NES-92, Iran Radio, July 9, pp. 54–55.

states, India acted swiftly in October to censure an Indian chemical company for exporting a potential chemical weapon precursor (trimethyl phosphite) to Syria without a license and halted a second shipment that was on the way. At the end of the year, India signed the international convention outlawing all chemical weapons.

A number of sour notes occurred in India's relations with Arab states. The Indian press and parliament were indignant at clandestine "smuggling" of young Indian Muslim girls as brides to Persian Gulf states and of even younger boys as "camel jockeys" for a barely reputable Persian Gulf sport in which many of the preteen boys died or were permanently disabled. The Indian government tried to avoid an open diplomatic argument with the Arab states involved, and trade in children is unlikely to end soon. The year also ended on an embarrassingly discordant note for India's reputation in the Islamic world, as noted earlier, when most Islamic states lodged strong protests against the Indian government's inability to prevent the destruction of the Babri mosque in Ayodhya and the death or injury of thousands of Indian Muslims in subsequent nationwide rioting in early December.

India and a "Resurgent Asia"

After decades of being on the "wrong side" of virtually every issue of major importance to most of the rapidly developing East and Southeast Asian states (the Korean war, the Vietnam war and relations with Vietnam in general, support for the Phnom Penh regime in Cambodia in the 1970s and 1980s, and security ties with the Soviet Union, as well as broad economic development strategy), India has in the last few years been determined to show the countries of this region that it has turned a policy corner once and for all.

Its primary motivations have been economic—learn from those doing well, trade with those with the most rapidly growing markets, and seek investment from those with money to invest—but its overall objective has been to make itself a more welcome economic and political partner for the rest of Asia.

Nevertheless, most Asians continue to be uncertain about how to deal with India. India is clearly not yet a fully accepted part of what other Asians think of as "Asia." ASEAN was willing to accept India as a "dialogue" partner on economic and security issues in 1992, but India's expression of interest in joining the Asia-Pacific Economic Cooperation forum thus far has met with a cool reception. As preliminary plans developed in 1992 among East Asians and Southeast Asians to establish an important new semiofficial regional security forum in 1994 for the Asia-Pacific (tentatively to be called the Council for Comprehensive Asia-Pacific Security), Indian planners and intellectual strategic studies circles again seemed to have fallen outside the frame of reference and to have been either ignorant of or indifferent to the pending plans.

Southeast Asia

Southeast Asia exemplifies a virtually virgin field in which Indian foreign policy attempted, with only partial success, to sow seeds for greater economic and political cooperation in 1992. The failure of Prime Minister Rao to stop over in the region in May, en route to or from Japan, did not help, although this was partially aided by his visit to Bangkok early in 1993. Nevertheless, Indian economic and security ministers visited the region, and there were repeated public calls for increasing exports to the region.

Several Indian companies have had investment ventures in Southeast Asia for a number of years, primarily in Malaysia, Indonesia, and Singapore. The number of ventures is increasing rapidly, and the Indian government's decision in 1992 to relax constraints on foreign investment by Indian companies is accelerating the process. A substantial Indian diaspora community has been in the region for over a hundred years and, in the case of Thailand, for centuries. Many have retained family contacts, particularly in South and West India, and this is likely to remain an important link in developing foreign economic relations in the future.

The Indian Defense Ministry and some academic writers on Indian strategy have also begun to think about closer security ties, seeking cooperative relations with Asian states that may have some common security interests, particularly with regard to China. The specific results of this policy are difficult to assess.

India's close relations with Vietnam are no longer a problem, as Vietnam has itself become an acceptable "partner" for most of the Southeast Asian states. India sent a battalion of troops to Cambodia (as did Pakistan) to participate in the U.N. peacekeeping effort and made small contributions for rehabilitation in Cambodia.

For their part, after decades of ignoring Southeast Asian perceptions of India as a potential threat, Indian planners have begun trying to change regional impressions of Indian intentions. The Defense Ministry has held or proposed naval exercises and military exchanges with Australia, Malaysia, Indonesia, Thailand, and Singapore. This is beginning to help ease regional concerns that had been growing particularly rapidly at the end of the 1980s about Indian force-projection capability and strategic objectives.

Enhancement of India-U.S. military cooperation was a particularly important element in encouraging other regional states to relax their concerns about an Indian "threat." The Indian defense minister visited Southeast Asian countries in February and explained India's determination to improve its relations with its neighbors in that area, and although some suspicion still remains, these efforts are beginning to bear fruit. The India-Malaysia security cooperation memorandum signed early in 1993 was another positive element in shifting perceptions of India in the region. And New Delhi's cohosting with the U.S. army in January 1993 of a regionwide conference of army leaders to discuss a broad range of current "army management" problems will almost certainly contribute to a perception of India in the rest of Asia as a regional state.

China

The central theme in India's discussions with China during the year has been to ease and improve relations wherever possible, even if underlying suspicions remain on both sides. Virtually frozen for nearly three decades after the 1962 China-India war, relations have been slowly thawing since Rajiv Gandhi's visit to China in December 1988. By the time Chinese premier Li Peng returned that visit in 1991, both sides had agreed on a consular treaty and an exchange of consulates in Bombay and Shanghai, expansion of trade, and easing of border tensions. This trend continued through 1992.

In February both sides again confirmed a position they had articulated over the previous four years: that the border issue was complex but should not prevent an expansion of socioeconomic, cultural, scientific, educational, and military cooperation. They agreed on broadening existing exchanges in the areas of management, administration, training, civil services, and education; on improving telephone "hot lines" between military border posts to deal with any problems that might arise; on paying closer attention to prior notification of military exercises in border areas; and on establishing a new schedule of semiannual military liaison meetings at key border passes in June and October to review and anticipate specific issues.

In July the first India-Tibet border pass was opened to trade since the end of the 1950s, symbolically marking a new point in the easing of border tensions. This set the stage for the upgrading of security relations as the Indian defense minister visited China in July. The Chinese chief of staff was to have returned that visit by the end of the year but did not, perhaps because of shifts in the Chinese military establishment, including of the chief of staff, after the Chinese Communist Party congress in the fall. Both sides agreed to move ahead with limited military interchanges that were not clearly defined. There was, however, discussion of mutual port visits by naval ships at an unspecified time.

Much more significant to some Indian observers was China's agreement at the end of the year to abandon its earlier refusals to discuss specific reduction of forces on both sides of the border and to negotiate the demarcation of an actual line of control at several contested points along the eastern end of the China-India border. It was unclear how far the Chinese would move on both these issues, but Indian officials saw the shift in Chinese positions as evidence that Beijing and its military commanders were increasingly willing to deal flexibly with concrete problems on the ground. Indian officials also noted that China had been relatively relaxed in its border negotiations with Bhutan, granting it a number of disputed areas along the northern Tibet-Bhutan border although remaining relatively unyielding where the western Bhutan border came close to the China-India frontier. Although some Indians were relatively encouraged, they agreed it was premature to suggest that the two sides were doing more than inching their way toward an eventual firm agreement demarcating their overall border.

Moreover, reservations continued to exist on both sides about how far China-India cooperation could extend. China's military support for Pakistan remained unchanged and included the transfer of upgraded tanks with night-vision equipment (courtesy of Sino-Israeli technology exchange), missiles, and fighter aircraft. Indian military strategists continued to write about long-term threats from China. Occasionally they speculated that India should focus its strategic attention on building collaboration with East and Southeast Asians in deterring China. Chinese proponents of a stronger navy argued that Indian naval expansion represented a "threat" requiring increasing Chinese capabilities. Chinese protests continued from time to time over the Dalai Lama's activities in India, and Chinese sensitivity to any popular political movement in Tibet remained a continuing issue in which New Delhi could find itself inadvertently entangled.

India is not at all sure what kind of relationship it will develop with China. The two countries probably look at one another as both potentially huge markets and major competitors for foreign investment and international trade. China is at present far ahead in both areas. It has "won" the competition that Indians and Americans alike wrote about in the 1950s and 1960s, but many Indians are convinced that they will ultimately be the tortoise that catches up.

Japan

If Indian policymakers were intermittently active during the year in pursuing President Venkataraman's parliamentary call to place greater strategic emphasis on relations with Asia, the high point of this strategy occurred during Prime Minister Rao's state visit to Japan in June. Rao told the Japanese that the economic success of the Asian newly industrialized countries, Japan, and ASEAN had drawn Indian attention and that Indian economic liberalization was based on those models.[10] In one speech during his visit Rao observed, "[India, Japan, and China] make up a good combination for a new Asian identity as a self-contained entity that also enables the continent to play an increasingly important role in world affairs. . . . We would like to interact more and more with other Asian countries for mutual benefits."[11]

On another occasion, he said, "At a time when traditional markets are becoming increasingly protectionist, this region must find sources for continental dynamism from within the region itself."[12] India's rising middle class of 200 million, Rao told still another audience of Japanese industrialists, was far larger than the whole population of Japan and could provide a "stable and growing" market while Europe and North America turned toward protectionism.

All these comments hinted that India was looking to link itself with some future "Asian trade group" should the world divide itself into rival trading blocs in the event of a breakdown in international trade negotiations. Other Indian officials, however, implied that India would look to special relations with the European Community as well. The reality is that India lies uncomfortably between prospective trade groups and is uncertain whether it might find itself out in the cold entirely in a "worst case" trade war.

The Japanese response thus far has been polite but careful. During Rao's Japan visit, a joint council to promote science, technology, research, and development was established, but business leaders carefully noted the importance of India's improving its investment climate further, particularly the infrastructure of communication, health, transportation, and power. Moreover, there were cultural problems on both sides. Japanese and Indian officials had begun early in the year to discuss the possibility of building model towns with facilities specially designed to attract Japanese corporate executives and professionals, including Japanese restaurants, hot baths, and golf clubs. But this reminded many Indians of old colonial enclaves, and in July the

[10] *India News* (Indian Embassy), June 16–30, 1992, Vol. 31, no. 12, p. 5.

[11] Ibid.

[12] Ibid.

prime minister was obliged to reassure parliament that any such towns would be "fully accessible" to Indians. Since "full access" was just what Japanese business executives hoped to avoid, the initiative faded. The Chinese, on the other hand, although equally unhappy at Japanese requests for similar separate areas in the Dalien area of North China, decided early in 1993 that the economic benefits of huge Japanese investments outweighed memories of the past.

Japanese business leaders were also frank in telling Narasimha Rao that they would begin to look at India once Japan's economy began to recover but that short-term prospects were less bright. Indeed, one of the major Japanese banks in New Delhi closed its office in the second half of the year. While some of the Japanese investments in India are doing well, particularly Suzuki's car venture with Maruti Industry—which plans to begin exporting small sedans to Europe in 1993—the pace of proposed Japanese investment in India is still low compared to that in East and Southeast Asia. Nevertheless, it has risen rapidly in the last three years, from roughly $2.2 million in 1990, to $20–25 million in 1991, to $188 million in 1992 (January–November).[13]

The Japanese, however, are frequently more cautious than other investors when confronted with possible political instability; it will be important to watch whether the communal riots and political uncertainty at the end of 1992 are having an effect on the Japanese view of the Indian investment climate.

Could an Indian-Japanese-Chinese power structure underpin a new Asian geopolitical structure? This seems to have little prospect in the foreseeable future, at least in a formal and organized sense. Japan and potentially India have some claim on new permanent seats in the U.N. Security Council, and China is already a permanent member. All three nations have major military forces and potentially significant naval forces. But the likelihood of a common axis of political-economic-security interests linking all three Asian states is small, at least in the coming decade.

Nonetheless, awareness that the three represent the major foci of military power in Asia has clearly been one element in the increasing interest of the U.S. Defense Department in building new relations with India, as well as in reviving its interrupted military contacts with China. All three countries are actual or prospective major trading partners for the United States and other industrial nations as well as the objects of increasing U.S. foreign investment.

[13] SEA Newsletter, November 1992, Vol. 1, no. 8, p. 6. Secretariat for Industrial Approvals, Department of Industrial Development, Ministry of Industry, Government of India, New Delhi.

The Economic Policy Agenda

Consistent with President Venkataraman's parliamentary speech, India intensified efforts to improve and broaden relations with major economic centers of the world. The objective was both to promote exports to hard-currency areas and to attract investment in and technology transfers to India. This policy, started under Rajiv Gandhi, represented a fundamental reorientation of Indian foreign policy priorities after the end of the cold war.

"Economics" had clearly become the center of Indian foreign policy priorities beyond the subcontinent itself. Prime Minister Narasimha Rao visited all three major industrial regions—Asia, the United States, and Europe—in 1992 and made a presentation at a major international economic conference in Davos, Switzerland, early in the year. The economic reforms announced since his appointment as prime minister had aroused intense interest within foreign investment circles. Rao's overarching focus on all these trips, therefore, was development, trade, finance, and investment, not security and political issues.

The prime minister's trip to Davos (which the Foreign Ministry insisted on managing instead of the Finance or Commerce ministries, despite the high-priority economic objectives of the trip) was unfortunately handled. His presentation was vague, detailed information on investment opportunities and proposed changes in the regulatory and macroeconomic environment was not available, and a question-and-answer session attended by the cream of the world's banking and investment community was cut short. Nevertheless, it was the first time any serious attention had been paid to India as an important prospective economic "player."

Prime Minister Rao's visits to France and Japan, as well as visits to India late in 1992 and early in 1993 by the Russian president, the British, German and Spanish prime ministers, and a series of French ministers, all focused heavily on economic opportunities between India and these countries. Unfortunately, Rao was without a full-time foreign minister for most of 1992 and without a commerce minister for the second half of that year, which, while not critical, almost certainly reduced India's ability to pursue its international economic goals with a number of countries.

Foreign Pressures

India's reform budget presented in February 1992 was greeted by the International Monetary Fund (IMF) and World Bank with enthusiasm for its commitment to lowering the budgetary deficit and repaying India's foreign debt in 1992–93. The IMF and World Bank strongly supported India's economic programs during the year, expressing general approval of India's request for $9 billion in credits over the next four years and providing $3 billion (from the IMF) in September as support for current structural adjustments in the economy.

This confidence seemed to have been justified at the end of 1992 by the 4 percent growth in the economy (up from 1.2 percent the previous year), 4 percent growth in industrial production (in contrast to negative growth in 1991–92), and strong agricultural growth of 5 percent. Private capitalization of new investment tripled in 1992 over 1991, despite a major scandal on the Bombay stock market that severely undercut confidence in the market for a period. The government succeeded in bringing inflation down from over 13 percent at the beginning of 1992 to under 7 percent early in 1993, and in meeting its target for budget reductions. Overall export figures showed over 10 percent growth to the hard-currency areas even while exports to the former ruble area were plummeting.

Nevertheless, Indian leaders and economic bureaucrats have had to fight a continuing public-relations battle throughout the year against critics from both left and right, who continue to charge the government with "knuckling under" to international financial institutions and selling out Indian business and national honor. That battle will clearly continue in 1993, and critics will seize on any failures, slippages, or concessions to foreign pressure. During 1992 these included U.S. threats to penalize Indian exports of pharmaceutical products for violations of patent rights or for dumping. India moved delicately in making some changes in its patent law during the year, but the issue is still a politically sensitive one.

GATT

India remained one of the staunchest opponents of the compromise proposal offered by Arthur Dunkel, Secretary-General of the General Agreement on Tariffs and Trade (GATT) at the end of 1991 as a means of reconciling conflicts on a broad range of issues in the Uruguay Round of GATT negotiations, although it quietly moderated its position on several issues during the year. India increasingly found itself isolated on virtually all the key issues it had raised, particularly in the interest of "developing nations." One by one virtually all of those states, led by Brazil—which had earlier joined with India on North-South related issues, demanding special trade access for less-developed states—dropped out as their own particular national interests were accommodated sufficiently. In part it looked as though India was maintaining its position to defend itself against domestic critics until the last moment, when, if an agreement was ultimately concluded among all other participants, India could then also join without appearing to have "caved in."

The $2–3 billion stock and bond scam in Bombay in the spring of 1992, which involved several foreign banks (U.S., British, Australian, and German) as well as major Indian banks, slowed government plans for bold reforms in the banking industry that would have opened banking significantly for both foreign and Indian private bankers. But early in 1993 the government resumed these reform efforts in its 1993–94 budget.

A host of other domestic reforms encouraged foreign investors in a broad range of sectors from capital industry to consumer goods to negotiate projects in India. Critics on both sides of the Indian political spectrum were swift, however, to condemn investors in consumer areas like soft drinks and breakfast foods for bringing unneeded technology to India, threatening traditional Indian domestic producers, and planning to drain profits from the country. The government stood up to all these accusations, but it is uncertain whether, should a BJP government come to power in the next few years, it would continue to honor the investment approvals that have been given.

Prospects

The overwhelming priorities of most Indians are jobs, better living conditions, national economic growth, and domestic tranquility. Foreign policy issues are a low priority even for sophisticated urban Indians other than as they appear to support this domestic agenda. India's foreign political and economic relationships are thus deeply linked to the ability of any Indian government to manage its internal economic and security dilemmas. The current Congress Party government in New Delhi led by Narasimha Rao remains committed to economic liberalization policies that are likely to have popular support so long as they do not dramatically threaten millions of public-sector jobs and they offer serious prospects for raising living standards in both rural and urban India.

Broadening India's economic and political links with the rest of the world is acceptable to most Indians, so long as the process is measured, carefully managed, and raises standards of living. The performance of the economy in 1992, the first full year of the new strategy, should strengthen the government's hand in continuing to pursue this strategy in 1993, but much more and identifiably popular consequences will be needed by 1994 to sustain it.

Strong forces within the country, including the BJP and its Hindu nationalist supporters, are suspicious of foreign investment except in certain limited high-technology areas, as well as of Indian links with international financial institutions. Even more important, the domestic environment being created by these forces threatens India's relations with both the Islamic world and the West, if communal violence and human rights abuses linked to police and paramilitary repression of such violence spread. The government risks being caught in a trap in which its domestic opponents may hurt it three times—first by weakening domestic order, next by compelling the government to use violence that appears excessive, and finally by damaging India's economic prospects.

Domestic communal unrest—aside from long-ongoing disturbances in Kashmir, Punjab (where order has in fact substantially improved since early 1992), and Assam (where the government also reached agreement with a major militant group, which promised to reduce violence there at the beginning of 1993)—thus far has been primarily limited to major cities in the North and West. Economic growth was not seriously affected in 1992, although disturbances in Bombay did constrain exports at the end of the year, and growth would probably have been even higher had the multibillion dollar banking scandal not disrupted capital markets for a considerable portion of the year.

Nevertheless, should there be a change of government in New Delhi, new elections in 1993, continued rise of the power and influence of the BJP, or greater labor unrest, both economic reform and the positive international perception of India as a modernizing state that has been growing over the last five years and particularly since 1991 could suffer serious damage.

Domestic political instability and a prospective shift in power toward the BJP would aggravate tensions on the subcontinent, not only between India and Pakistan but with most of India's other neighbors as well. A long-scheduled summit of South Asian leaders under the South Asian Association for Regional Cooperation (SAARC) for mid-December was postponed twice after the December and January riots in India, and regional concerns about communal violence and internal stability in India are growing. When the summit finally took place in Dhaka, Bangladesh, in April, there were few concrete results other than a loose agreement on a potential tariff preference area for South Asia.

The rise in political and social violence has not yet seriously damaged India's image as an increasingly attractive trading and investment partner. But the OECD (Organization for Economic and Cooperative Development) estimates at the end of 1992 predicting Indian economic growth at 4.5 percent or more in 1993 are clearly contingent on domestic political stability as well as ongoing foreign and domestic investment and continuing good crops.

Prime Minister Rao's political position is weaker at the beginning of 1993 than a year earlier. He will focus even more heavily on domestic policy and give less priority to foreign policy, including foreign travel, than in the preceding year. He has appointed a new full-time foreign minister, Dinesh Singh, who had previously held the position during Indira Gandhi's prime ministership in the early 1970s, and whose views on India's new economic-directed foreign policy are still unclear. Alternatives to Rao's leadership within the Congress Party center on politicians 15 to 20 years his junior whose careers have focused on local politics, whose vision of India's future is uncertain, and whose domestic political bases are regional, not national.

At the start of 1993, India's ties with most of the major powers were substantially improved from a year earlier. Problems with Russia have been sorted out, relations with China are improving, and links with Japan, the United States, and major European Community states have been strengthened. A BJP-dominated political administration might continue many of these policies but would almost certainly be more "nationalistic" than the current Indian administration. It would probably be less willing to compromise with China or other neighbors on territorial issues, more confrontational with Pakistan over Kashmir, and more assertive of Indian influence throughout the subcontinent. It would probably be less willing to reduce military expenditures than the current government (which has barely kept pace with inflation in the 1993 budget) and would likely be more vigorous in pursuing high-technology weapons programs, including nuclear and missile development. It might resume naval expansion, which could set back relations with Western states including the United States and revive concerns in Southeast Asia about India's long-term geopolitical agenda. And its ties to the international financial institutions would be strained.

But this is a worst-case picture. If domestic political and economic developments keep pace even with the current government's cautious expectations, and the threatened cracks in internal stability do not widen, India's image as a prospective important economic "player" will steadily come into sharper focus in American, European, and Asian business and financial circles. India's credibility as a major partner for Asian states and the European Community, as a contributor to international security, and as a prospective permanent member of the Security Council will grow as its economic weight increases to match its physical size and population. The potential is there but remains at risk from internal threats.

3
Economic Reforms: Birth of an "Asian Tiger"

Jay Dehejia*

When Indian finance minister Manmohan Singh presented his third budget on February 27, 1993, all members of parliament, including those from the opposition Bharatiya Janata Party (BJP), listened in silence. This surprised many, because the opposition had announced its intention to disrupt all proceedings following its abortive political rally in New Delhi the previous week. BJP leaders had been agitating since December 6, 1992, the day when the mosque at Ayodhya was demolished by their supporters, who swore to bring down the government and press for new elections. The BJP's silence during the budget presentation indicated its support of the economic reforms that were initiated in July 1991. The budget speech confirmed that the government had overcome short-term economic problems: inflation was down to a manageable 7 percent, while economic growth for 1992–93 had moved up to 4 percent from a low of 1.2 percent the previous year.[1] In essence the government has brought about fiscal discipline and moved forward with much-needed structural reforms.

Dr. Singh's speech, while taking due credit for the changes that have occurred during the last two and one-half years, clearly recognized the problems that lay ahead. The government's confidence was apparent in its announcement that the rupee would be fully convertible on the trade account and that customs and excise duties had been substantially reduced. Singh took account of the financial scandal that had rocked the markets and announced major initiatives in the financial sector. As was expected, no significant changes were announced

* I would like to thank Jagdish Bhagwati, Jairam Ramesh, Rita Nangia, Raunaq Singh, Lalit Thapar, Mani Shankar Aiyar, Isher Judge Ahluwalia, Deena Khatkate, and Dharma Kumar for their insights and suggestions during the preparation of this paper.

1 These figures and all others in this chapter, unless otherwise noted, are taken from *Economic Survey*, Government of India, New Delhi.

in personal and corporate tax structures; Singh stated that these would have to wait for another occasion. Several comments were made about the plight of the poor and the working class, and plans were announced for substantial increases in the social sector and rural development programs. Education and health were given special mention, along with women's issues and child welfare programs. Implementation of all these projects will increase government expenditure; however, this is both politically astute and consistent with the long-term economic reforms planned for the country.

In the past, Indian industrial policy was enlarged and maintained by the state as its sole promotor, owner, and regulator. The consensus among the country's political leaders, intellectuals, and business people was that the achievement of the nation's most basic goals—growth, social justice, and self-reliance—required a centrally planned industrial strategy. While these attitudes and beliefs may have been acceptable in the 1950s and even in the 1960s, India's public-sector enterprises have today become a major liability. Like the sizable, gas-guzzling, low-mileage American cars of that vintage, Indian public-sector industries soaked up huge amounts of capital, while earning little or no returns.

After the 1991 elections, the government decided to accept the reality that the country's economic thinking had to change quickly and firmly in order to ensure a better quality of life for its people. The path has not been easy, but the administration has demonstrated that perseverance can bring about significant results. This chapter highlights the recent changes that have taken place in the areas of industrial and financial reforms, privatization programs, and trade policy, indicating the issues and benefits that have accrued. Pessimists may say that all of the work that has been done by Prime Minister P. V. Narasimha Rao's administration since July 1991 can be reversed by future governments, but it would be extremely difficult, if not impossible, to revert to the thinking of the old guard. Barring unforeseen issues arising from the Ayodhya crisis and the winter 1993 Bombay riots and bombings, Indian economic reforms will continue to propel the country into the mainstream of global economic growth.

Highlights of Economic Reforms

India is close to achieving its commitment to the International Monetary Fund (IMF) and donor countries to bring down inflation to around 6 percent within a year. Chief Economic Adviser Ashok Desai stated recently, "Mechanisms are now in place and programs are on track to reduce the fiscal deficit on both the revenue and expenditure accounts, and to bring down inflation."[2] Inflation as measured by the wholesale price index, which was as high as 17 percent in August 1991, was down to 8.6 percent during the latter part of 1992, and came down further to 6.9 percent by February 1993. In the absence of complications from the Ayodhya crisis, the country is moving smoothly and surely toward its medium-term goal of reducing inflation to around 4–5 percent. To achieve this goal, the government requires the full support of all major political parties; the IMF and donor countries continue to be concerned that political pressures may lead to compromises in government policies.

India has lived beyond its means for many years, leading to a balance-of-payments crisis, rising prices, and high rates of interest. Since taking office, the present government has worked consistently toward reducing budget deficits. With implementation of specific government policies, the fiscal deficit was reduced from 8.4 percent of GDP in 1990–91 to 5 percent by February 1993 in spite of concessions given to both the industrial and the agricultural sectors. Initially, the government shelved its plan to reduce subsidies on all fertilizers, but subsequently, in August 1992, it eliminated subsidies only on phosphate and potassic-based fertilizers, which accounted for a substantial portion of fertilizer subsidies. Among the measures being taken to reduce the deficit are increased collection of taxes and excise duties, a squeeze on government expenditure and capital spending, and reduced subsidies to loss-making government-owned public-sector units. Also aimed at deficit reduction was an 18 percent hike in the price of petroleum goods announced in September 1992, which would allow the oil companies to accrue a further $1 billion during the current fiscal year.

Substantial reduction in defense expenditures is difficult owing to the threat of regional conflicts, real or imagined, as well as other global issues. Nor is reduction feasible for interest payments that are dependent on previous borrowing; of the total Rs. 56.6 billion expenditure increase in 1992–93 over 1991–92, interest payments alone account for Rs. 47.5 billion. (In mid-1993, Rs. 31 equaled US$1.) The government's decision to index capital gains for inflation and rationalize the tax code for personal incomes and wealth gains is a sure way to encourage investments in the productive sector, rather than in gold and real estate. Revised estimates for 1991–92 show that the total tax revenue generated has moved up to Rs. 693 billion, an increase of 22 percent over the previous year. During the same year (current ac-

[2] Interview with Ashok Desai, chief economic adviser, Department of Economic Affairs, New Delhi (December 1992).

count) expenditure increased by 15 percent to Rs. 864 billion. Also, the government's internal debt has been reduced from 27.9 percent of GDP to 27.1 percent. These are positive moves, and if they can be continued without creating suffering for the poor and the lower-middle class, the country will be set on the right course for the medium to long term.

The total government expenditure for 1992–93 has been fixed at Rs. 1,229 billion, a 7.1 percent increase (in nominal terms) from the previous year. Defense spending has been marginally reduced, as has capital spending on power, oil exploration, agriculture, and other development projects. It is expected that private investors will increase capital spending in these areas. The government is also encouraging foreign and private-sector domestic investment in power and oil exploration and other basic infrastructure projects.

India's balance-of-payments situation has been dismal over the last few years. The Persian Gulf war of 1991 worsened the situation because nonresident Indian remittances from the region stopped, and India had to pay higher "spot-market" prices for its gulf oil. The Reserve Bank of India reported that the first half of the fiscal year 1991–92 was marked by an external-payment crisis, foreign currency reserves having declined to $1.1 billion despite heavy borrowing from the International Monetary Fund. However, there has been a turnaround from October 1991. Excluding the revaluation of gold holdings, India's foreign exchange reserves, combining foreign assets and "Special Drawing Rights" (SDR) from the IMF, rose by $3.1 billion compared with a fall of $1.1 billion during 1990–91. Foreign currency assets at the end of December 1992 were $5.46 billion, with SDR holdings at $4 million and gold reserves valued at $3.4 billion. This improvement has no doubt been facilitated by help from bilateral and multilateral sources. The government also set up a "Remittances in Foreign Exchange (Immunities) Scheme" and Indian Development Bonds, both of which were instituted to attract "black" money accumulated abroad by Indians.[3] It is estimated that in recent years there has been an annual capital flight of around $2 billion. Some of this money appears to be coming back, however slowly.

At the Aid India donors (United States, Canada, Japan, and West European countries) meeting held in Paris in June 1992, aid commitments went up by $500 million to a record level of $7.2 billion. This is a sure sign that donor countries are confident that India can move in the right direction; their commitment is predictive of excellent prospects in the medium to long term. Several countries were concerned

---

[3] "Black" money refers generally to money not declared to the government.

with elements of India's governmental expenditure in the fields of defense and nuclear development. Certain programs, such as the World Bank development and restructuring programs for the transport and finance sectors, were held up. Some German and Japanese aid was also cut, pending India's confirmation of speedy reforms.

While the government is proud of its achievement in moving its foreign exchange reserves from around $1 billion during June 1991 to $8.88 billion by December 1992, the World Bank puts this into perspective by pointing out that the increase has resulted primarily from one-time gains and is unlikely to be replicated in succeeding years. India received $2.3 billion from the immunity schemes launched last year for nonresident Indians; another $1 billion was brought in by the foreign banks as a result of the losses they incurred as part of the financial scandal, while the rest was infused by multilateral agencies like the IMF. Much of this increase in reserves is unsustainable unless exports begin to pick up quickly. The Planning Commission maintains that in order to avoid the balance-of-payments problems of the past, growth rates of imports must be kept below 8 percent, while exports must grow in excess of 14 percent. This is a tall order for an economy that is moving from inward-looking growth to an export-led industrial policy. The finance minister himself stated publicly that it would be at least four years before India achieved significantly higher growth. In the short term, it is expected that there will be an imbalance between inflows and outflows of foreign currency.

Recent studies on India's balance of payments indicate that the country could slide back into another short-term "crisis" situation. The World Bank estimates that India will require at least $10 billion over the next five years to cover debt service and import growth requirements. At best, foreign investment is likely to bring in $1 billion a year. The World Bank argues for a sustained and increased level of external grants and low-interest loans. Before the expiry of its current standby agreement, India is keen to finalize the conversion of its $7 billion loan from the IMF into the extended fund facility in order to ease the repayment burden. Additional low-cost loans are expected from the World Bank and the Asian Development Bank. It is anticipated that during the coming year India will require additional foreign currency infusion of at least $2 to $3 billion. Nonresident Indian funds could be one solution; commercial loans may be another possibility, although international credit agencies have not upgraded India's rating at this time. Another area of foreign exchange funds inflow could be through an acceleration in foreign investment.

India thus faces a challenge that must be met head on; it should not allow the naysayers to browbeat it into reversing its reform policy. Except for a few people in parliament who may continue to believe in torpedoing much-needed reforms, the government has the support of all sections of the opposition on the need for economic reforms.

Initiatives and Issues

Certain major events that occurred during 1992 and early 1993 need further analysis if we are to understand the moves being made by the government, with the general agreement of the opposition parties, and the impact that these moves have had on growth. Occasionally these announcements appear contradictory, and implementation seems too slow, but an administration working within democratic norms and with openness, unlike the closed society in China, may have to take a circuitous and occasionally painful route to reach its goal.

Indian policymakers and implementers recognize that millions of people live in acute poverty and suffer grossly inadequate access to the resources required to give them a chance for a better life—education, health services, infrastructure, land, and credit. According to the World Bank, "The essential task of development is to provide opportunities so that these people, and the hundreds of millions not much better off, can reach their potential."[4] Recognizing these goals as an integral part of economic growth, the government is orchestrating strategies to implement change. There is general consensus that the way forward is not through ad hoc economic changes, or the socialist political thought of previous governments that led to emphasis on self-reliance, import substitution, and "export pessimism"; rather, it is through an open attitude and initiatives in the private sector. Such a strategy has been to take significant controlled strides, in contrast to the about-face in countries of Central and Eastern Europe on the one side, and the spurts and halts of China on the other. Within the Indian context, the administration is making the bolder moves required to free itself from the shackles of government controls and allow market forces not only to fuel the economy but also to improve the quality of life for its 850 million people. Strongly embedded vested interests will have to be overcome to ensure that the country leaps into the 21st century.

The party manifestos of both the Congress Party and the BJP agree that economic liberalization is the key to real economic growth. The 1992 budget was passed by a comfortable margin, with the BJP supporting the government on all economic changes except those consid-

[4] *Development and the Environment*, World Development Report, 1992, p. 4.

ered "anti-poor," "anti-rural," and "anti-middle class." The Janata Dal (JD), Socialist Janata Party (SJP), and Left Front spoke out only against those elements of the proposals that were linked with cutbacks on subsidies, especially those relating to subsidized pricing of fertilizers. Another stumbling block was the closure of "sick" industries that entailed massive layoffs. In his 1993 budget speech, the finance minister asked his colleagues in parliament for their support in approving the reform agenda for the coming years. He went on to proclaim that the government will take steps to minimize the burden of adjustment on the poor and the working classes.

In a flurry of positive and eloquent announcements since July 1991, the government has taken steps to decontrol the financial sector, reform the industrial sector, and encourage global trade. Measures have also been initiated to encourage private domestic and foreign investment in oil exploration, oil refining, power generation, communications, and national roads. A major factor contributing to these initiatives was the firm nudge provided by the IMF and Group of Seven (G-7) donor countries in the face of India's well-recorded foreign exchange and balance-of-payments crises.

India's leaders have taken the necessary giant steps toward joining the global village of the 1990s. A centrally planned structure, with heavy orientation toward public-sector production, has given way to private-sector initiatives within the context of a market-driven economy. In the 1970s some liberal conditions were introduced for entry and expansion in the capital-goods sector. During the 1980s, partial decontrol of pricing brought about a dramatic response in both investment and output, especially from the cement industry. In the late eighties, domestic and foreign investment in the area of telecommunications manufacturing was opened to the private sector.[5] The apprehension remained, however, that these changes could be reversed with little advance warning. Foreign investors generally stayed aloof, and local industrialists concerned themselves with New Delhi's regulations to the detriment of their corporations. There had to be a change in attitude toward the private sector at the highest levels of government.

Dr. Singh fully recognized that while changes can be announced, they still have to be implemented by those very persons who have been running, or obstructing, the process for more than 40 years. He and his top management team are working swiftly to remove barriers as and when they surface, thereby reconfirming to industrialists and

---

[5] Isher Judge Ahluwalia, "Structural Adjustment and Productivity Growth in India," *Productivity*, New Delhi, Vol. 33, no. 2 (July–Sept. 1992), pp. 201–08.

entrepreneurs around the world that the country is genuinely seeking a new way to economic growth. In his February 1993 budget speech, Manmohan Singh announced that he had asked all central and state government ministries to set up a special review group to ensure that in the new environment, changes are made at all levels to promote development and investment. Referring to such developments as the breakup of the Soviet Union and the onset of a privatization and liberalization process in Eastern Europe, the finance minister commented that "change is writ large across the globe in all continents; old rivalries have vanished; ideologies have been overturned; there is a spirit of exuberant experimentation everywhere. India too is changing with the world."[6]

The moves made in the last three years may be perceived as too bold and too dramatic by those industrialists who have lived and worked in conditions under which the Planning Commission made the decisions on what the population required and the Department of Industries gave permission to start new factories or expand existing ones. Opposition could come from trade unions, which have ensured high wages for unproductive urban workers in the organized sector, and from the many corrupt *babus* (low-level civil servants) in both the central and state governments. Such interest groups could, at the slightest provocation, take the opportunity to derail the economic reforms. These fears can best be addressed by quoting noted economist Jagdish Bhagwati: "The reforms are being unfolded in a *blitzkrieg* of successive moves that both give them a momentum and keep the opposition off balance. This strategy is reminiscent of the 'bicycle theory': just as you keep cycling so as not to fall off, you should keep going from reform to reform to prevent the opposition from concentrating forces at any static target of opportunity."[7]

Can these reforms be completed within a reasonable time frame without undue hardship to the general population? The World Bank suggests that "a minimum of five years would probably be necessary to carry out the reforms, while a program of more than seven years would probably be too slow."[8] The present government believes optimistically that real turnaround can be achieved within three to five years.

A further issue is whether economic growth can eradicate the nation's poverty. The latest statistics indicate that around 35 percent of

[6] Manmohan Singh speaking at the Bank of England, September 17, 1992.

[7] Jagdish Bhagwati, *India's Economy: The Shackled Giant* (Oxford: Clarendon Press, forthcoming), p. 87.

[8] "India: An Industrializing Economy in Transition," World Bank Country Study, December 1989, p. 39.

the population today is considered poor, compared with 60 percent during the mid-1960s.[9] Though the extent of the decline is disputed, it is clear that poverty is on the decline. It is tragic, however, that owing to the rapid annual population growth, the absolute number of people living below the poverty line has declined only marginally. The poor have inadequate access to basic social services, and they lack employment and other income-generating opportunities. The 1991 Government Industrial Policy paper stated, "Government is pledged to launching a reinvigorated struggle for social and economic justice, to end poverty and unemployment and to build a modern, democratic, socialist, prosperous and forward-looking India. Such a society can be built if India grows as part of the world economy and not in isolation."[10] Many observers believe that the growth strategies will have a positive impact on the standard of living and increase the income level of the population as a whole. The finance minister's 1993 budget speech reconfirmed the government's firm position of working diligently toward the goal of removal of poverty.[11]

In contrast to the false starts in the industrial sector, the Indian agricultural sector has, for the last 20 years, maintained an acceptable blend of entrepreneurial skills and timely government intervention. The "green revolution" has had the benefit of serious private-sector participation, with the government assisting farmers with input subsidies, expanded irrigation, better seed quality, innovative pricing strategies, and, when required, massive imports of food grains and edible oils. As a consequence, the country has been able to maintain a surplus of food supplies.

Monsoons, however, play a major role in food production, especially in the lesser-irrigated areas. The June 1992 scare that the rains had failed after three consecutive excellent years fortunately proved to be wrong. The government took the precaution, however, of purchasing 3 million tons of wheat from Canada, the United States, and Australia, bridging the gap between demand and supply. Priority must be given to ensuring appropriate distribution of food across the country.

The government has decided to keep a watchful eye on the agricultural sector, as one-third of the GDP and two-thirds of the population still depend on agriculture, and the overall standard of living cannot be improved without sustained agricultural growth. During 1992–93,

---

[9] *World Bank Annual Report 1992*, p. 131.

[10] Government of India, Ministry of Industry, *Statement on Industrial Policy*, New Delhi, July 24, 1991 (cyclostyled copies distributed in parliament).

[11] For a detailed discussion of poverty in India, see Alan Heston, "Poverty in India: Some Recent Policies," in *India Briefing, 1990*, ed. Marshall M. Bouton and Philip Oldenburg (Boulder: Westview Press, 1990).

agricultural production recorded a high 5 percent growth, though output had grown only marginally until 1990. Government procurement pricing strategies have diverted production toward commodities like sugar and oil seeds, rather than essential commodities like wheat, rice, and cotton. A combined strategy of higher grain prices and decreased subsidies, as announced in the 1993 budget, must be implemented quickly so that there is a balance of food-grain production and exportable cash crops. The "green revolution" will be given a further boost as new technologies spread rapidly, bringing with them better farming methods, canning, freezing, freeze-drying, and the like.

Exports of horticultural products are also expected to increase. India has a large number of small- and medium-sized farms, in which a substantial amount of the work is performed manually. In addition, farm communities employ family members and transient labor during peak periods, leading to income generation for many people. "Given the employment intensity of processes of production, increased agricultural exports will have a favorable impact on rural incomes, thereby helping to reduce the incidence of poverty."[12]

In the short time since early 1991, the impact of India's economic changes has already been felt. These initiatives have not only maintained the momentum, but generated quantum leaps of economic growth. Economic indicators have shown a steady though not dramatic growth during the past several years: 5.2 percent during 1989–90 and 5.6 percent in 1990–91. GDP at constant (1980–81) prices grew by a modest 1.2 percent in 1991–92 and showed a remarkable improvement to 4.2 percent in 1992–93. The industrial sector has not picked up as briskly as expected due to the severe import compression during 1991–92. This reconfirmed the view given in the IMF's September 1992 report.

Barring the occurrence of events such as the Ayodhya incident, the winter 1993 Bombay riots and bombings, and the pressures brought on by "power-hungry" politicians, the impact of liberalization and government reforms will be likely to yield encouraging results in 1994 and beyond. Economists in India believe that a GDP growth of 6 percent can be achieved during 1994. This is not unrealistic if one notes, by comparison, that China is expected to top the list of fast-growing countries with GDP growth at 11.2 percent, having risen rapidly from 6.9 percent in 1991 and 4.7 percent in 1990.

---

[12] Finance Minister Singh speaking at the Society for Promotion of Wastelands Development, New Delhi, June 17, 1992.

Financial Reforms and the Indian Stock Exchanges

The Indian stock market has been active for more than 100 years, with stock exchanges in 20 cities around the country and the Bombay Stock Exchange (BSE) as the market leader. After the initial euphoria of the 1991 budget, the bullish stock market was expected to return to normal. Instead, the Bombay index went up to 1,973 by the end of 1991 (as compared to 100 in 1978–79) and rose to 4,000 by the middle of 1992. During 1990, Bombay alone averaged 45,000 trades a day, which equaled trading on the London Stock Exchange, and during 1991 and early 1992, trading activity was twice that rate. On the domestic front, public issues moved up dramatically from 154 to 253 companies in a single year, with activity increasing from Rs. 26.5 billion to Rs. 50 billion in that same 12-month period ending June 1992. Additional stock infusion by existing stockholders went up from 188 to 251 companies, though the monies generated remained at the same level of Rs. 64 billion. Fifteen million households, or one in every two urban homes, actively take part in the capital markets; until three years ago, there were only 2 million participants.

The "bubble" caused by the excitement of changes in policies should have burst with the end of speculative buying. No one, however, expected a financial scandal of major proportions. For many years, government-owned banks have been instructed to lend money to preferred projects and to the agricultural community, even if such loans were likely to be unproductive. At the same time, these banks were judged on the basis of their profits. During the 1980s, political parties representing the rural communities brought pressure on the banks to forgive substantial loans to the agricultural communities. These contradictory forces impelled banks to find new ways to maintain or improve their profitability, and innovative stockbrokers like Harshad Mehta and Hiten Dalal found the mechanisms to help these banks. They assisted banks to transfer securities away from low-yielding government bonds to the more lucrative stock market. There was also a widespread abuse of the system; a panoply of regulations, far exceeding the ability of the administration to enforce them, led to a serious misuse of funds by both the state-owned banks and foreign banks operating in India.

The basis of the 1992 financial scandal was large-scale insider-trading activity. In addition, unscrupulous stockbrokers and bank employees exploited Indian banks, which were forced by their trade unions to continue the age-old, inefficient manual bookkeeping, making use of money for up to 18 days (a float), and diverting funds from the banking system to the individual accounts of brokers. The scandal began to unravel during the reconciliation process at the end of the 18-day period; one discovery led to another, resulting in the arrest of certain prominent stockbrokers. Although Harshad Mehta was targeted by the press, he was but one among many stockbrokers who took advantage of the situation.

As part of the financial reforms instituted during 1992, the government decided to "introduce new norms for income recognition, and provisioning bad debts and the prescription of new capital adequacy requirements in line with internationally accepted Basle Committee norms."[13] The Securities and Exchange Board of India (SEBI), a statutory body formed in January 1992, and the Reserve Bank of India (RBI) have given assurances that the problems will be rectified without delay. The RBI set up a committee headed by its deputy governor, R. Janakiraman, to "scrutinize the procedure adopted by . . . the RBI in regard to the maintenance of the book of accounts (subsidiary general ledger, or SGL) and other related matters and suggest remedial measures to tone up the responsiveness of the system."[14] The total loss to the banks is estimated at Rs. 35 billion and is likely to move higher.

A joint parliamentary committee (JPC) is reviewing and assessing several aspects of irregularities in the banking and securities transactions. Members of this committee appear committed to identifying the basic issues underpinning the diversion of funds from low-yielding government securities to the stock market, and the weaknesses in the internal control mechanisms within both nationalized and foreign banks. Membership in this parliamentary committee cuts across party lines, with the Congress Party, the Bharatiya Janata Party, the Janata Dal, and the Communist Party of India–Marxist all taking an active part. Initial hearings, more akin to inquisitions, gave many the impression that several members had already made up their minds and appeared to be seeking facts that fitted their version of the verdict. The JPC chairman, Ram Niwas Mirdha, insists that the committee will complete its task by the middle of 1993. Discussions with JPC committee member Mani Shankar Aiyar, Congress Party member of parliament, confirm that the JPC will deliver to the government clear guidelines for much-needed financial reforms. He admits that apportioning blame cannot be ruled out, though this is not the primary objective of the JPC.

While charges and countercharges will continue for some time as politicians use this issue to censure the government, it seems likely

[13] Manmohan Singh, 1993–94 budget speech delivered to parliament, February 27, 1993.

[14] Janakiraman Committee reports issued in May, July, and August 1992.

that the financial scandal will soon be left behind, without any major repercussions on the growth of India's market-led development program. It is true that small investors were badly affected by the scam; the government must ensure that SEBI can prevent the recurrence of such irregularities.

The government felt it prudent to ensure that financial reforms are properly structured and consistent with other moves being made to open the country to domestic and foreign investment. The 1991 announcement that foreign investors could participate in the Indian stock exchange system was followed by the issue of specific guidelines in which four major elements were covered. Registration with the Securities Exchange and the Foreign Exchange Regulation Act remains valid for 5 years; all types of financial transactions are open to foreign investors; no restrictions are placed on the volume of investment, although a ceiling of 24 percent of issued share capital exists for groups of foreign institutional investors, of whom no single one can own more than 5 percent; and there is no lock-in period for holding stocks, although the tax rate provides an incentive for holding stocks and shares for more than a year. The government proposed a tax of 20 percent on dividends and interest, and 10 percent on long-term capital gains. The short-term capital gains tax rate of 45 percent was brought down to 30 percent starting in April 1993.

It is unlikely that sophisticated global investors will now neglect the opportunity to invest in India, where growth rates of over 6 percent could be sustained for a decade starting in 1993 and corporate earnings could grow at 25 percent over the next five years. As the country's capital markets mature, new money is expected to come in from foreign institutional investors. A modest estimate predicts an inflow of $500 million within the first six months of 1993. Of the Bombay Stock Exchange's 6,260 listed stocks with market capitalization of $60 billion, at present only 1,000 are actively traded; an under-researched market could be of interest to many pension funds and foreign financial institutions. An element of realism may also enter the Indian markets with the advent of foreign investors. Lower inflation, better-than-average rains, and steady improvement in the foreign exchange reserves appear to have bolstered the confidence of investors starting from the middle of 1992.

As part of the financial-sector reforms announced during 1992, the Reserve Bank of India issued guidelines for setting up private-sector banks as public limited companies. The government announced its intention to allow private-sector investment in nationalized banks and decided to reduce by one percentage point the minimum lending rate for commercial advances. As inflation abates, it is expected that this floor rate of 17 percent will also be reduced. As part of the capital market reform, the government gave its approval to financial institutions and banks to set up the National Stock Exchange of India (NSEI), with the Industrial Development Bank of India acting as the nodal agency. NSEI is expected to serve as a model exchange, integrating stock markets all over the country by providing nationwide stock-trading facilities and electronic clearing and settlements. The process of reforms has only just begun; we should expect further changes in the near future.

Industrial Reforms

The most striking achievement of the reforms of 1991 and 1992 has been that commercial considerations, rather than government mandates, are now the determinant in all investment decisions, including ownership, location, local content, technology fees, and royalty. The approval authority in the Directorate General of Technical Development within the Ministry of Industries has been eliminated. Controls on the import of capital goods have also been removed, and the many regulatory bodies responsible for clearance of domestic and foreign project proposals have been dissolved or reconstructed. The speed with which projects are now approved by the government and its agencies is remarkable. States now compete with each other to attract new investments. Investors, both domestic and foreign, can start new production facilities in the manner best suited to them. Foreign investors can own 51 percent of the equity, or more in certain instances. Market forces, and not the central government's Comptroller of Capital Issues, determine the price at which commercial paper is bought or sold. Companies issuing capital are now required to disclose to SEBI material facts and specific risk factors associated with their projects. The concept of industrial licensing, together with its cumbersome procedures for setting up operations, has been abolished, except for a short list of industries of security, strategic, or environmental importance and "luxury" consumer products. This negative list identifies those industry sectors and specific operations that need government approvals, and in the intermediate future these may remain within the purview of the government sector.

The Monopolies and Restrictive Practices Act has been amended to eliminate prior approval for both expansion of existing industrial units and the establishment of new industries by large business houses. Also abolished are the procedures by which the government required companies to increase local content, often beyond economic limits, by securing approval for its "phased manufacturing program." As part of the modifications announced during 1991, the government directed that all foreign exchange requirements for a project must be met through the foreign-currency earnings of the company. During the second half of 1992, this restriction was removed, because it affected the payment of dividends in foreign currency. The government has also eased regulations for Indian companies to raise money in foreign markets. Foreign institutional investors are encouraged to participate in Indian companies through the stock exchange. The whole concept of "self-reliance," as defined by previous administrations to mean that all products and services had to be produced or procured locally, has been changed. Today, the government has clearly enunciated that exports of competitive products must increase in order to allow freer imports of goods and services. The 1993 budget announcements of reduction in taxes and duties will help promote exports of value-added products and reduce import barriers.

Import liberalization that brought several items under a special simplified import scheme was announced in October 1992. This move allows exporters access to quality material for their own use, or for sale on the market at a reasonable premium—a method used to reduce "black" money cash transactions in foreign currency. The government took the initiative to reduce smuggling and the movement of foreign currency outside the formal exchange control system by allowing the import of gold by nonresident Indians upon the payment of nominal customs duties. It is estimated that earlier around 200 tons of gold was smuggled into the country each year. Legitimizing such imports has resulted in 80 tons being officially repatriated between April and December 1992, while an additional 40 tons is expected to be legally imported in the first quarter of 1993; this implies a legalized entry of over $15 billion during 1992 alone. Apart from the gold that has been converted into bracelets, chains, bangles, and the like, hoarded gold in India is estimated to be around 7,000 tons, valued at $93 billion. If half of this could be brought into circulation, India could save at least $2 billion a year on interest payments alone.[15] However, in a milieu where gold ornaments are a woman's dowry and a guarantee of security, gold mobilization is a remote dream.

Manmohan Singh indicated that policy changes, together with a change in attitude and perspective, had created a favorable atmosphere and built confidence within the business community, both domestic and foreign. He believed that delicensing had already created

---

[15] S. Gurumurthy, "In Quest of a Friendlier Gold," *Statesman*, December 3, 1992, p. 1.

competition, thereby benefiting consumers, both rich and poor.[16] The finance minister is justified in thinking that expanded choices allow consumers to get more value for their money and a wider selection of products. Between August 1991 and January 1993, the government approved $2.3 billion in new foreign-equity investment, as compared with $200 million during the previous five years. An indication of what might be achieved is provided by the fact that since 1978, when reforms first began, China has attracted $3 billion in foreign-equity investment annually, with Chinese from Hong Kong and Taiwan playing an important role in project-related equity investments.[17] The Indian ministry of industry reported that during 1991–92, more than 7,400 investment intentions were filed—more than double the number for the previous two years combined. Foreign investors are no longer treated as exploiters. Companies are allowed to use their foreign brand names (which was not the case for consumer products sold in the domestic market), buy property, open branch offices, and accept deposits. The Foreign Exchange Regulations Act has been modified to reflect these and other positive moves by the government.

Notwithstanding the laudable changes in New Delhi, problems continue at the state and local levels. Many Indian businesses that led a comfortable life under controlled conditions without competition, as well as petty bureaucrats who held on to their negative power for more than 40 years, prefer to cling to the old ways. Minor items like securing power and water connections can cause undue delays in project implementation. In some cases, more than 40 separate state and local community approval certificates are necessary prior to starting an operation. Several industrialists noted that as competition increases, senior ministers and officials in progressive states are rectifying the situation. The ambiguity over the plethora of "new improved" approval mechanisms gives "the lower-level civil servant at the state level the power to delay programs, and low-level corruption continues to thrive."[18] An ironic outcome of the reforms is that corrupt government officials now seek assignments in the Customs Department, in place of the Industries Ministry, using import controls rather than industrial controls as their power base.

[16] Finance Minister Singh, in conversation with *Business India's* Ruchira Gupta, talks about priorities of the reform agenda and how far it has permeated the bureaucracy. *Business India*, July 6–19, 1992, p. 55.

[17] "India and China Compared," paper written by Adviser to the Vice Chairman of the Planning Commission Jairam Ramesh, for the Indian Planning Commission, unpublished.

[18] Interview with Ramesh Chauhan, chairman, Parle Industries, New Delhi, December 1992.

Infrastructure Privatization

Modifications in several areas of infrastructure operations were announced during 1992. The operation of toll roads as part of the national highway system, thus far under the sole purview of the government, is now open to the private sector. This announcement needs to be followed up with major modifications to several interlinking acts of parliament that are more than 100 years old. Ownership of land is in the hands of the states, and approvals for right-of-way, toll charges, profit margins, and other such issues can cause significant delays. Industry and trucking companies will also need to change their age-old outlook and use toll roads in place of the present dilapidated highway system.

The government continues to take ad hoc measures to attempt a patchwork of improvements in the telecommunications sector. India has only 7 million telephones providing basic voice service. Both industrial and agricultural sectors demand full-feature service to keep pace with the fast-changing world. Successful implementation of the new economic policies requires high-quality telecommunications services; the government has yet to develop a clear strategy with a speedy implementation plan. After several false starts, the Indian Telegraph Act of 1885 is currently being modified to allow private-sector participation in the operation of various services; a government committee is preparing the new act for submission to parliament. This promising start needs to be followed up with a liberalization program that would allow competition from the private sector in the operation of both basic and value-added services, thereby improving the services offered to business and residential subscribers and helping the export promotion drive. These and other issues and opportunities were discussed at the November 1992 workshop held by the Industrial Credit and Investment Corporation of India and sponsored by the World Bank.[19]

During 1992 the government issued a "menu" of power generation projects that are now available for investment by the private sector. However, the distribution of that power is still in the hands of State Electricity Boards, and problems persist on power loss, pilferage, and inefficient distribution. The Uttar Pradesh State Electricity Board is the worst offender, with as much as 18 percent lost through pilferage. The government is considering several changes to ensure that private-sector power generating and power distribution schemes are established to alleviate the problems of power shortages around the coun-

[19] Deliberations at a symposium titled "International Experience in Telecommunications Reform and Its Implications for India," New Delhi, November 21–22, 1992.

try. In his budget speech, the finance minister announced major tax incentives for investment in the power sector. He also mentioned that the government will increase its capital outlay by 22 percent to Rs. 51.7 billion. The government has decided to allocate time and resources to improve the basic infrastructure to reap the benefits of the new industrial policy; the private sector must be encouraged to invest in infrastructure projects, which generally have long gestation periods. Utilities, telecommunications, roads, and railway sectors must be restructured and liberalized at the earliest opportunity. Recent empirical research in economics demonstrates that public infrastructure can play a significant role in improving productivity and growth.[20]

Trade Liberalization

Concurrent with changes in the investment climate, basic modifications have been introduced to encourage trade and ease export-import regulations. A five-year trade policy was announced in 1992 to demonstrate the manner in which liberalization will progress. In essence, except for a few items covering less than 5 percent of imports, trade will be freed from licensing and nontariff barriers. All capital goods, intermediate products, and most raw materials will be license-free, and cumbersome import permits will not be required. Manmohan Singh announced in his 1993 budget speech that the government would reduce import duties for all projects to 35 percent. In addition, he announced import-duty reductions for a number of specific cases. Overall import duties have been reduced from 110 percent to 85 percent. These modifications to the trade policy are steps in the right direction; however, more needs to be done to ease restrictions. International trade economists suggest that India set up a two-tier structure with duties of 25 percent for capital goods and 40 percent for other items; only then will trade expand sufficiently, allowing the balance of payments to be brought under control. The primary intent would be to increase value-addition for exportable products, while maintaining domestic consumption at acceptable levels.

The 30 percent devaluation of the rupee in May 1991 was accompanied by the currency being made partially convertible; 60 percent of export earnings were convertible at market rates, while the remainder was convertible at the official rate. In February 1993 the finance minis-

[20] Richard H. Clarida and Ronald Findlay, "Government, Trade, and Comparative Advantage," *American Economic Review*, Papers and Proceedings, May 1992, pp. 122–27. David Canning, Marianne Fay, and Roberto Perotti, *Infrastructure and Growth*, unpublished manuscript, Columbia University, New York, June 1992.

ter announced that, effective immediately, the rupee would be made fully convertible on the trade account. Dr. Singh expects the rupee to be accepted as an international convertible currency unit within three to five years; this is based on the assumption that the financial and structural reforms take root and that unforeseen internal political squabbles do not delay timely implementation.

As part of the 1992 budget reforms, the government announced fiscal benefits to trading companies; foreign companies may, if they so wish, own 100 percent of the equity. Several other important changes were recently announced. The banned list of exportable items was considerably shortened, a large number of import items were decontrolled, and a significant group of imports were placed under "Open General Licensing Scheme," thereby allowing companies the freedom to import raw materials, components, or parts without restriction and central government intervention. Import restrictions were eased by reducing from 50 percent to 25 percent the cash deposit required by the importer. These initiatives are bound to improve foreign-trading activity in the country.

India's inward-looking policy of the past had reduced its share of the world market from 2.4 percent in 1951 to 0.5 percent in 1991. According to economist Isher Judge Ahluwalia, "had we maintained our share in world exports at the 1950 level, our exports in 1990 would have been Rs. 1,161,690 million. . . . In one year alone we could have earned $32 billion."[21] Trade initiative was stymied by the Indian government during the immediate postindependence period when it was believed that the government would be able to perform that task better. Also, Indian industry found selling to domestic markets more lucrative than exporting high-quality products to Western markets. Government-controlled foreign-trading corporations were set up and all trade was channeled through one or more of these agencies. Corruption increased and consumers were unable to obtain the best products or raw materials at the lowest price or at the right time.

Indian imports accounted for 11 percent of GDP during 1989–90, while exports were 8.2 percent. During the fiscal year 1991–92 the trade deficit was $1.5 billion, which was a significant improvement from $5.9 billion in the previous year. While exports fell in dollar terms to $17.8 billion, imports also fell substantially to $19.4 billion, representing a drop of over 19 percent. During 1992–93 imports have moved up; however, exports are only showing a marginal improvement. Export promotion and import substitution is essentially the suc-

---

[21] Isher Judge Ahluwalia, "Trade Policy and Industrialization in India," Exim Bank Commencement Day Annual Lecture, Bombay, March 5, 1992, p. 3.

cess formula to be adopted by those framing the reform policies. According to Ratan Tata, chairman of Tata Sons, "value-addition, and promotion in niche markets where Indian skills have an edge is the only way that Indian industry will increase its global market share."[22]

India has seen a shift in trading patterns, both in its partners and in products and commodities. The Soviet Union accounted for over 16 percent of India's exports. Such trade fell dramatically during 1991 and 1992 as the Commonwealth of Independent States (CIS) countries, especially Russia, curtailed their bilateral rupee/ruble trade agreement. India and Russia have agreed to denominate all future bilateral trade in U.S. dollars, and discussions were concluded in January 1993 on how the previous accounts are to be settled. Major problems have been created for exporters of garments, leather goods, and consumer products who have been unable either to organize barter agreements or to obtain convertible currency from CIS importers. Such agreements have, however, been reached on a government-to-government basis for the export of tea, coffee, and certain other commodities in exchange for oil and special equipment. Russia offered India an $850 million credit to buy arms equipment, and it has also proposed a joint India-Russia defense equipment agreement to manufacture Russian tanks and aircraft with a view to earning foreign convertible currency from Third World export markets. Trade between India and Russia appears to have only short-term political and economic implications; as their industrial sectors mature, realistic trade and technology transfer initiatives will emerge.

Trade with Europe and the United States has not increased significantly in dollar terms, and recession in the West has further impacted India's exports. India and the United States have tried to improve and expand bilateral trade. However, the issue of intellectual property rights in the pharmaceutical industry has brought further sanctions from the United States under the "Super 301" trade provisions, resulting in the loss of tariff preferences. High-level discussions are presently in progress between the two countries. The official Indian government view is that intellectual property rights and other issues need to be resolved as part of the continuing multilateral GATT talks. The United States objected to India's sale of an experimental nuclear plant to Iran, and it also complained about rice sales to Cuba. A more serious problem related to India's import from Russia of rocket technology that could be used to deploy nuclear warheads over large distances. The United States instituted a two-year ban on trade with and technology transfer to the Indian Space and Research Organization.

---

[22] Interview with author, Bombay, December 1992.

Annually, India exports around $1.5 billion worth of textiles and garments to the United States; recently the United States demanded reciprocity in the textile trade. These incidents, however small, are seen by the Indians as intimidation by a superpower. With a change in administration in Washington, the Indian government would be well advised to restart serious negotiations; initial contacts between the Clinton administration and the Indian government began soon after the U.S. presidential elections.

India has been a traditional exporter of commodities and relies heavily on exports of tea, jute, and other agro-based products for much needed foreign exchange. As other sources of supply are being identified and consumption stabilizes around the world, the country is not able to maintain a reasonable share of the world's market, and these traditional exports have shown a dramatic decrease. Jute and jute products, which accounted for 20 percent of the exports in the 1960s, are down to just 1 percent, while tea, which accounted for 19 percent of the exports, is now only 2 percent. On the other hand, engineered goods, cut diamonds, shrimp and fish products, chemicals, leather goods, and software exports have increased substantially.

Indian imports have shown a trend similar to that of Indian exports—a change both in countries and products. Major resources that were used for import of food grains and consumer products have been reduced substantially, while there has been an increase in the foreign-currency requirement for raw materials and semifinished products. Imports of fertilizers, edible oils, paper, and steel continue at the same levels as before. During the coming years, with the improvement of the manufacturing sector, it is expected that imports of capital goods will increase, leading to increased use of locally available raw materials for manufacture of finished goods.

Some of the trade liberalization directives are confusing and do not appear to meet any stated objectives, especially when seen in light of the other moves made by the government in the last three years. Three areas of concern are worth mentioning. (1) Indian exporters were traditionally provided with subsidies to encourage them to increase exports, not unlike exporters in the United States or Europe. These subsidies were removed during 1991. At the same time the government set up "exim scrips," a tradable paper allowing companies to import items or sell the paper to other companies that might need foreign exchange for their imports. These exim scrips were allowed to be freely traded on the market. Premiums on these scrips quickly declined after the initial rush, with exporters losing out on the subsidies as well. (2) Exporters were permitted to convert their foreign exchange earnings at the official rate, while imports had to be converted at the market rate. These exporters continue to pay very high import duties for capital goods required for improving their production techniques. The government will need to review this situation to ensure export growth for engineered products. (3) Rapid changes in rules and regulations for companies deemed to be "export houses" create confusion. Companies deemed to be 100 percent export organizations are allowed to sell anywhere from 25 to 50 percent of the output in the domestic market, depending on the industry sector. Serious investors are concerned that these directives may also change in the near future and are therefore waiting for further signals from the government.

Public-Sector Enterprises

As reforms were implemented to attract both domestic and foreign investors in the private sector, government companies also came under scrutiny. India's severely constrained budgetary circumstances, together with pressure from the IMF, were used by the government to change the management and operation of the public-sector companies. The government has also reaffirmed its policy against keeping "sick" companies open. The problem of the public-sector units (PSUs) is large by any standard; there are 246 PSUs in a "state of near-paralysis."[23] Some have near-obsolete technology, while others have severe overstaffing problems. A 1991 announcement allowing 49 percent private-sector participation was quickly followed up by announcements of varying degrees (up to 20 percent) of government disinvestment in many loss-making companies. This program of further divestiture is being continued in 1992, with profit-making public-sector companies being offered by auction. The September 1992 announcement of the third round of disinvestment in government-owned companies should net the treasury $500 million. The government target for the fiscal year ending March 1993 is $1.2 billion. During the previous rounds in 1991, $1 billion was raised, helping to reduce the fiscal deficit from 8.5 percent to 6.2 percent. During the first stage of stock sales in PSUs, the Krishnamurthy Committee recommendations were followed, and shares for groups of companies were sold in "bundles" to selected Indian financial institutions; this strategy, however, obscured the strengths and weaknesses of individual companies. This time, shares have been offered to anyone authorized to trade in the Bombay Stock Exchange, whether banks, financial institutions, mutual funds, or registered brokers. In theory,

[23] *Business India*, September 28–October 11, 1992, pp. 97–100.

foreign financial institutions could also have participated in these transactions, and one may expect this in the future.

Public and parliamentary discontent on the possible underpricing of the first round of shares, offered only to financial institutions, led the government to review its methodology for the next round. The two options were either to go directly to the public or to auction off large blocks to institutions. The government went with the second alternative as less cumbersome and also likely to raise a higher value on sales. During the February 1992 PSU stock sale, the bids were, on average, 35 percent above the floor price, the minimum having been fixed by Industrial Credit and Investment Corporation of India. Share prices in these companies must be watched during the coming year to determine if the government's auction decision was prudent and accepted by the public at large, or if trading in these scrips is restricted and speculation limited.

The auction method raises the distinct possibility of collusion between bidders to preserve a lower price. A move to restrict a full disclosure of the financials, as required by the rules of the Securities Exchange Board of India, may continue to shield the PSUs from much-needed scrutiny and a true evaluation of their performance. Many in India believe that this type of restrictive selling defeats the government's stated intention to involve the public in a meaningful manner in public-sector reform. The possibility has also been raised of reserving 5 percent of the shares in PSUs for the employees of the company being divested. The idea that employees should see the price of their company's shares in the morning papers may be new to India, but is commonplace around the world. Guidelines are eagerly awaited on issuing such shares to the employees in PSUs.

Restructuring of the entire public sector is a massive undertaking. With strong trade unions and a narrow majority in parliament, this issue needs to be solved with prudence and tact, though it is an issue that needs immediate attention and must be resolved during 1993. Princeton University specialists Henry Bienen and John Waterbury caution: "Beneficiaries of the status quo may be able to paralyze the reform process before future beneficiaries of that process can be organized to support it."[24] Although India's many advances may appear dramatic and consequential to both domestic and foreign institutions, many more breakthroughs are necessary. The most crucial are reforms in the labor market, involving retraining, reemployment, and the "exit" policy.

---

[24] Henry Bienen and John Waterbury, "The Political Economy of Privatization in Developing Countries," *World Development*, Vol. 17, no. 5, pp. 617–32.

The "Exit" Policy

India's strong labor unions make it imperative for the government to enunciate an "exit" policy, defining procedures for companies to lay off employees as and when required either on account of adverse economic conditions or inadequate plant utilization. The 1976 Industrial Disputes Act, which is still in effect, requires companies with more than 100 employees to obtain the permission of the state government to lay off personnel. It is expected that amendments to the act will be forthcoming during 1993. Since obtaining permission was generally a lengthy procedure that could take several years, private-sector companies frequently bypassed the rule, merely closing down units and leaving employees stranded without fund payments and other benefits. Public-sector units usually reverted to government funds to continue paying salaries to redundant employees; such continued losses led to further reliance on budgetary support, resulting in increased fiscal deficit. While the problem is acute in the public sector, it also burdens the private sector. Companies that have the authority to set up production and hire workers must also be given the liberty to close establishments and fire unproductive personnel.

A ray of hope may be seen as private-sector industry leaders and trade unions begin to sign contracts with productivity-based wage increases and joint agreements for laying off excess workers. The same cannot be said of the public-sector companies. A job in the government, its agencies, or its companies is thought of as a job for life. With the privatization of government-controlled operations such as hotels and companies in communications and the energy sector, a solution to the labor problem is of utmost urgency. The banking industry has the most powerful labor unions, making labor issues in the banking sector some of the most difficult to resolve, but they must be tackled before privatization of this sector is contemplated. "Regimes engaged in structural adjustment can generally sense the limits to which labor can be pushed. As breaking points are approached, they may try to renegotiate social pacts and associate organized labor with austerity measures."[25] Trade and industry reforms have eliminated jobs for several hundred thousand white-collar workers at central and state government levels; none of them have been let go. The finance minister believes that the government can rely on natural attrition to reduce the number of civil servants; however, this is unlikely to happen soon.

The Indian socialist structure and the politically derived policies of the previous governments gave trade unions the advantage, ensuring

[25] Ibid.

that workers could not be fired. The government acquiesced, and in many cases actually acquired unprofitable "sick" companies from the private sector. Public-sector companies, which collectively employ more than 2.3 million people, believe that employment rather than profit is their primary motive for existence. In fact, several ancillary units were set up by such PSUs to meet the demand of further employment. The Indian parliament expects to discuss the Industrial Relations Bill after the 1993 budget session. Rakesh Mohan, the economic adviser to the ministry of industry, comments: "Nowhere in the world do workers lose their jobs without adequate compensation. Our laws must be flexible. I think 'exit policy' is a horrible phrase. It is a policy for industrial restructuring and rehabilitation."[26] Whatever the exact phrase used in this connection, it is imperative that quick action be taken on the question of employment termination.

A National Renewal Fund has been instituted with $67 million from the government budget and $333 million to be recovered from the sale of PSUs. Private-sector companies have shown interest in participating in such a scheme. This fund will be used to cover the redundancies that exist in "sick" units and that will arise from the forthcoming restructuring of PSUs. A broad set of guidelines has been announced, according to which workers will be divided into three categories on the basis of age. The oldest group will be given compensation toward retirement; the middle group will get a smaller compensation together with a retraining plan; while the youngest will be given assistance in finding new jobs. The business community eagerly awaits the government's specific action plan.

In the meantime, many of these companies have instituted their own voluntary retirement schemes, leading to an enormous cash outflow and the possible loss of their best employees. In fact, several formerly profitable PSUs are presently in the red. In addition, the government decided to withdraw its traditional monetary support, thus bringing most of these companies to a grinding halt. Official estimates indicate that during 1992, central government companies have laid off more than 300,000 employees at an average cost of $7,500 each; at this rate, the government would have to find a minimum of $2.5 billion over the coming two years. As the National Renewal Fund is not yet fully operative, these companies are borrowing monies at 12–15 percent interest, leaving many with no cash for their working capital.

A recent World Bank study of 82 government companies estimates that 22 will have to be closed down and the remaining 60 privatized in a phased manner. In excess of 450,000 employees will be affected

---

[26] Rakesh Mohan, *Business India*, September 28–October 11, 1992, p. 44.

by these moves, and the World Bank estimate of retrenchment costs is in the range of $1.7 billion. The government needs to consider critically the implications of this enormous cash drain and the accompanying human suffering. Parliament must ensure that the objectives of a "market-led economy" are met with the least disruption in the medium and long term.

Conclusion

Economic reforms cannot be viewed in isolation; they are linked closely with the political, cultural, and social changes taking place in India's heterogeneous society. The economic reforms are not moving at the speed that many expected; this is the price to be paid for an open democratic community in which consensus and majority approval in parliament are necessary. It is important that diverse forces in all sections of India's society, not just the elite, move together toward a better, healthier, and more socially just world community. It is now necessary to implement the shift from a subsidy culture to an investment culture, and the government must take on the responsibility for improving basic needs of the population like education, housing, clean water, health, and nutrition.

India has come a long way from the days when nonalignment and socialist political thought were considered the cornerstone for global success. Civilization and ancient culture were given paramount importance, and the country was judged by the way its democratic system functioned. In the dynamic world of today, with the breakup of the Soviet Union, the freeing of countries in Central and Eastern Europe, slow moves toward the integration of the European Community, and the inception of the North American Free Trade Agreement, India also needs to make changes and move toward a freer economic society. Old reference points have disappeared; new markers must be found to ensure a sustainable progress within the context of a changed world order.

Domestic investment has picked up pace, with $5 billion committed during 1992 alone; in the next five years, such investment is likely to reach $22 billion. Coupled with the foreign investment that is slowly trickling in, India is on the right track to catch up both domestically and externally. The solid start that has been made needs to be consolidated with assistance from all sections of society; financial and sectoral reforms must continue and not get bogged down by extraneous circumstances.

The Ayodhya incident may have severely set back India's move toward rejoining the world economic order. Economic reforms must not take a back seat, however, but continue to be implemented side by side with the necessary social and cultural reforms. India has the potential to become another "Asian Tiger"; let the birth process not be too painful.

4
The Constitution, Society, and Law

Granville Austin

Indians inaugurated their constitution on January 26, 1950, and they commemorate the occasion as Republic Day. The annual parade in New Delhi down Rajpath, once called Kingsway, thrills onlookers with smartly marching soldiers, the colorfully caparisoned camel corps, schoolchildren's pageants, and army helicopters dousing the crowds with rose petals. The choice of date was not coincidental. January 26 was the day in 1930 when the Congress Party adopted the "Pledge Taken on Independence Day," which established "complete independence" as the party's goal.[1]

The process of formulating the Indian Constitution began in December 1946 when the Constituent Assembly convened in New Delhi. The Assembly found its justification in Mohandas K. Gandhi's pronouncement, years earlier, that *swaraj* (freedom and self-rule) could not be a gift of the British, but must spring from "the wishes of the people of India as expressed through their freely chosen representatives."

That month the Assembly set the tone for the work it would complete three years later when it adopted the Objectives Resolution, written and formally proposed by Nehru. Expressing what would become the philosophy of law for India, it declared that the Indian Union derived its power and authority from the Indian people. It said that there should be "secured to all the people of India justice, social, economic and political; equality of status, of opportunity, and before the law; freedom of thought, expression, belief, faith, worship, vocation, association and action, subject to law and public morality." The resolution went on to state that adequate safeguards should be provided to minorities, depressed and "backward" classes, and underde-

[1] For the text of the pledge, which also said that it is "the inalienable right of the Indian people . . . to have freedom and to enjoy the fruits of their toil," see *Jawaharlal Nehru: An Autobiography*, 1958 reprint (London: Bodley Head), p. 612.

veloped and tribal areas. The integrity of the territory of the republic should be maintained. And this ancient land should make its "full and willing contribution to the promotion of world peace and the welfare of mankind."[2]

The Assembly drafted provisions embodying this philosophy and designed for pursuing these goals. They may be summarized as a trinity: protecting and enhancing national unity and integrity, establishing the institutions and spirit of democracy, and fostering a social revolution to better the lot of the mass of Indians. As important as the goals themselves was that the framers believed (and Indians today agree) that the three were inextricably intertwined. Social revolution should not be sought at the expense of democracy, nor could India be truly democratic unless a social revolution had established a just society. Without national unity, little progress could be made toward democracy or social and economic reform. And without democracy and reform, the nation could not hold together. The circle was complete. Enthusiastic and optimistic though Assembly members were, they did not believe the constitution would achieve all this. They did believe, however, that it could light the way.[3]

The Constitution, Briefly

The more than 370 articles and 10 schedules of the constitution fill 309 pages in the 1989 edition published by the Ministry of Law and Justice. The bulk of the articles provide the administrative framework for the country's governance. Indians inherited nearly 300 years of British administration, including a general blueprint for a constitution in the 1935 Government of India Act passed by parliament in London. Rather than draft a constitution of broad principles and legislatively reenact the lengthy administrative provisions of the 1935 Act, the Constituent Assembly modified that act to suit itself and added elements it wished to have in its own constitution.

The Indian Constitution is two constitutions in one: a constitution for the national government and a constitution for the states, with

[2] For the Objectives Resolution, see *Constituent Assembly Debates*, Vol. 1, no. 5, p. 59. For an account of the framing of the constitution, see Granville Austin, *The Indian Constitution: Cornerstone of a Nation* (Oxford: Clarendon Press, 1966).

[3] Assembly members were not insulated from the country's problems. The Constituent Assembly wore two hats. As the Constituent Assembly (Legislative), members functioned as the nation's provisional parliament. Because the Westminster model prevailed, as it would in the constitution, the ministers of the government were members of the Assembly, which dealt daily with national affairs. As the Constituent Assembly (Constituent), the same persons framed the constitution. Typically, the Assembly sat as the parliament in the morning and drafted the constitution during the afternoon.

provisions largely parallel to those of the national constitution. Both are based on the Westminster model, with the president functioning as head of state and governors appointed by the president fulfilling an analogous function in the states. Each establishes a legislature, council of ministers, administrative structure, and so on. The national parliament has a directly elected House of the People, the Lok Sabha, and a Council of States, the Rajya Sabha, elected by state legislatures. Each state has a number of representatives in the Rajya Sabha proportional to its population—unlike the equal representation of states in the U.S. Senate, but like the Senate in that only one-third of its membership is elected in any one election. The constitution establishes a national civil service that operates in the states and allows them to establish their own civil services. Part XI of the constitution establishes the relations between the central and the state governments. The legislative jurisdictions of each are detailed in a schedule containing three legislative lists: the Union List, the State List, and the Concurrent List, upon whose items both the center and the states may legislate, with the center having precedence. For example, on the Union List are defense of India, atomic energy, railways, interstate trade and commerce, and many taxes and duties—97 in all. On the State List are public order, local government, agriculture (including land revenue and agriculture income taxes), and state public services—a total of 66 items. On the Concurrent List are criminal law and procedure, economic and social planning, and education—47 items in all.

Other parts of the constitution establish the Supreme Court and the high and subordinate courts in the states and deal in discrete sections with central and state financial matters, trade and commerce, elections, the language of the union and the regional languages, special provisions with respect to several states (particularly in the Northeast), and the amendment of the constitution.

The constitution's three grand, mutually dependent goals are clearly discernible. Unity and integrity are mentioned in the Preamble and are provided for in the very first article, which establishes India as "a Union of States". They also appear as goals in the centralized character of the provisions for center-state relations, especially the Emergency Provisions, to be discussed later; in the legislative lists; in the unified judicial system and national civil service; in the provision for an official language (Hindi); in the restrictions allowed to be placed on the freedoms of speech, assembly, and association "in the interests of the sovereignty and integrity of India"; and in single citizenship. In contrast to the United States, where an individual is a citizen of, say, both Vermont and the United States, an Indian is a citizen of India only.

Democracy also appears in the Preamble and is established through parliamentary government at the center and in the states; through the judicial system; through the Fundamental Rights and the provisions against discrimination elsewhere in the constitution; in the goals of social and economic egalitarianism in the Directive Principles; in the Fundamental Duties (added by the 42nd amendment of 1976); and, most of all, in the provision for universal adult suffrage (the voting age was reduced from 21 to 18 by amendment in 1988).[4]

The social revolution, with its especially close relationship to democracy, is given special emphasis in the Preamble, which is a direct descendant of Nehru's Objectives Resolution. The people of India, it says, having formed a "sovereign democratic republic," resolve to secure for all: "justice, social, economic and political; liberty of thought, expression, belief, faith and worship; equality of status and opportunity; and to promote among them all fraternity assuring the dignity of the individual." The words "and the unity and integrity of the nation" were added to the Preamble by amendment in 1976, as were the words "socialist secular" after "sovereign." Although the latter two words had long expressed national goals, their insertion was a device to serve the purposes of the state of emergency that Indira Gandhi had imposed on the country a few months previously.

The Fundamental Rights and the Directive Principles of State Policy are in Part III and Part IV of the constitution. The Rights are those "negative rights" well known since the 18th century, including the right to equality before the law and equal protection of the law; no discrimination on the grounds of "religion, race, caste, sex, place of birth"; and the "freedoms" included in Article 19. This article grants the freedoms of speech, expression, and peaceful assembly, of movement and residence, to form unions and associations, to practice any occupation, and to "acquire, hold, and dispose of property." The 44th amendment (1979) moved property from the Fundamental Rights portion of the constitution to a new Article 300A: "No person shall be deprived of his property save by authority of law." Holding property became a constitutional right but not a fundamental right. The Rights also abolish "untouchability" and allow the government to give special treatment in government employment to "backward" classes of

---

[4] The 42nd amendment added a new Part IV-A, "Fundamental Duties," to the constitution. Still controversial, they are considered essential by some and window dressing by others. They include the duty of each citizen to abide by the constitution, to cherish the noble ideals of the freedom struggle, to defend the country and uphold its unity, to promote harmony among India's peoples, to protect and improve the environment, and to develop the scientific temper and humanism and the spirit of reform. The Duties are nonjusticiable.

citizens. Article 22 is unusual. It allows for preventive detention (several preventive detention laws were on the books at the time), and it establishes curbs intended to prevent abuse of such laws.

Little of all this may sound revolutionary to the American reader. But in a society as firmly traditional and hierarchical as India's, where status depended on caste, occupation, and/or control of agricultural land, all the Rights were revolutionary. There might have been an approximation of equality among those at the very top of society, but not elsewhere. For many Indians, that a low-caste person (let alone an "untouchable") or a woman should be treated socially or by the law as the equal of a higher-caste individual or a man was quite literally unthinkable. Through the Rights and the Principles and through universal suffrage and representative government, with neither the communal electorates nor the restricted franchise of British times, Constituent Assembly members intended to break the traditional mold of their society.

The Directive Principles were as revolutionary or more so than the Rights—although they were not to be justiciable, only "fundamental in the governance of the country," a distinction ripe for controversy. For the Assembly's constitutional adviser, B. N. Rau, the Principles were "positive rights . . . moral principles for the authorities concerned." For Assembly member T. T. Krishnamachari, they were "a veritable dustbin of sentiment."[5] Nevertheless, the Principles contain a mixture of social revolutionary (including classically socialist) and Hindu and Gandhian provisions—and, as we shall see, they have greatly affected constitutional developments by becoming yardsticks for measuring governments' successes and failures in social policy.

Among the social revolutionary principles were "that the ownership and control of the material resources of the community are so distributed as best to subserve the common good"; "that the operation of the economic system does not result in the concentration of wealth and means of production to the common detriment"; that there should be a uniform civil code; that free and compulsory education up to age 15 should be provided within 10 years; and that children and the health and strength of workers should be protected and maternity relief provided. Amendments would add more principles, among them that the legal system should provide legal aid; that there should be worker participation in management; and that the government should endeavor to improve and protect the environment.

---

[5] See B. N. Rau, *Constitutional Precedents,* third series (New Delhi: Government of India Press, 1947), p. 22. For Krishnamachari, see *Constituent Assembly Debates,* Vol. 7, no. 12, p. 583.

The Hindu and Gandhian principles were fewer. They included the organization and empowerment of village *panchayats*; prohibition of intoxicating liquor and injurious drugs; "and prohibiting the slaughter of cows and calves and other milch and draught cattle."

Arduous and painstaking though the drafting process was, Indians have since found it desirable to amend the constitution. Indeed, it has been amended so often (some 70 times) that critics in India and elsewhere have claimed that the constitution has been reduced to a "scrap of paper." The text of the constitution can be changed in three ways. One way is by simple majorities in each house of parliament. Technically, such changes are not "amendments," even though they may alter the definition of citizenship in the constitution and may change the boundaries of a state. Article 368 of the constitution provides for amendment in two ways. The first is by a majority of the members of each house with a two-thirds majority of the members present and voting. The second method of amendment is by passage as in the first method plus ratification by the legislatures of one-half of the states. The constitution requires this latter method if an amendment affects certain "federal" articles.

The two dozen or so amendments made by simple majority have dealt with administrative matters—changes in state boundaries and the creation of new states along with citizenship issues. Some 14 other amendments have dealt with matters of policy, ranging from one that said that the nondiscrimination provisions in the constitution should not prevent special treatment for "backward" groups to other amendments affecting the distribution of essential commodities, taxes, and education. Thus, about half of the amendments have made adjustments to the constitution without weakening it.

The effect of other amendments is arguable. A few have struck at the heart of democratic government. The amendments arising from property issues have had an unforeseen detrimental effect on the Fundamental Rights and the constitution itself, as will be discussed later.

The Constitution's Antecedents

The constitutional history of pre-British India has two major threads, politics of empires and concepts of governing. The elements of the former (imperial rule through local chieftains), though fascinating, are not singular to India. The content of the latter is astounding. For 2,500 years the Vedas, the Upanishads, the Shastras, the writings of Kautilya and Shankara and of the Buddhists and the Jains, and the epic myths of the Ramayana and the Mahabharata (widely read and performed today) proclaimed or explored the processes and ethics, indeed the very origins, of society and government. The concept of *dharma* (or cosmic law, right action, and duty as expressed in the Dharmashastra) was to regulate all human activity.[6] Kings had defined responsibilities toward their subjects, who had a moral right to revolt against a bad king. Public opinion, according to some ancient texts, expressed itself through popular assemblies or councils (*sabha*s and *samiti*s). "Rama's [Ram, the hero of the Ramayana] noble example of devotion to duty, to his father, and to his people, as well as Sita's [Ram's wife] long-suffering fidelity to Rama, have been looked to as religious and ethical ideals down through the ages."[7]

When the British arrived in India at the beginning of the 17th century, in the shape of the Honourable East India Company, they brought English law and administration with them, first limited to themselves and then extended gradually to Indians. A series of Regulating Acts established executive authority and courts. Pitt's India Act in 1784 tightened the British government's control over the company and enlarged the governor-general's authority in India. An act of 1833 opened the company's civil service to Indians, although more on paper than in reality. In the watershed year of 1858 (the year after the "mutiny" or India's first war of independence, depending upon one's viewpoint), the Crown took over the East India Company to rule India through a secretary of state, who replaced the authorities who had supervised the company's activities. The Indian Councils Act of 1861 expanded the governor-general's legislative council, and in 1862 Governor-General Canning appointed three Indians (of maharaja or equivalent rank) to the council. The 1892 Indian Councils Act conceded the principle of elections both to local councils and to the Central Legislative Council, which was to include Indians.

In 1885 moderate Englishmen and middle-class Indians formed the Indian National Congress. Its demands included the development of self-government through expanded and elected legislative councils in the provinces and the holding of examinations for the Indian Civil Service in India as well as in England (to allow more Indians to compete for positions). In England the Congress began lobbying for its demands and published a newspaper, *India*. Upper-class and land-

---

[6] The Dharmashastra is "the Indian classical 'science of righteousness'" as based upon the Vedas and the recollections of sages from the writings of lawgivers like Manu and others. It is a collection of oughts and ought-nots, in large part from oral tradition. As such, it is very much customary law. J. Duncan and M. Derrett, *Introduction to Modern Hindu Law* (Bombay: Oxford University Press, 1963), pp. 2–3.

[7] Quotations and examples from William Theodore De Bary, general editor, *Sources of Indian Tradition* (New York: Columbia University Press, 1958), p. 212. See also U. N. Ghoshal, *A History of Indian Political Ideas* (Bombay: Oxford University Press, 1959).

holding Muslims founded the Muslim League in 1906. This period also produced a host of influential Indian political thinkers and the inevitable conflict between incrementalists and revolutionaries.

These developments provided the foundation for those that began in 1909, which led directly to the Indian Constitution. Secretary of State for India John Morley told parliament that the India Councils Act (the Morley-Minto Reforms) of that year would not lead directly or indirectly to parliamentary government in India, but it certainly did so. The act reserved a seat for Indians on the governor-general's Executive Council and resulted in Indians being on provincial executive councils. The act greatly expanded provincial legislative councils and allowed for the inclusion of many Indians. It also established representation by religious communities. The Indian Statutory Commission, reporting in 1930, found that such representation was not a cause of communal friction, but it was convinced that "separate communal electorates serve to perpetuate political decisions on purely communal lines."[8]

The 1919 Government of India Act (the Montagu-Chelmsford Reforms) went much farther. More important than its details were the sentiments underlying them: the "gradual development of self-governing institutions with a view to the progressive realization of responsible government in India as an integral part of the British Empire."[9] The act gave provincial legislatures authority over internal law and order and other subjects and stipulated that the governor's cabinet be chosen from among elected members of the legislatures. In New Delhi (the capital having been moved there from Calcutta in 1911), membership of the Central Legislative Assembly was greatly expanded. The Congress Party first accepted these reforms and then rejected them as inadequate.

The great changes brought about by the Government of India Act of 1935 were preceded by the report of a British investigating commission, a Round Table Conference held in London between Indian representatives and the British, and energetic politicking within the Indian independence movement. The 1928 Nehru Report, named after Jawaharlal Nehru's father, included a list of Fundamental Rights that was a direct precursor of the constitution's Rights and some of its Directive Principles. Following this was the Congress's "Resolution on Fundamental Rights and Economic and Social Change," adopted in

---

[8] *Report of the Indian Statutory Commission, Volume I: Survey* (London: H. M. Stationery Office, Command Paper 3568), p. 30.

[9] W. H. Moreland and Atul Chandra Chatterjee, *A Short History of India*, 4th ed. (London: Longmans, Green, 1957), p. 455.

1931 at Karachi. This is the immediate ancestor of the Principles; its motif was that "political freedom must include the real economic freedom of the starving millions."[10]

The 1935 Act and its implementation between 1937 and World War II was the great rehearsal for independence. The act established a federal structure, including the apex Federal Court, which became India's Supreme Court. Authority over certain subjects at the center was transferred to Indians, and there was full parliamentary government in the provinces, eight of which the Congress came to govern after its victories in the 1937 elections. (The British Governor-General and governors, however, continued to have extraordinary powers, including rule by ordinance.) The act had 478 provisions or "sections" and 16 schedules, setting the example for length the Indians would follow. (Several of the sections and schedules, however, pertained to Burma, which the act "separated" from India.)

National Unity and Integrity and the Constitution

The heritage of the past and the conditions of the present tilted Constituent Assembly members toward a strongly centralized constitution. The British had ruled from the imperial capital, written national codes of law for India, and included both countrywide and state constitutions in the 1935 Act. British domestic government, much admired by Indians, was unitary, and British political parties were centrally commanded—unlike the powerful parties in U.S. states. The Indian National Congress, for itself and as leader of the independence movement, adopted this central-command structure; powerful personalities submerged their differences to rid themselves of the British.

Events at independence reinforced existing sentiments and patterns. The vivisection of the subcontinent into Pakistan and India focused India's leaders on preserving the unity of that which remained India. Some 500 feudal so-called Princely States, which had neither been under direct British administration nor joined the federation envisaged in the 1935 Act, had to be brought into the new India. A spirit of unity had to be built to unite the diversities of religion, language, and region.

Nehru asked, "How shall we promote the unity of India and yet preserve the rich diversity of our inheritance?" He and leaders since

[10] D. Chakrabarty and C. Bhattacharya, *Congress in Evolution* (Calcutta: Book Company Ltd., 1940), p. 28.

have seen great dangers in "communalism," defined as including Hindu-Muslim extremism, "linguism," "casteism," and "provincialism." "Secularism," a sense of Indianness above subordinate loyalties, has been the ideal to counter the other "isms." Because "secularism" envisages a society more homogeneous than India's may ever be, failure to achieve it may have raised unwarranted fears. Although there have been genuine internal threats to national integrity, groups' demands for "independence" or "autonomy" often seem to have been bargaining chips for a better economic or political deal from overbearing or corrupt central or state governments, rather than genuine secessionist sentiment. (Hindu extremism in the Babri mosque affair falls outside this category.)[11] Invoking constitutional mechanisms like Emergency and President's Rule (discussed below) to control dissatisfaction may actually foster alienation.

India has so far managed threats to unity from the connection between language and subnationalism in several ways. Using foresighted provisions in the constitution, the states in 1956 were reorganized on a linguistic basis. Fifteen languages are "recognized" by the constitution. And the divisive issue of a "national language" was sidestepped by anointing Hindi as the "official language" of government while keeping English for many official purposes. Proceedings of the Supreme Court and the high courts are to be in English, although the president may authorize Hindi to be used in a high court. Subordinate courts use local languages and English. Regional languages have considerably displaced English in state governments.

Beyond what may be called social unity, India needed an economy that united its assets and brought development to its backward areas with some measure of evenhandedness. Most leaders believed that this demanded centralized economic planning and management and central government collection of many revenues for distribution among the states. So, for a variety of reasons seen as compelling, the constitution that Assembly members drafted was top-down, heavily centralized "federalism."[12]

The centralized character of the constitution is especially evident in its Emergency Provisions. These empower the president (on the ad-

[11] In 1963 a constitutional amendment, catalyzed by Tamil separatism coming after the 1962 India-China war, empowered government to curtail freedom of speech if it endangered the "sovereignty and integrity of India."

[12] Indicative of sentiment during the framing, and largely still, are the words of Rajendra Prasad, chair of the Constituent Assembly and the republic's first president: [I do not attach importance to the label] "whether you call it a Federal Constitution or a Unitary Constitution . . . as long as the Constitution serves our purpose." *Constituent Assembly Debates*, Vol. 11, no. 12, p. 987.

vice of the cabinet and the prime minister) to proclaim an "emergency" in all or part of the country because of war, external aggression, or armed rebellion. Under an emergency, the central government can direct—in effect, take over—the state government, and parliament can legislate on items in the state legislative list. The president may also modify the provisions for the distribution of revenues and can suspend both the "freedoms" of the Fundamental Rights and the right of citizens to appeal to the courts for their enforcement. The first nationwide external emergency, proclaimed in 1962 after the Chinese attack in the Northeast, continued until the end of 1967 despite loud criticism that the external dangers justifying the emergency had long since disappeared and that preventive detention under it was being abused. The second nationwide external emergency, proclaimed in 1971 on the occasion of war with Pakistan, was still in force in June 1975 when Prime Minister Indira Gandhi had the president declare an internal emergency. She then ruled dictatorially until forced from office by the 1977 winter election. Except during the last emergency, normal government processes typically continued, but the threat of unitary government hung over the country, and there were frequent charges of abuses of civil liberties.

A more frequently used emergency provision has been President's Rule. Under this, the president—"on receipt of a report from the Governor or otherwise" that a state cannot be governed according to the constitution—may assume the power of the state executive and declare that parliament may supervise or assume the powers of the state legislature. Parliament may then empower the president to legislate for the state. Proclamations resulting from President's Rule must be placed before parliament for approval.

As security has deteriorated, there has been a large increase in the number and size of centrally commanded police and paramilitary organizations. The presidentially appointed state governors have come to be seen often as "agents of the center." Other constitutional provisions have a centralizing aspect. For example, parliament has the power to adjudicate disputes of interstate river waters.

President's Rule was invoked sparingly until 1967. Since then it has been used increasingly with various justifications. It has been invoked when state coalition governments were unstable as well as after the actual breakdown of government during violent turmoil. Punjab and Jammu and Kashmir are current examples of the latter use of President's Rule. After 1967, Prime Minister Indira Gandhi (Jawaharlal Nehru's daughter) frequently employed President's Rule in questionable circumstances—as did the Morarji Desai government that succeeded her in 1977.

Overcentralization also resulted from the Congress Party's dominance and its central-command structure. Many state chief ministers and members of parliament came to owe their positions to Mrs. Gandhi's favor. She and her son Rajiv, who became prime minister after her assassination in 1984, made and unmade chief ministers, changed the composition of state cabinets by transferring ministers to the central executive, and otherwise toyed with state governments and local Congress committees. This personalization of power—drawing sustenance from an ancient reverence for sages that has become a cultural characteristic of adulation and sycophancy toward prominent persons—extended far beyond anything contemplated in the constitution.

Perceived overcentralization recently has produced reconsideration among politicians and intellectuals of the constitution's provisions and practices under them. Considerable, if as yet seldom defined, decentralization is increasingly thought of as the way to hold the country together.

Democracy, the Social Revolution, and the Constitution

Believed by Indians to be inseparable and as both means and ends, democracy and the social revolution may be considered together. They pose a well-known paradox: the democratic and social reform processes that are ultimately to bring about an equitable society upon which stable democratic government can rest will, on the way toward these goals, put both democracy and socioeconomic change at risk. They will do so by producing instability in the form of conflict and sharper oppression as the have-mores oppose the rise of the have-lesses and the have-nots.

A reform document, the constitution purposely engages this paradox. The Preamble, the Fundamental Rights and Directive Principles, and the special provisions to assist disadvantaged segments of society explicitly and implicitly call for reform. The special provisions for the disadvantaged and representative government with adult suffrage establish processes to pursue reform. Both these means and ends are revolutionary in a society where status is based on hierarchical position and possession of landed property, and where primary loyalties are to family, clan, caste, and region, more or less in that order. Reform also comes hard and slowly where individuals' economic survival genuinely is at stake because there are few institutional safety nets. The rich and middle ranks of society fear reform that would endanger their economic condition, and the lowest ranks are wary of pressing for reform for fear that retribution would increase their destitution.

The first great reform was to improve the lot of millions of Indians by giving "land to the tiller." When several courts struck down such legislation on the ground that compensation for property taken from landholders was inadequate, they ignited a constitutional confrontation over judicial versus parliamentary "supremacy" that would last 30 years. Beginning in 1951, constitutional amendments attempting to deny recourse to the Fundamental Rights (of which property was one) to gain adequate compensation for land taken "for public purposes" evoked a 1967 Supreme Court decision entrenching the Rights (the Golak Nath Case).[13]

Charging that the courts were blocking the social revolution (whereas the state governments' unwillingness to implement their own land-reform laws was more to blame), parliament responded in 1971 with two amendments. These said that parliament could amend *any* part of the constitution; that the amount of compensation for compulsorily acquired land could not be questioned in court; and that government policies to implement the two classically socialist provisions in the Directive Principles could not be challenged as violating the Fundamental Rights. (As mentioned above, these two provisions are that the distribution of the ownership and control of the material resources of the community shall serve the public good, and that wealth and the means of production shall not be concentrated to the public detriment.)

Under attack in these and other ways, the Supreme Court in 1973 handed down a remarkable decision. It upheld portions of the two amendments while asserting that when amending the constitution parliament could not damage its "basic structure," which the court did not define (the Fundamental Rights, or Kesavananda Bharati, case).[14] Judicial review of constitutional amendments now had a firmer foundation than before, and the court later reaffirmed the 1973 ruling. Prime Minister Indira Gandhi immediately struck back by appointing a presumably accommodating judge to be chief justice (to replace the chief justice about to retire), superseding three judges who would have become chief justice according to the convention of seniority (the infamous Supersession of Judges incident). The centrality of property issues to the social revolution and the amendments to the constitution resulting from property's being among the Rights eroded the stature of the Rights and of the constitution more broadly. Although many of these issues had been resolved by 1979, parliament

[13] *I. C. Golak Nath v. State of Punjab, 1967 Supreme Court Reports*, Vol. 2, p. 762.

[14] This case is formally named *Kesavananda v. State of Kerala, 1973 Supreme Court Reports*, p. 1461 ff.

by amendment that year removed property from the Fundamental Rights.

On June 25, 1975, in the name of implementing unrealized land and other economic reforms and citing domestic turmoil, Mrs. Gandhi had the president declare an internal emergency. She postponed parliamentary elections due the next year and had parliament—her creature since 1971 and now tamed by the arrest of some opposition members and the walkout of others—enact a number of amendments that were clearly anti-democratic. The government behaved in a manner equally so—with the Supreme Court seldom applying a brake. Eighteen months later, apparently believing that she and her Congress Party were popular enough to be reelected, Mrs. Gandhi called elections. The Congress lost massively. The new parliament repealed, and an awakened court struck down, the most egregious amendments enacted during the Emergency. Although the Emergency did little to spur the social revolution, it taught Indians a so-far indelible lesson in democracy's fragility.

Economic reform and social change beyond land reform also involved the constitution and its institutions of law and regulation. India needed to build a manufacturing base (which had been discouraged by the British) for its own sake and to provide jobs for those leaving the land. Heavy industry was to be in the public sector and there was to be a joint public-private sector for light industry and consumer goods. Each sector was to be guided by a sense of the public interest. The public sector was controlled directly from government ministries and the Planning Commission. A massive regulatory structure emerged, partly grounded in the Soviet experience, but principally resulting from the leadership's distrust of private industry and commerce. This, in turn, derived partly from the leadership's intellectual socialism and Fabianism and partly from Indians' experience with private commerce, which had a reputation, if not a record, for market manipulation, hoarding, food adulteration, and other "anti-social" practices.

Emphasis on a planned economy and regulation to effect balanced growth fostered the overcentralization discussed earlier and stifled entrepreneurship, a strong element in the culture. Nevertheless, a private sector grew, as initiative, sometimes assisted by corrupt practices, triumphed over obstacles. Private enterprise was ready, quite literally, to capitalize upon the "liberalization" quietly permitted by Mrs. Gandhi in the 1980s (her behavior was far less socialist than her rhetoric) and by her son Rajiv when he became prime minister. The government of the current prime minister, P. V. Narasimha Rao, is openly implementing a liberal economic policy, but the business leaders, politicians, and bureaucrats who benefited from heavy regulation are letting go reluctantly. Outsiders wishing to do business in India will need skill and great patience to do so successfully.

The considerable economic development that has taken place has not created enough jobs to absorb those who cannot make a living on the land. Although labor unions in major manufacturing have become strong, worker exploitation has been more the norm despite the provisions in the Directive Principles calling for protecting "the health and strength of workers . . . [and] children . . . the right to work . . . just and humane conditions of work . . . a living wage . . . [and] a decent standard of life." Yet economic development has spread and deepened democracy in much of the country. During the 1970s and 1980s the appointment to the Supreme Court of "activist" judges like P. N. Bhagwati, Krishna Iyer, Chinnappa Reddy, and others produced a number of judgments protecting workers and citizens more broadly. In a potentially far-reaching ruling, one of these expanded due process, which is not explicitly contained in the constitution, as a criterion for the fairness of administrative process.[15] Some rulings have been implemented, others not. Supreme Court activism has declined since these judges retired from the court. The court has infrequently used contempt of court procedure against government agencies to enforce implementation of its rulings.

Visible improvements in the political position of religious and ethnic minorities and Scheduled Castes and Tribes and other "backward" classes (OBCs) have also been due to constitutional provisions.[16] Reservation of seats for them in parliament's lower house and in the state legislatures, proportional to their percentage in the state's population, has brought them into public life. Educational levels have been greatly increased by affirmative action programs establishing percentage quotas for them in the civil services and government-supported educational institutions.

A constitutionally mandated commission to monitor the conditions of such groups and to recommend how they might be improved published a report in 1980 that was resuscitated in 1990 by then–prime minister V. P. Singh. He proposed to implement the Mandal Commis-

---

[15] This was the case in which Maneka Gandhi (the wife of Sanjay Gandhi and daughter-in-law of Indira) claimed that the issuance of a passport (hers had been impounded by the government) was a fundamental right (the right to practice a profession), which could be denied only by procedure. Thus, whether the law had been followed (due process) was involved. See *Maneka Gandhi v. Union of India, 1978 Supreme Court Reports*, p. 597 ff.

[16] The Scheduled Castes were "untouchables," and the Scheduled Tribes, noncaste indigenes. Both classifications date from British times.

sion recommendations by reserving 27 percent of government jobs and university admissions for OBCs on top of existing reservations for Scheduled Castes and Tribes.[17] A firestorm of protest erupted among students fearful of diminished educational and job opportunities for themselves, and agitated disagreement arose among various castes about the commission's classification of OBCs and whether or not their group should be included to receive preferential treatment.[18] A more important issue is the continued employment of caste categories in a society constitutionally dedicated to the withering away of caste through "secularism." The Supreme Court in 1992 upheld the principles the Mandal Commission had established, leaving important details for negotiation, including the application of criteria such as a means test to screen out individuals born into "backward" classes but who had achieved advanced economic and social status, particularly through education and the acquisition of agricultural land.

Women's lot overall is such that the Backward Classes Commission suggested that women constituted a "backward" class. A woman's rights and position are that of the men of her station—only less so. A woman is subordinate to her husband and to her mother-in-law. A poor woman's wages are less than a man's in industry. A lower-middle-class wife may risk "dowry death," particularly in the Northwest. In run-ins with the police, a woman lacking high social status is more likely to be abused than a man. Female infanticide is banned, but still occurs. On the other hand, improvements begun soon after independence continue. The Hindu Marriage and Succession Acts have given women property rights and other rights as well. The Law Commission has submitted 14 reports on women's rights. The Committee on the Status of Women has been following up on its report, *Towards Equality*.[19] Women now vote in numbers equal to men, are elected to parliament and state legislatures and serve as ministers, are active as lawyers, and make up 20 percent of the officers in the Indian Administrative Service. Upper-class women suffer few socioeconomic restrictions. Village women have shown themselves to be feisty, attacking the grog shops that serve their husbands' alcoholism, partici-

[17] *Report of the Backward Classes Commission* (New Delhi: Government of India, 1980), chaired by B. P. Mandal.

[18] The Mandal report also has raised matters of definition: Are castes and classes the same? Are the "backward" classes to be composed of certain castes? The report defines backwardness according to caste. In the view of the author of this chapter, certain castes (and caste frequently means occupation) may be fairly grouped as a class, "backward" or otherwise.

[19] *Towards Equality*, Report of the Committee on the Status of Women (New Delhi: Government of India, 1974).

pating in protest movements alongside men, and making their dissatisfactions public to a degree little imagined 40 years ago. Yet women have far to go toward equality.

Representative government and the social revolution have been mutually reinforcing. Adult suffrage, in addition to changes in landholding patterns and improved agricultural techniques and resources (irrigation, fertilizers), has created a band across rural Indian society of comparative economic well-being and power called the middle castes. (Paradoxically, many are OBCs, according to outdated criteria.) In parallel, the manufacturing, merchant, government service, and professional castes and classes have expanded with the growth of the economy, giving the country a rural-urban lower-to-upper-middle class of perhaps 300 million persons. This *broad* middle class is well represented in state legislatures, in parliament, and in all major parties. This leaves perhaps 100 million individuals near the edge of poverty and nearly half the population of 850 million poor to destitute, although even among the poorest, economic conditions have improved somewhat over the last 40 years. Although this enormous block of poor persons has representatives in parliament and the state legislatures, its political influence is small. The constitution's abolition of "untouchability" and the anti-discrimination provisions within the Fundamental Rights have had beneficial effects, although society remains very discriminatory.

In an important development, private voluntary organizations devoted to charity, to consumer and social causes (for example, environmental protection), and to the protection of civil rights are giving voice to segments of the population previously unable to affect governing processes. Greatly aiding this, the Supreme Court has given "standing" to third parties to represent in the courts individuals and groups of citizens with grievances. This has opened a new area of the law called public interest, or social action, litigation, which is examined more closely in the next section.

India has seen two transfers of power, one from the British to the Indians and the second from the upper classes/castes to the middle ranks, but not a third transfer: power sharing with the bottom half of society. This will come about, but it will take a long time. Meanwhile, as the bottom cries "upward" and those above cry "back," there will be turmoil and some violence as elements within society test both the goals and the institutions of the constitution.

The Constitution and the Legal System

India has an extensive legal system operating under the constitution and in aid of it. Its roots are ancient, its development modern. So far, the legal system has shown both notable successes and inadequacies in meeting its responsibilities. This section first examines the legal-judicial system as it is today and then looks at its historical development and the intersection of law and society.[20]

At the top of the structure is the Supreme Court. It is an appellate court with original jurisdiction on constitutional, federal, and human rights issues and has the authority to issue writs of habeas corpus and mandamus, among others. Appointments to the court are made by the president (that is, by the government, i.e., the law minister and the prime minister), usually from among high-court judges, after consultation with the chief justice of India, who may consult other judges. Below the Supreme Court are the high courts, typically one in each state. These are not state courts, although they have close relationships with state governments. They, too, have the authority to issue writs, and they supervise the subordinate judiciary below them. The president appoints these judges after consultation with the chief justice of India, the chief justice of the high court concerned, and the governor of the state. Appointees come from both the bar and the state's judicial service.

The top level of the subordinate judiciary is the District Court in the district's headquarters town, or elsewhere—each state being divided into a number of administrative units called districts. When dealing with civil matters, this is called the District Court; when dealing with criminal matters, it is the Court of Session; otherwise, nomenclature may vary from state to state. The civil courts are established by state legislation, although the parliament may act on them and their staffing is provided for in the constitution. The criminal courts are provided for in the Criminal Procedure Code. One judge may preside over both district and session courts, with the aid of other judges. Below the District Court is the Court of the Subordinate Judge, First Class, or the Civil Judge, Senior Division. The lowest court is the Court of the Civil Judge, Junior Division, sometimes also called the Court of the Subordinate Judge, Second Class, or the Court of the

---

[20] For this section, the author is particularly indebted to Courtenay Ilbert, *The Government of India* (Oxford: Clarendon Press, 1916); Marc Galanter, *Law and Society in Modern India* (New Delhi: Oxford University Press, 1989); Krishan S. Nehra, *The Judicial and Legislative Systems in India* (Washington: Library of Congress Law Library, 1981); the generous counsel of P. M. Bakshi, longtime member/secretary of the Indian Law Commission; and the tutelage of many others.

Munsiff. Below the Court of Session are Judicial Magistrates, First and Second Class, and Metropolitan Magistrates. In either civil or criminal matters, cases go to the lowest court in which they are eligible. Criteria for the jurisdiction of the courts are the seriousness of the offense on the criminal side and the money involved in civil cases. (For example, a Court of Session will hear cases of treason, murder, rape, extortion of a confession, and defamation of the president.) Appeals may be made upward to the high courts. Attempts have been and still are being made to establish village courts called judicial *panchayat*s for petty cases. These elected bodies have been established in some states more than others and have the appeal of a grass-roots justice and harmonious dispute resolution—with emotional and historical links to ancient, traditional government. But both bench and bar have tended to scorn this process. Unresolved questions of the "law" to be employed (local usage and statute law) and how to protect the *panchayat* courts' independence from village influences have impeded their development.

The hierarchy of courts is supplemented by tribunals and special courts that are increasingly active. The matters that go before them include consumer grievances; landlord-tenant, land revenue, income tax, and labor disputes; and family matters. Restraint of trade disputes go before the Monopolies Commission.

Under the British, the head of government in a district had both executive and judicial roles. He was called the district magistrate or the "collector," because one of his original functions was to collect revenue. Today, the collector or district magistrate is entirely an executive official. If he or she is also an executive magistrate, he or she has the power to detain individuals to keep public order (usually under the Criminal Procedure Code or one of the central or state acts permitting preventive detention), but such detentions are outside the criminal/civil justice system until the detention is considered by an advisory board upon which a high-court judge sits.

District judges are appointed in two ways. They may be promoted by the high court from within the state's judicial service or be appointed from the bar if they have had seven years experience as an advocate. In either case, appointments are made nominally by the governor (effectively, the state ministry) in consultation with the high court. Appointments to lesser judgeships in a district include consultation with the state Public Service Commission, which conducts, with high-court assistance, the examinations for joining the state's judicial service. Candidates are required to have a Bachelor of Laws degree. District judges and to a lesser extent judges of lower courts now attend government-organized retraining courses.

To understand the legal education of judges and advocates in India, one must be familiar with the bar council system. The Advocates Act of 1961, which resulted from bar committee recommendations, provided that the Bar Council of India should maintain a common roll of advocates having the right to practice in any court, including the Supreme Court; should designate senior advocates according to merit; should create autonomous bar councils in each state; and should prescribe uniform qualifications for advocates. For the latter there was created the Legal Education Committee of the Bar Council, which among other things was to set standards of legal education in consultation with universities. As a result, since 1968 the 130 or so law schools in India must offer a three-year course using the Bar Council's prescribed curriculum in order to grant a Bachelor of Laws degree—which must be preceded by a Bachelor of Arts or Bachelor of Science degree. (A number of universities also offer a Master of Laws, and fewer, a doctorate.) To be admitted as an advocate, an individual must have an LL.B., be over age 21, and be an Indian citizen. There are no bar examinations as there are in the United States. With the exception of Calcutta, there are no solicitors in India, with the result that there is little pretrial fact finding or discovery. Some senior advocates (equivalent to English barristers) have "juniors" to assist them. A bar council, particularly that of the Supreme Court, may have considerable influence on judicial affairs. Councils discipline their members; lawyers may not be disciplined by the courts.

Although the moral law of India dates to the Hindu Shastras and Muslim *shari'a* law, today's statutory law and judicial processes are British with Indian modifications. During their early years, the British in India primarily had to govern themselves. For example, in 1669 the Crown authorized the East India Company at Bombay, through its court of committees, to make basic laws, ordinances, and constitutions for their own and the inhabitants' good government, which they did using British law. As the company, and after 1858 the Crown, expanded its territories, law followed. Initially the British wished to avoid entanglements with indigenous disputes and legal systems, but practicality and their "civilizing" mission drew them in. They found bewilderingly varied legal texts, sources, traditions, and procedures among the Hindu and Muslim communities. Although Shastric and *shari'a* law supposedly prevailed, disputes were settled by a mixture of classical texts and local custom and usage in a variety of tribunals. A dual system of laws, British and indigenous, evolved. Where they overlapped and indigenous law was involved, the British appointed Hindu and Muslim "experts" to expound the law to British judges. The result was that the "law" could vary with what the "expert" thought it to be and the British judge's interpretation of what the "expert" told him. British deviations from indigenous systems were confined largely to laws and practices "no civilized government could administer," such as *sati* (widow self-immolation) and the harsh Muslim criminal penalties like execution for heresy and apostasy.[21]

Deciding that it was "expedient that, subject to such special arrangements as local circumstances may require, a general system of judicial establishments and police, to which all persons whatsoever . . . may be subject" should be constructed, the governor-general appointed two law commissions, which sat between 1833 and the 1880s.[22] The great Anglo-Indian Codes resulted: the Indian Penal Code of 1860 and in succeeding years the Indian Councils Act, the Criminal Procedure Code, the Civil Procedure Code, the Indian High Courts Act, the Succession Act, the Evidence Act, the Contracts Act, and others. Modified from time to time, these became the national laws of India. Because the 1950 constitution provided that all laws pre-existing it remained in force unless repealed, the codes, with modifications, are the law of India today. The British mainly left personal, or family, law to adjudication by the various communities unless the individuals concerned opted to place themselves under British law. Law and its administration in the so-called Native States (ruled by feudal princes and not part of British India) were left largely to the rulers of these states.

The law of torts (or civil wrongs) as administered by the British was practically English law, but it was never codified in the manner of the great codes. Under the constitution, government may sue and be sued; however, judicial rulings have established that government may not be sued for injury done in exercise of its "sovereign" functions, but only for wrongs done by government servants in the course of business. An individual may sue if a product causes him harm or if an environmental hazard harms him. But actions under tort are seldom undertaken for a number of reasons: contingency fees are barred; ad valorem court fees must be paid; and magistrates' awards are low (there are no juries). There is no body of tort law, and lawyers are not trained for tort cases. As one result, "claims are diverted into requests for specific relief and into criminal complaints," as the case of the Union Carbide toxic gas leak from its plant in Bhopal has demonstrated.[23]

---

[21] Ilbert, *Government of India*, p. 355.

[22] Ibid., p. 86.

[23] Marc Galanter, "Legal Torpor: Why So Little Has Happened in India after the Bhopal Tragedy," *Texas International Law Journal*, Vol. 20 (1985), pp. 273–94. See also Marc Galanter, "When Legal Worlds Collide: Reflections on Bhopal, the Good Lawyer, and the American Law School," *Journal of Legal Education*, Vol. 36 (1986), pp. 292–310.

To enforce law, the British established a hierarchy of courts so like the present Indian system that it need not be described here. The district courts handled civil matters and criminal matters as a sessions court. Lower courts handled lesser cases. Magistrates were of the first, second, and third class, and the cases they could try were categorized in civil cases by the monetary awards sought and, in criminal cases, by the severity of the crime involved. The 1935 Act established the Federal Court. Although this was the direct parent of the Supreme Court and had jurisdiction in federal matters, could render advisory opinions to the governor-general at his request, and took appeals from the high courts, it was not a court of last resort. Appeals could go from it to the Privy Council in London. As this system developed, the changes made in who might sit as judges and appear before the courts as attorneys progressively involved Indians.

Trial by jury in India began in 1623, but it was never a major element of British-Indian jurisprudence. It was part of criminal, not civil, procedure and never had the sanctity it enjoyed under common law in Britain or under the constitution in the United States. The major recodification of the Criminal Procedure Code in 1898 said that criminal trials originating before high courts should be by a jury of nine and that the court could direct the use of a jury in criminal cases transferred to itself. Trials in Courts of Session should be by jury or with "assessors" (advisers to the judge on matters of fact). The code also provided that a "European or Indian British" accused could call for the majority of the jury to be either Europeans and Americans or Indians.

During the early years of independence, trials by jury seldom took place—never in seven states and only in some districts in others. The Law Commission, in a major report on judicial reform (1958), recommended that trial by jury be abolished. Citing the opinions of state governments, witnesses heard, and even Mahatma Gandhi, the commission gave as its principal reasons that competent jurors were hard to find, jurors were "approachable," juries were expensive, and such trials took longer than trials by a judge alone. The jury system had resulted in failures of justice, and it was a "transplantation" from England that had "failed . . . to take root in this country."[24] With the major rewrite of the Criminal Procedure Code in 1973, jury trial disappeared entirely.

How do the constitution, the judicial system, and the imported but modified laws fit Indians? Paradoxically, they may fit Indians ill while

---

[24] Law Commission of India, *Fourteenth Report, Reform of Judicial Administration* (New Delhi: Ministry of Law/Government of India, 1958), pp. 864–73.

suiting them well. They may fit them ill because both representative government and the judicial system run contrary to the oppressive hierarchy of a still largely traditional society and its norms. They may suit Indians well because Indians desire to change much that has been customary in their society and believe that the institutions and laws of the constitution give them the opportunity to do so. Indians also look to English and U.S. legal precedents regarding fundamental rights, especially, and to U.S. and Commonwealth legal precedents in federal matters. Yet there is a wealth of evidence that there have been major dysfunctions in the working of the constitution and law. Do these indicate that Indians have taken the wrong road toward an equitable society? Or are they only potholes in the road to eventual success? A look at developments gives some answers.

Clearly, laws altering property ownership along with technological advances in agriculture, industry, and commerce since independence have benefited many, the new middle castes/classes in particular. Just as clearly, some 40 percent of Indians have been left behind socially and economically, typically with only rhetorical invocation of the Directive Principles of State Policy. Politically, the underprivileged are better off, increasingly using the vote and reserved representation in legislatures and the bureaucracy to bring advances for their kind.

Land ownership—with its associated status and influence—continues to elude this 40 percent of society despite enactment of much land-reform legislation. Removing protections for property ownership from the Fundamental Rights leaves unaffected those who have no property. And it is unlikely to affect the small landholder, for the question, even for communists, has been how much property is enough, not whether ownership of private property should be eliminated. Acquisitiveness in India is as strong or stronger than the better-known Hindu asceticism.

Under the Fundamental Rights, Indians in the main enjoy liberty and exercise their "freedoms." Speech and the press are vigorously free. So is religion, and great attention has been given to protecting the religious rights of minorities. Yet where religion and law confront each other in India, as they have since the British came, there have been disasters. The inability of politics to contain and the law to prevent the destruction of the Babri mosque in Ayodhya by militant Hindus in December 1992 is an extreme example. More germane here is the confrontation between religiously derived personal law and the secular constitution, one of whose Directive Principles is that a common civil code should be developed for the country. During the early 1950s, Prime Minister Nehru led a campaign in parliament to enact the Hindu Code Bill, which would have supplanted the customary law of the Dharmashastra. Marriage and divorce, inheritance, the rights of individuals in joint families, and much else would have been affected. Resistance outside and within the government (including from President Rajendra Prasad) prevented passage of an omnibus bill, but parliament did pass a series of acts (known collectively as the Hindu Code) making many of the larger bill's changes. In deference to Muslim sensitivities in the wake of partition, the government did not attempt a similar secularization of Muslim personal law, evoking from Hindu militants over the years charges of "coddling" Muslims. (For a current manifestation of this dispute, see the discussion of the Shah Bano case in Chapter 1.)

Exercise of the freedom of association varies. Labor unions in big industries considerably protect their members; laborers in small industries typically are not protected, and employers would strongly resist formation of unions. Agricultural labor unions have not developed despite Congress Party rhetoric favoring them. Caste-based, religious, and other kinds of associations provide charity and scholarship assistance. Citizens' rights groups provide some measure of protection to consumers, judicial prisoners, and the environment.

Personal liberty is both widely enjoyed and severely violated, but government is not the primary offender. Denial of one citizen's liberty by another is India's greatest problem. Among the denials of liberty by government have been torture and brutality against persons awaiting trial, prolonged imprisonment without trial, ill treatment of the convicted, and excessive use of preventive detention. These have evoked more critical reports than remedial measures. Recently Amnesty International has become active on such illegal practices in India. Preventive detention, adopted from the British, has long been an issue. The Fundamental Rights of the constitution provide for preventive detention and include protections against its abuse. But national and state laws have whittled away at these protections, particularly through legislation designed to protect internal security. Detention has been used against genuine terrorists and to imprison both political opponents and alleged criminals against whom government believes it cannot win a conviction. Many judges, otherwise supporters of civil liberties, consider preventive detention a "necessary evil" in a society where intimidation of witnesses can be more the rule than the exception.[25] Civil liberties organizations to fight against abuses were established in the early 1950s and have recently become more numerous and influential, but the need for reform far exceeds their capacity to fight for civil rights.

---

[25] Retired Supreme Court and high-court judges in interviews with the author.

The two greatest liberty issues come from the structure of society: denial of one citizen's liberty by another, and access to the judicial system. One product of hierarchy in Indian society is the oppression of its lower ranks by those above. When the lower ranks seek civil and social liberties and economic betterment, they frequently are denied these, forcefully and otherwise, by dominant groups. The very system that allows such repression impedes its remedy. India does not have a Civil Rights Act, American style. The codes are said to make illegal acts by one citizen infringing the liberties of another, but their employment for this seems to have been limited. It is reasonable to predict that the awareness of democracy and its liberties that is budding throughout India will make this a prominent issue as the country progresses to a more equitable society.

In many of the same ways, hierarchy inhibits access to justice for many Indians. Americans will recognize the parallels with the poor's access to justice here and with our health-care system. Health care exists, but can you gain access to it, and, if you can, can you pay the bill? Position and poverty effectively exclude many from the judicial system in India. The poor are further disadvantaged because the subordinate courts, where they typically would take a case, are especially subject to higher-caste influence—and sometimes cash, according to popular perception.

New forms of process are ever so slowly protecting civil liberties and increasing access to justice. Called "social action litigation" (SAL) and "public interest litigation" (PIL), they have resulted from the Supreme Court's having given "standing" to third parties to lodge or enter a case on behalf of an individual or a group of citizens. Examples have been defenses of the rights of destitute children, tribal peoples, slum dwellers, bonded laborers, other exploited workers, prisoners in custody, and those affected in the Bhopal disaster. Also, legal aid has become a statutory right. The government has created a legal-aid agency, but this has experienced the financial undernourishment known to similar state and national agencies in the United States. These new processes, products of citizen outrage and the ingenuity of activist judges in landmark decisions (prior to which these judges sometimes invited the cases to be brought), have had both spectacular successes and been subject to misuse. Although far from institutionalized, they have come to stay in Indian jurisprudence.[26]

---

[26] See Marc Galanter, *Law and Society in Modern India*, pp. 290–91; and "From Public to Proxy," *Sunday Times* (of India, Bombay edition) September 6, 1992, p. 13.

Conclusion

India's record in constitutional and other legal affairs is mixed. The pertinent question, "Would any other system of governance and law have worked better?," is unanswerable. Traditionalists and neo-Gandhians—like the Constituent Assembly member who protested that in the constitution he heard not the music of the *veena* but that of an English band—have offered few suggestions for changing the constitutional structure beyond the decentralization of power and citizen empowerment in the village. Desiderata in any secular democracy, these stand high on current India's intention list. India's great attorney general M. C. Setalvad speculated that India's classical governing institutions, left by themselves to time, would have evolved into something like modern democracy and law.

Indians—at least those to whom it was available—embraced English law even in British times. In it they saw freedom from their traditional forms of constraint. Indians go to court today in droves for satisfaction in the dispute immediately at hand, to exercise power, and to win socioeconomic change. Democracy as well as law is exercised in the courts. The result is not always ideal, democracy being a garden in which both weeds and roses bloom. And the poor's access to justice is inadequate, sometimes just plain bad. Yet despite limited access to justice, the lack of flexibility of case-based law in a changing social environment, the judicial system's poor administration, and the tarnishing of the courts' reputation from actual and perceived corruption, the judiciary (tribunals and other forums included) maintains a higher reputation than any other element of government.

Indians are far from reaching the declared goals of their constitution and the best employment of its institutions. But they have been working at it for only 43 years. (Recall American law and politics in 1830.) No other people has faced such uncongenial circumstances for pursuing at the same time economic development and a civil society. The paradoxes as well as the grandeur of their three great goals beset Indians everywhere. The necessity to build unity from diversity brings forth forces for decentralization. The goal of resolving deep socioeconomic conflict by creating an egalitarian society produces interim-term conflict as the have-nots seek their share of society's goods and the haves protect their dominant position. Representative government allows for adjustments in power, while favoring the dominant. Democracy's ideals of fairness and disinterested public service war with the drive for personal, family, and group financial survival in a society lacking institutional safety nets.

India is a democracy with troubles. But the breeze of democracy is blowing. Constituencies for democracy, for the rule of law, are strong. Voters, both the literate and the illiterate; the press, both the reasoned and the scurrilous; entrepreneurs, both the sound and the shady; pressure groups, both the malignant and the best intentioned; elected representatives and officials, both the civic-minded and the corrupt; civil servants, both the timeservers and the constructive changers; corporate bodies, both governmental and private; governments, both national and state; the armed forces—all these groups prefer democracy to any alternative. Their dissatisfactions with their democracy and its attendant legal system are an affirmation of them, not a denial. When democracy and access to justice come more slowly than can be borne, the breezes will rise to violent winds. But the malleability of Indian society allows change. The society adjusts to events and forces. Therein lies India's hope.

5
Social Movements and the Redefinition of Democracy

Smitu Kothari

> We have for over a century been dragged by the prosperous West behind its chariot, choked by the dust, deafened by the noise, humbled by our own helplessness, and overwhelmed by the speed. We agreed to acknowledge that this chariot-drive was progress, and that progress was civilization. If we ever ventured to ask, "progress towards what, and progress for whom," it was considered to be peculiarly and ridiculously oriental to entertain such ideas about the absoluteness of progress. Of late, a voice has come to us bidding us to take count not only of the scientific perfection of the chariot but of the depth of ditches lying across its path.
>
> —Rabindranath Tagore

In the closing weeks of 1992, a large contingent of police and government officials moved into several villages in the northernmost part of the state of Maharashtra in India. Armed with bulldozers, they came to evict forcibly residents who were slated to be in the submergence zone of what is arguably India's most controversial development project—the Sardar Sarovar dam on the Narmada River. The villagers stood their ground. Supported by people who had gathered there from all over the country, they reaffirmed their pledge to resist displacement. Despite the use of force and intimidatory tactics, the police were unsuccessful in their eviction efforts.

These tenacious villagers are part of a unique movement that has been gathering momentum in the valleys of one of the most sacred rivers in India. This ground swell, like other popular assertions across the length and breadth of the country, is challenging some of the most fundamental givens of postcolonial India: parliamentary democracy, nation building, and rapid economic development as the means of achieving progress and equity.

The Sardar Sarovar Project (SSP), located in Gujarat state, is expected to irrigate 1.9 million hectares of land and provide 1,450 megawatts of electricity. The project, if completed, will submerge 13,744 hectares of forestland and 11,318 hectares of agricultural land and displace over 400,000 people from their traditional habitats.

Shifting from an earlier stand of seeking comprehensive resettlement, a majority of people in the submergence area have been opposing the dam since 1988. Over the past five years, representatives of these rural communities and of independent social action groups working among them have traveled beyond their local contexts to meet with successive prime ministers, chief ministers, and a galaxy of regional and national bureaucrats and administrators. They have also met with members of other organizations and movements from across the country and played an important role in forging new independent national formations that are redefining autonomous political action in the country.

It is significant that these representatives have also ventured beyond the national boundaries; in addition to participating in official government hearings on the role of international aid and of the World Bank in this project, held in Japan, the United States, Germany, and Canada, representatives have linked up with organizations in more than 20 countries in an effort to create wider public awareness and to influence governments. In late 1992 full-page advertisements in the *New York Times* and Britain's *Financial Times*, signed by over 900 organizations from countries all over the world, openly challenged the World Bank's involvement in this project.[1]

Much of this activity is unprecedented. Several years earlier, in 1989, the Japanese government, relenting to growing public pressure, withdrew its commitment to provide a loan for the project. Subsequently, several European countries and the European Parliament called on the World Bank to withdraw from the project. In response to this pressure, the World Bank was forced to constitute, for the first time in its history, an independent review of the project.[2] After an eight-month investigation, the review concluded that "the project is deeply flawed" and called for the World Bank "to step back."

Despite this unequivocal conclusion, along with national and global pressures and the growing evidence that the project had serious economic, social and ecological problems, the Indian governments (state and central) and the World Bank remained committed to the project.

---

[1] *New York Times*, November 25, 1992; *Financial Times*, November 25, 1992.

[2] *Sardar Sarovar: The Report of the Independent Review* (Canada: Resources Futures International, 1992).

However, because of the pressure generated by the report of the independent review, in October 1992 the executive board of the World Bank set conditions for its continued involvement. These included a series of social and environmental studies that the Indian state and central governments had to complete by March 31, 1993. By early March, it was becoming evident that the governments were going to be unable to meet even these minimum conditions. Citizens' pressure in Europe, Japan, and the United States also gave clear indication that those countries' executive directors in the World Bank were going to vote in April against the bank's involvement in the project. At almost the last minute, in a desperate attempt to save face, the Indian government informed the bank that it did not want the remaining undisbursed loans.

The Gujarat government has continued to propagate the project as being essential for meeting the crucial water needs of the state. With over 70 percent of its districts drought-prone, the project has been heralded as the "lifeline of Gujarat." However, the government's own data show that over 80 percent of the most severely affected areas of the state will not get even a drop of water.[3]

Critics argue that not only are there more sustainable and cheaper means of achieving water security in a much wider area than the SSP provides for, but also the massive costs of displacing over 400,000 people along with their cultures and habitats can be avoided. Critics also point out that as the populace of Gujarat is socially stratified, the water will primarily benefit industry and upper-caste farmers. Also cited is the enormous cost of the project: current estimates range from $4–5 billion. This works out to a staggering $1,000 per irrigated hectare. Several alternatives that are relatively more equitable and less socially and environmentally disruptive have been available since the 1950s—plans that would not only ensure stronger local control but cost between one-third and one-tenth of this.

The controversy has raised crucial questions regarding the "politics of development." Who benefits? At whose cost? Who decides who will be displaced or what constitutes "progress"? What should be the mechanisms of securing the participation of communities whose entire life-support systems will be fundamentally altered by these developmental projects and processes? These questions have been at the center of the efforts of the local movement in the Narmada Valley as it has mobilized a global campaign in its favor.

---

[3] Narmada Development Department, *Planning for Prosperity: Sardar Sarovar Development Plan* (Gandhinagar, Gujarat: Sardar Sarovar Nigam Limited, November 1989), p. 250.

Today it is increasingly accepted that these movements and other efforts by citizens' groups to build horizontal linkages transcending local and even national boundaries represent a watershed for India's exploding nongovernmental sector. In fact, in many parts of the country, these assertions are contributing to the process of redefining governance as it has been conventionally understood. These movements have also underscored one of the many crises of the modern Indian state: that, despite efforts to be a "nonpartisan arbiter" and despite a complex system of providing funds, programs, and patronage to the poorer sections of society, the state is incapable of creatively accommodating these "claims from the grass roots." It has continued to try to appropriate these claims, and occasionally it has been successful in doing so. However, where this appropriation has failed, the government has attempted to undermine and eventually crush the dissenting activity.

This chapter assesses the historical and contemporary processes that are reflected in the diverse array of independent social and political activity in India. It is divided into five parts: a historical contextualization of social movements in contemporary India; an overview of the different movements; a description of the relationship between these movements and the state; some ongoing debates within these movements; and an analysis of the movement in the Narmada Valley. At the outset, two clarifications are necessary.

Most of the movements that have mass participation resent the externally imposed classification "nongovernmental organization (NGO)." They consider it a negative identification. While a wide range of terms that groups use to define themselves has evolved in every Indian language, some commonly accepted ones are "social action groups," "political action groups," and, similarly, "social movements" and "political movements." Equally, there continues to be confusion regarding the term "voluntary." While voluntarism has been an integral feature of Indian social life throughout history, it has significantly changed in identity and character as the modern nation-state system has consolidated. In the more recent past, the term (particularly "voluntary agencies" or VOLAGs) has come to connote organizations that are officially registered under the Societies Registration Act of 1860. Significant confusion continues to prevail in the literature, with different nomenclatures being used interchangeably.

Another confusion invariably arises as to what is meant by social and political action groups and movements. One could legitimately consider Hindu "chauvinist" organizations or linguistic mobilizations to be social action groups or mass movements. Here, however, we are narrowing the definition of these terms to include only those initiatives that are struggling for social justice through cultural and political means and for structural changes toward that end (and even this assumes commonly accepted meanings of what constitutes justice and change).

In the past decade, there has been much greater acknowledgment both in the media and in academia of the important roles movements like those in the Narmada Valley play in the processes of democracy. D. N. Dhanagare, a prominent Indian sociologist, stated that the emergence of "a large number of action groups who have been trying to educate, conscientize and mobilize different marginalized sections, particularly the oppressed poor, is *the most important development in India since the 1960s*."[4]

There is, however, little appreciation of the diversity, scale, and creativity or the longer-term political role that these groups are playing. For the media particularly, these groups are "watchdogs" acting as important correctives to regressive or lawless state policies. Among academics, there is a slow recognition of a more fundamental role that some of these groups and movements are playing in challenging the state, other vested interests, and economic and social injustices. Equally, many see them as innovators, not only attempting to sustain entitlement and strengthen control over local production processes but also collaborating with other similar groups to play a role at the national, regional, and global levels. There is also a growing acknowledgment of their representing and bringing into being more democratic institutions and processes of governance.

The primary focus of this chapter on social movements and action groups is on the struggle and support activities (and to a lesser extent on the single-issue-based activities that work toward systemic transformation), because such efforts are not dependent on development project cycles and therefore require a longer-term commitment. This is not to underestimate the importance of the activity undertaken by the more conventional developmental groups. In fact, this activity plays an important role in bringing immediately realizable benefits: improved medical support, adult literacy, and more secure access to water, to name just a few. Also important is the shedding of a deep-seated belief that oppression is part of one's *karma*, that is, that it is inherited. Often, the realization of economic rights facilitates the capacity to make demands for delivery of services and for implementation of laws that guarantee protection against oppressive conditions.

---

[4] "Action Groups and Social Transformation in India," *Lokayan Bulletin*, Vol. 6, no. 5 (Delhi: Lokayan, 1988) (author's emphasis).

What may thus be achieved is personal or collective empowerment, a process that creates conditions for raising the larger issues of structural oppression, whether within the home, in the fields, or in the workplace.

Historical Context

Movements in Preindependence India

Historically, voluntarism encompassed not only efforts within the community (self-help, management of commons, and provision of civic amenities) but also efforts outside it (relief in times of calamity, community kitchens for the poor, and philanthropy). Numerous institutions provided channels for voluntary activity. These ranged from the *panchayat*s (village councils) to the *gurukul*s (community-owned schools).

In the 19th century, significant social-reform movements, including those seeking religious reform, drew on this spirit of voluntarism. Some notable examples are the Brahmo Samaj (1828) and Arya Samaj (1875), which opposed child marriage and practices like *sati*. Both these movements mobilized voluntary participation of people from various communities and castes. This period also witnessed other activity challenging religious and social injustices. Social reformers and critics like Jyotiba Phule (1827–90), Bal Gangadhar Tilak (1866–1915), and, later, Babasaheb Ambedkar (1891–1956) were successful in widespread mobilization toward this end. Significant examples from the mid-19th century include initiatives in support of widow marriage and intercaste marriage, spearheaded by people like Ishwar Chandra Vidyasagar and K. C. Sen. Other well-coordinated voluntary efforts were the social-service initiatives undertaken by the Servants of India Society.

The last two decades of the 19th century saw the deepening of the nationalist movement and the slow emergence of women articulating a greater consciousness of their rights. Various independent organizations were set up by women, many of whom had earlier crossed structural barriers and gone abroad to study. Several important magazines like *Stree Darpan* became public forums to highlight women's concerns.

Similar initiatives were taken up by specific groups with distinct social or religious identities, for example, by the Christian community and by caste groups like the Nadars and the Vayanars. Christian volunteers penetrated interior areas of the country to provide education and health care and, of course, to propagate the faith. In addition to the institutions of the church, numerous organizations were set up to further such activity. This legacy continues until today but with a wider range of ideological thrusts. Some of the most self-consciously political agendas that challenge entrenched power interests are being promoted by Jesuits and other Christian groups.

An example of caste mobilization for economic and social "uplift-ment" is the Nadar community in Tamil Nadu. A historically "un-touchable" caste, Nadars made tremendous efforts in the 19th century to achieve economic mobility. Intricate networks were then set up to enhance the social status of the caste. A complex of community centers, inexpensive hotels, and trading networks was also set up, which, in turn, helped to generate significant political clout for the community (to the point that, in the 1960s, one of its members, Kamaraj, was chosen chief minister of Tamil Nadu). The case of the Nadars may not be representative, but it is nevertheless indicative of voluntary efforts made by individual caste groups for furthering the interests of their community as a whole.[5]

This period (1840–80) also saw the slow crystallization of resistance to colonial rule, compelling the colonizers to institute legal controls over this activity. In the first modern effort to regulate and monitor voluntary associations and other groups, the British legislated the Societies Registration Act in 1860. Arguably, for these social-reform organizations, whether or not they were linked to the anti-colonial resistance, "the colonial state became a frame of reference for defining their scope of activities and their legal identity."[6] While some voluntary activities began to be increasingly perceived as anti-state, several others pushed the state to adopt progressive social legislation. For many, the thin line between political autonomy and co-optation by the state became thinner.

However, popular mobilization against British policies was not restricted to seeking reformistic responses. In numerous parts of the country, by the middle of the 19th century, communities had mobilized to oppose colonial intrusion. This opposition was significantly manifest in tribal areas where communities did not acquiesce quietly in the face of external intervention. There were protests and rebellions against colonial laws such as the Forest Act of 1876. While adherents of the newly emergent colonial science of forestry had begun to blame

[5] Smitu Kothari, "There's Blood on Those Matchsticks: Child Labour in Sivakasi," *Economic and Political Weekly*, Vol. 18, no. 27 (July 2, 1983).

[6] See D. L. Sheth and Harsh Sethi, "The NGO Sector in India: Historical Context and Current Discourse," *Voluntas: International Journal of Voluntary and Non-Profit Organisations* (Manchester, U.K.: Manchester University Press), Vol. 2, no. 2 (November 1991).

the agrarian system of forest dwellers for decline in forest coverage, tribal peasants in India were waging struggles against state intervention in forest resources based on their own moral economy. Gadgil and Guha have aptly described this conflict as between the political economy of profit and the moral economy of provision.[7]

The Jainti hill tribes revolted in 1744, the Bhils in 1846. The Naikads revolted in 1858. The Koya tribals revolted successively in 1862, 1879, and 1880. The rebellions in Bastar in 1876 and the Rampa rebellion in the Godavari district were just the first glimmerings of the successive forest *satyagrahas* against the Indian forest department after 1878.[8] In Jharkhand, the recorded history of resistance movements dates back to as early as 1600 A.D. The well-documented ones among them, such as Tika Manjhi (1780), the Kol Revolt (1831), the Santal Hul (1855), and the Birsa Revolt (1900), are only landmarks in a continuous genealogy of dissent in areas like Jharkhand.[9]

By the early 1900s, the nationalist struggle had begun to mobilize the dispersed social-reform movements as well as the disparate acts of resistance (encompassing a wide range of ideological persuasions) against British rule into a more coherent movement. Gandhi and other leaders creatively blended local issues (for example, the planting of indigo or the appropriation of natural resources or the price of salt) into the anti-imperialist national struggle. Simultaneously, thousands of people were inspired to undertake voluntary work ranging from health and education to spreading awareness of social injustices. There was a virtual explosion of new organizations. Gandhi's effort was in that sense an embodiment of restoring centrality to voluntarism and the community. This was critically evident when, on the eve of independence, he sought the dissolution of the Congress Party and its conversion into a national force of activists committed to the task of realizing the general material and spiritual well-being of India's people. While this call was substantially disregarded, several people went further, founding in the process the Sarvodaya (Welfare of All) movement.[10]

---

[7] Madhav Gadgil and Ramchandra Guha, *This Fissured Land: An Ecological History of India* (New Delhi: Oxford University Press, 1992).

[8] Richard Grove, "Colonial Conservation, Ecological Hegemony and Popular Resistance: Towards a Global Synthesis" in *Imperialism and the Natural World*, ed. John MacKenzie (Manchester: Manchester University Press, 1990), pp. 15–50.

[9] Smitu Kothari and Pramod Parajuli, "No Nature Without Social Justice," in *Issues in Global Ecology*, ed. Wolfgang Sachs (London: Zed Books, 1993).

[10] Jayaprakash Narayan, *Total Revolution* (Patna: Allied Press, 1977); T. K. Oommen, *Protest and Change: Studies in Social Movements* (Newbury Park, CA: Sage, 1990).

On the other hand, influenced by Marxist-Leninist politics and by the workers' struggles in Europe, by the 1930s India's socialist and communist groups were able to provide a further channel for popular mobilization. While some of the organizing eventually got subsumed into political parties and the nationalist movement, with *kisan sabhas* (peasant associations) and trade unions providing the main organizing forums, the work of people like Godavari Parulekar (among peasants and tribals) in Maharashtra or Muzaffar Ahmad (among urban and rural scavengers and other oppressed communities) in Bengal inspired many young people to volunteer for this activity.[11]

The Postindependence Period to the Present

The first two decades in the postindependence period were marked by an ebb in the activities of social and political groups and movements. India's first prime minister, Jawaharlal Nehru, sought the participation of various voluntary bodies in the process of "nation building." This strategy was in keeping with Nehru's belief that the state must be the agency to facilitate the formation and strengthening of democratic institutions and generate social change. What emerged, however, was a broad network of patron-client relationships sponsored by the Congress system of state patronage. Numerous independent initiatives were subsumed within the ambit of the state. The Khadi and Village Industries Corporation and the Handloom Board are representative examples of this.

By the 1960s it was becoming evident that both the state-directed policies and the dominant model of economic development were gradually creating greater immiseration of the marginal populations of rural and urban areas. The euphoria of nation building and the hope that independent India would rapidly transform iniquitous social and economic relations were both gradually eroding. What compounded the sense of disillusionment and frustration and created the eventual ground for mobilization, particularly of marginalized and poor communities, was the fact that the conventional political formations—parties, trade unions, and farmers' unions and associations—were relatively ineffective in responding to endemic structural questions as well as to the adverse impacts of a fundamentally top-down capitalist development. The democratic institutions of the country were at best only peripherally able to respond to these realities. Even Gandhian

[11] For a brief treatment of a variety of popular mobilizations by party and nonparty groups, see Ghanshyam Shah, "Grass-Roots Mobilization," in *India's Democracy*, ed. Atul Kohli (Princeton: Princeton University Press, 1988), pp. 262–304.

organizations experienced a decline in their political purpose as they became increasingly dependent on governmental subsidies and grants.

It is this reality that in the late 1960s first inspired hundreds of primarily middle-class young people, many from the universities, to forgo the traditional options available to them (to become urban-based professionals or politicians or even to stay unemployed) and instead to go to the communities of oppressed and marginal people and join the struggle against social injustices. For most of these activists, this meant initiating mobilization to foster structural changes or to widen "the everyday forms of struggle," while for others, it meant active political mobilization to confront established power relations. For still others, the task was defined as a more efficient delivery of the numerous official programs aimed at alleviating poverty or creating some local assets for the poor. All these efforts were also aimed at bringing to the center of the political process the struggles of subordinate and peripheral populations.

For many, political activism was not new. They had been involved with the parties of the left, particularly the Communist Party of India–Marxist (CPM) because of its stated commitment to comprehensive land reforms and other radical measures. Others had been active in socialist parties and formations. Socialist leaders like Ram Manohar Lohia provided a significant political critique to the policies and programs of the ruling Congress Party. By the mid-1960s, however, there was a slow disillusionment with the Communist parties, particularly with what was perceived as a decline toward reformism, the appeasement of middle-class and rich farmers, and a greater emphasis on the industrial proletariat (and their gradual integration into the capitalist market economy). In early 1967, some of the most radical cadres supported a peasant uprising in the Naxalbari region of West Bengal. This was the founding process of the Naxalites and the Marxist-Leninist Party, followed in 1968 by a national level organization, the All-India Coordination Committee of Communist Revolutionaries (AICCCR). While the Marxist-Leninist Party has, in the intervening 25 years, split into several factions and diversified its political strategies, the radicalism continues to provide a significant base for activists frustrated with reformist politics—either of the governmental or the non-governmental kind. (Today, the activity is based primarily in three states—Andhra Pradesh, Bihar, and Maharashtra.)

While a majority of Naxalite groups supported an "annihilationist strategy" (either as an offensive or defensive weapon), several among them eventually gave up these methods and embraced electoral or social-movement politics. The latter activity ranges from popular mobilization to human rights work. While this "spin-off" resulted in numerous initiatives, two examples of groups that have significant influence today are the Indian People's Front (whose activities range from mass mobilization to publication, mostly in North India) and the constituent members of the Federal Front (a national coalition of groups working among both landless and marginal tribals and peasants as well as urban poor).

The Naxalite movement was also to have a profound impact on the radical traditions of social and political movements and their supporters and support organizations. Other events that influenced a radicalization of activism were the Jayaprakash Narayan (JP)–led Bihar movement, a struggle for "total revolution" and a "partyless democracy" and against the growing authoritarianism of Indira Gandhi's Congress rule, culminating in her imposition of a state of emergency in June 1975.

Following the Emergency and the defeat of the Congress at the center, there was hope that the new government, which represented socialist and leftist politics, would undertake the necessary transformations. This was not to be. While some attempts were made to decentralize power and render policymaking more transparent, within 19 months factionalism and disruptive politics forced the government to collapse, making way once again for the Congress. Throughout this period, a lot of important organizing activity in different parts of the country with landless labor, marginal peasants, and slum and pavement dwellers continued, regardless of the changes at the superstructural level. A representative example is the Chattra Yuva Sangharsh Vahini, a nonparty force of students and youth inspired by Jayaprakash Narayan and formally established in 1978 to further the struggle for his conception of total revolution. Vahini activists have been at the forefront of many significant rural struggles for the rights of the underprivileged and disadvantaged.

In an overall sense, the experience with the Emergency and its aftermath was fundamentally politicizing. Political awareness expanded and rural and urban struggles widened. In the urban areas, numerous new organizations were established to work with subjugated groups like women, slum and pavement dwellers, and child and unorganized laborers. Some notable examples are:

- Self Employed Women's Association (SEWA), which works among unorganized female labor in both urban and rural areas (SEWA has also initiated the formation of the first bank owned entirely by these women, who are the shareholders);
- Society for the Promotion of Area Resource Centers (SPARC), which works among slum and pavement dwellers in Bombay; and

- Committee for Working Children (CWC), which started its work among the working children in the shops and establishments in Bangalore, then expanded its activities to include a shelter and a major rural program.

Also included among urban initiatives are groups that support ongoing struggles in other parts of the country: documentation groups such as Bombay Urban and Industrial League for Development (BUILD) and Centre for Education and Documentation; human rights groups such as the Committee for the Protection of Democratic Rights and the People's Union for Democratic Rights; research and catalyzing groups such as Lokayan and Participatory Research in Asia (PRIA); single-issue groups such as the Centre for Science and Environment, the Forum Against Oppression of Women, the Centre for Women's Development Studies, and Medico-Friends Circle.

The ideological orientation of these urban and rural groups and movements encompasses a broader range than that of political parties. Extending from neo-Gandhian to Marxist-Leninist and drawing from sources as diverse as liberation theology and the more indigenous ideologies of people like Babasaheb Ambedkar and Mahatma Phule, this activity began both to challenge conventional ideologies and to contribute toward the definition of new ones. The organizational structure of these efforts—from cooperatives to party-like organizations to a dispersed but coherent association of individuals and groups—is equally diverse. Social movements thus criticize the centralization of power and policymaking. They also create the realization that the role of intellectuals is crucial to the empowerment of marginal groups, not in the conventional sense of providing leadership but by representing the best interests of the oppressed classes in a relationship of partnership.

Social Movements and Action Groups Today

While there are no clear indications of the number of independent groups (including NGOs and other welfare and charity organizations), estimates range from 50,000 to 100,000.[12] The Ministry of Home Affairs, which closely monitors organizations receiving foreign funds and therefore under the jurisdiction of the Foreign Contributions (Regulation) Act (1976, amended in 1984), has a listing of more than 15,000 groups. In

[12] This is an informed estimate based on several directories prepared by various departments of the government and by independent institutions. As yet, there are no comprehensive surveys.

1991–92, the total inflow of funds for these registered organizations was about $400 million. This does not include a sizable proportion of monies coming in from religious sources and from most of the United Nations system (UNICEF, UNDP, and so on).

One possible classification of independent groups in India is (1) welfare/charity—including religious and humanitarian activities; (2) developmental—including activities that help improve the social and material condition of the poor; (3) struggle-oriented—social action groups and movements; and (4) support—legal action, documentation, research, investigation, and so on. A fifth grouping is of single-issue organizations, for instance, women's organizations, environmental groups or those working exclusively with specific "target groups," such as handloom weavers and unorganized labor.[13] It is the last three that are the primary concern of this chapter.

Struggle-Oriented Movements

While it is difficult to do justice to the full mix of activity in which community-based groups are involved, the list presented below gives a sense of the diversity of participants and the range of activity. Unless indicated, besides the examples cited, similar movements are active throughout the country.

Tribals and Other Peasants. Community-based tribal and peasant groups are composed of those who oppose displacement and loss of control over productive natural resources, including commons. These community groups are challenging processes that create not just a crisis of survival but also threats to their cultural and social fabric. In addition, they are asserting demands for greater political and economic autonomy. Similar to the struggles around megaprojects like those in the Narmada Valley, most of this activity also challenges the dominant patterns of economic development.

Some representative groups are Kashtakari Sangathana (Organization of Toilers) and Bhoomi Sena (Land Army) in Maharashtra, and Mazdoor Kisan Sangharsh Samiti (Workers' and Farmers' Struggle Collective),

[13] Any such classification is fraught with problems. Often, organizations play multiple roles. Also, such division neglects the often fluid boundaries between these approaches as, for instance, when individuals or entire organizations shift from being instrumental agents of delivery for the developmental apparatus of the state to confronting local or societal structures and oppressions. Such a classification also does not give an indication of the range of ideologies, organizational activities, action strategies, and relationships with the wider political process—particularly the state and political parties.

Jharkhand Mukti Morcha (Collective for the Liberation of Jharkhand), and Lok Jagriti Kendra (Center for Empowering the People) in Bihar.

Lower-caste Groups (also called Dalits). Members of these communities fight against caste discrimination and various forms of bondage, and for permanent rights to lands on which they work as agricultural laborers, for strategies to strengthen affirmative action, and so forth. Some representative groups are the Association for the Rural Poor in Tamil Nadu and Bandhua Mukti Morcha (Front for the Liberation of Bonded Labor), working in different parts of the country. The Dalit movement has a long and important history in the contemporary political life of the country. Babasaheb Ambedkar, the chairman of the team that drafted the Indian Constitution, was also a Buddhist Dalit leader who inspired generations of Dalits to leave the fold of a caste-ridden Hindu community and struggle for an equal place in Indian society. Dalits all over India and more particularly in western India have some of the most vibrant organizations—from literary and cultural groups to those participating in political-party activities.

Urban Working Classes. These groups include those who are unorganized, generally lack security of tenure, and are targets of regular eviction. Also included are contract and construction laborers. Other urban residents are the poor who become victims of industrial and environmental disasters. In one dramatic example—Bhopal—several significant citizens' initiatives were taken. These ranged from medical surveys to campaigns for justice for those affected by the gas leak and the official indifference that followed. Other urban movements include those of organized workers, particularly those in the trade unions in mining areas like Dhanbad in Bihar and Madhya Pradesh, who have waged some of the most remarkable struggles in the recent history of the country.

Women. Women face not only discrimination within the family, community, and society but also legal discrimination in access to productive resources. A vast range of women's groups are active in the country's urban areas as well as in states such as Rajasthan and Kerala. Several struggles also focus on ecological questions as well as resistance to social problems like alcoholism. Representative examples are the Uttarakhand Sangharsh Vahini (Uttarakhand Struggle Movement) in Uttar Pradesh and the Appiko (Hug the Trees) movement in Karnataka.[14]

---

[14] The struggles of women are vast and diverse. Readers are urged to look at the excellent material generated by the women's movement, particularly in the past decade, and the chapter by Madhu Kishwar and Ruth Vanita, "Indian Women: A Decade of New Ferment," in *India Briefing, 1989*, ed. Marshall M. Bouton and Philip Oldenburg (Boulder: Westview Press, 1989).

Farmers. Farmers face the adverse impacts of the new economic policies that not only have reduced or withdrawn the subsidies to agricultural inputs but also threaten to increase dependence on transnational chemical and seed companies. A recent farmers' rally in Delhi (March 1–2, 1993) brought together more than 150,000 farmers from all over the country to express their opposition to the new proposals drafted under the General Agreement on Tariffs and Trade (GATT)—proposals that, for instance, would legitimize the foreign patenting of indigenous plant varieties and genes. Another group of relatively more affluent farmers held a smaller rally on March 31, 1993, expressing support for some aspects of the GATT proposals. An example of the former is the Karnataka Rajya Ryota Sangh (Karnataka State Farmers' Association) and of the latter, Shetkari Sangathana (Organization of Farmers), active primarily in Maharashtra. Both movements have extensive horizontal alliances with similar farmers' associations in different parts of the country.

Fishing Communities. Fisherfolk have been threatened by mechanized fishing and the increasing commercialization of the industry and export of fish. Federations exist all along India's coastline as well as on the banks of rivers and lakes. The better-known movements are the National Fishworkers' Federation and the Ganga Mukti Andolan (Movement to Save the Ganga).

Minority Communities. Members of minority groups are subject to a daily onslaught from fundamentalist forces both without and within their group as well as from the forces of the state, which frequently play a partisan role, for example, the role of the police in the recent communal riots or that of the army in states of the Northeast or in Kashmir. By far the most serious challenge facing the Indian polity is the growth of religious fundamentalism and bigotry as well as a crude nationalism that not only propagates a majoritarian state but also continues to neglect the fundamental structural discriminations inherent in the country's social fabric. Some important independent initiatives have taken place in an effort to intervene in the communalization process.

In the aftermath of Indira Gandhi's assassination in 1984, over 3,000 members of the Sikh community were killed in Delhi alone. Two major initiatives followed. Dozens of organizations in Delhi teamed up with scores of volunteers and founded Nagrik Ekta Manch (NEM; Citizen's Unity Forum) to provide relief and rehabilitation to the more than 80,000 survivors of the carnage. Simultaneously, the People's Union for Civil Liberties and the People's Union for Democratic Rights undertook an exhaustive investigation into who was responsible for the violence.[15] Both these initiatives went a long way toward providing solace and opening the avenues of justice for a beleaguered community.

Similar initiatives bringing together organizations and individuals and cutting across disciplines and political persuasion have taken place in cities where intercommunity conflict is a regular occurrence. Sampradayikta Virodhi Andolan (Movement to Oppose Communalism) in Delhi, Hyderabad Ekta (Unity), and Ahmedabad Ekta are three examples. A more recent effort is the formation of Independent Initiative, which has brought together some of the most respected academics, jurists, and journalists to monitor the defense of democracy wherever it is threatened. Two other efforts, the Kashmir Initiative and the Punjab Initiative, have attempted to highlight state repression in those two states and the wide range of draconian legislation that has permitted the lack of accountability of the state apparatus. Arguing that if the state does not abide by the rule of law, all semblance of civility breaks down, these groups have undertaken investigations, filed cases in court, held public meetings, and produced popular literature on the situation in these states. Both the initiatives have been criticized as being anti-national; it is argued that militancy and private terrorism merit the use of "strong-arm" measures and that these measures are in the interests of the unity of the nation.

One inherent problem of initiatives such as NEM and the Ektas is that while they have played a remarkable role in providing temporary succor, they have failed to provide a means for working with the communities in conflict in a more sustained way to create a permanent climate of amity.

More recently, the situation arising from the temple-mosque controversy has engendered a wide range of newer initiatives like the People's Movement for Secularism and the Secular Front in Delhi, and the various peace committees in Bombay and Surat.

An important debate has acquired a fresh momentum in this context. In the postindependence period, it was assumed by most of the ruling classes that the processes of industrial modernization and nation building (nurturing what might be called a positive nationalism) would gradually subsume the diversity of religious and other cultural identities. In fact, quite the reverse has happened, with boundaries around identities hardening. While most agree that religion should not be allowed to influence governance, the fact that dominant fundamentalisms and development processes that primarily benefit a few

[15] *Who Are the Guilty?* (Delhi: People's Union for Civil Liberties and People's Union for Democratic Rights, 1984).

create large-scale insecurities among other communities and identity groups is a cause of tremendous concern. In fact, it is these processes that are fueling the growing movements for political and cultural autonomy. Examples across the country range from the assertions of the Gorkha National Liberation Front (which after a protracted struggle was granted the rights to an autonomous region in eastern India) to similar "subnationalist" movements in Chattisgarh in the state of Madhya Pradesh or Kolhanistan in Bihar, and from the Jharkhand movement to the secessionist movements in Punjab and Kashmir. This range of movements also underlines the complexity of the action group universe as most of these movements also encompass demands for social and political justice.

Some Other Efforts

In addition to these struggles, numerous efforts are being made to secure legal and constitutional rights (including initiatives to repeal repressive and discriminatory legislation); to seek greater transparency (including the right to information and participation) in policymaking and planning processes; to assert the right to self-management and ownership of production processes; to achieve the right to work, housing, or socially relevant education; to secure a clean environment; and to gain access to cheaper health care (including significant mobilization for strengthening traditional healing systems).[16] Finally, cultural troupes and street theater groups play a crucial role in the process of building a movement. Among urban groups, a representative example is the Nishant Natya Manch (Theater Forum to Break the Silence), while other examples include Gurusharan Singh's group in Punjab, Gadhar's Jananatya Mandali (People's Theatre Group) in Andhra Pradesh, and Jan Sanskriti (People's Culture) in West Bengal, all of which perform in both urban and rural areas.

A wide array of urban activity, from legal support to comprehensive research and from documentation to communications support, supplements and expands the activities of these movements. In addition, several journals, magazines, and other publications report and analyze the activities and debates of these groups. Notable among

---

[16] Groups continue to contribute significantly to the policy process even though this is still seen as an activity over which the state wants to maintain total control. These initiatives range from playing a central role in the formulation of policies like the National Perspective Plan for Women to *Shramshakti*, a major policy document on self-employed women and other female laborers, to chapters in the Five Year Plan document to the Forest Policy. Similar impacts have been made in the fields of health and education.

those that are available in English are the *Economic and Political Weekly*, *Dalit Voice*, *Manushi*, *Social Action*, and *Lokayan Bulletin*.

National-Level Associations, Federations, and Coalitions

A major development in the past few years has been the formation of national-level associations. The range of initiatives is indicative of the fact that many groups working in local contexts or spheres of action feel the need to form coalitions that can further their political concerns on a wider societal level. These coalitions defy easy classification. Some older initiatives were either state-level (for example, FEVORD, Federation of Voluntary Organizations in Rural Development in Karnataka and Tamil Nadu), single-*event*-based (National Convention on the Forest Policy and the National Convention on Women's Rights), or single-*issue*-based (National Working Group on Displacement).[17]

Specific developments have also engendered collective responses. One of the best examples was the mobilization after the Bhopal tragedy in 1984. Doctors, lawyers, and other professionals teamed up with representatives of the victim communities to demand justice for the victims of the worst industrial disaster in history. Like the Narmada campaign, though on a smaller scale, horizontal alliances were created with trade unions working in Union Carbide factories elsewhere in the world as well as with grass-roots organizations such as the Highlander Center in the United States.

Several newer initiatives attempt to orient themselves to the longer term and are more politically self-conscious about the need for a structural reorganization of society. Five examples are the Jan Vikas Andolan (Movement for People's Development, a loose coalition of over 200 groups ranging from political movements to urban support organizations); Bharat Jan Andolan (a coalition of movements working almost entirely in the rural areas); the Federal Front (a coalition of primarily movement-based groups seeking a fundamental reorganization

---

[17] Responding to agitations against forced displacement in several parts of the country, and the scale of this phenomenon, a remarkable initiative was taken in 1987 by a group of activists, researchers, scientists, and lawyers. Called "National Working Group on Displacement," it facilitated over a dozen meetings across the country of activists and professionals with representatives of communities that had either faced or were going to face displacement. Because there was no national policy for those displaced by developmental projects, a legal subgroup drafted a policy statement that was subsequently used by the central government to draft a national policy in 1990. However, the government draft was thoroughly inadequate and has yet to be completed. Estimates of the number of people displaced by development since independence range from 15 million to 25 million.

of the polity); Azadi Bachao Andolan (Movement for the Defense of Independence), working to expose the adverse implications of the lending programs of the World Bank and the International Monetary Fund as well as other interventions in the economy that threaten livelihoods and ecosystems, particularly of poor communities); and the National Campaign for Housing Rights, a coalition of groups working in urban and rural areas and asserting a redefinition of the concept of housing. The Narmada Bachao Andolan (Movement to Save the Narmada, a national coalition of groups with a core set of three groups based in the valley) is another example. Similar coalitions exist at state levels: for example, Shoshit Jan Andolan (Movement of the Oppressed People), which consists almost entirely of groups working in the tribal areas of Maharashtra. Recently, there have been some efforts to collaborate across these initiatives, as many people in them recognize that fragmentation and disparate, uncoordinated activity are counterproductive.

Social Movements, Action Groups, and the State

The State and Democracy

Working with a state that is simultaneously strong and weak, a developmentalist state and one that legitimizes the erosion of livelihoods, a militarizing state and one that opens democratic possibilities makes the activities of groups and movements all the more challenging. What contexts justify collaboration with the state and when there should be resistance and opposition to it are the subjects of perennial debates. Dilemmas are created, for instance, when developmental initiatives are implemented by administrators sensitive to the demands of democratizing social action.

Many feel that the state is the biggest problem. However, most recognize that criticism of the state does not mean negation of it. In most cases when there are conflicts over natural resources, groups seek the mediation of the state. The state can also play the role of a buffer in the face of increasingly predatory transnational corporations. Yet, growing state lawlessness and partisanship for the interests of national and global elites require new and more creative ways of defining the mechanisms to ensure accountability. In addition to strengthening internal efforts, many movements and groups like those in the Narmada Valley are increasingly attempting to build pressures from the outside—both by using the institutional mechanisms of the United Nations system (such as the U.N. Commission on Human Rights) or by horizontally aligning themselves, across country boundaries, with other citizens' groups and coalitions. Critics have questioned the legitimacy of this approach. In fact, spokespersons for the state and a section of the media have charged that seeking accountability by invoking international human rights standards is anti-national activity. Movement groups, on the other hand, have argued that there are international covenants and conventions to which India is signatory and that there is a body of internationally recognized rights that India must respect. Additionally, when the current regime is clearly taking its directives on the new economic policies from institutions like the World Bank and the IMF, its charge of raising the anti-national bogeyman rings false. Other commentators argue that in societies like India's, the state monopolizes both violence and the right to define policy. In that sense, it also attempts to monopolize the decision on what constitutes "national interest." It is precisely these monopolies that are being challenged by the movements.

These questions gain all the more urgency because the experiences of the past 45 years have shown that by and large the state has attempted to mesmerize the poor by announcing numerous "developmental" programs without the requisite political will to implement them effectively.[18] A tenuous and fragile dependency has resulted, and where there have been protests, the state has resorted to other forms of co-optation or outright repression in the case of collective mobilization. In a paradoxical sense, the state can both protect democratic space and create conditions for narrowing it.

State Control Through Official Institutions

In the postindependence period, independent citizens' action was primarily seen as complementary to that of the government, and while dissidence existed, most of it was channeled through political parties. The government set up several agencies to facilitate voluntary action, for example, the Central Social Welfare Board, People's Action for Development in India (PADI), and the Council for Appropriate Research and Technology (CART).[19] By the early 1970s, however, with escalating dissidence and growing militancy in the countryside, including continuing secessionist movements in several parts of the

[18] The Garibi Hatao Program (1972), the plethora of rural development programs, elements of the 20-point program (1975), and the Jawahar Rozgar Yojana (1990) are some examples of programs that were well-intentioned reformist measures but did not address the basic social and economic inequities in the country.

[19] PADI and CART were later merged into one organization, CAPART (Council for Advancement of People's Action and Rural Technology).

country, the government introduced a series of new measures to control the spread of these organizations.

The Foreign Contributions Regulation Act was legislated during the Emergency (more stringent amendments were added in 1984), bringing all organizations receiving foreign funds under the direct gaze of the Ministry of Home Affairs. An instance of the control exercised by this measure was the decision in 1984 to ban 124 groups from receiving foreign funds. Over the past decade, dozens of groups have been similarly controlled; in most cases, the reasons for imposing the restrictions have not been valid because there was no evidence of activities that could be construed as unconstitutional. In each of these cases, the concerned group was involved in activity that was perceived by local or national vested interests as threatening to their political or economic hegemony.

The other strategy is to increase state patronage of some of these groups. Since the Seventh Five Year Plan (1985–90), there has been a significant increase in funds earmarked for expenditure through NGOs.

State Repression and Human Rights Organizations

A wider consciousness of the use of state repression and the escalation of "state lawlessness" began to congeal in the late 1960s, the early years of the Naxalite movement. The first human rights organizations—the Association for the Protection of Democratic Rights in West Bengal and the Association for Democratic Rights in Punjab—were formed during this period. The growth of this dimension of the movement has had a close correlation with the escalation of state repression. In 1975 the first national organization, the People's Union for Civil Liberties, was formed, followed soon thereafter by other initiatives all over the country.[20] Despite all the official rhetoric, the large-scale terrorization of poor communities asserting their constitutional rights continues unabated. Industrialists, landlords, contractors, and upper- and middle-class peasants continue to receive state protection to suppress any political mobilization of the poor. In addition, the state has, in the name of controlling secession and other militant activity, declared large parts of the country to be "disturbed areas."[21]

---

[20] For a compilation of reports prepared by these organizations, see A. R. Desai, *Violation of Democratic Rights in India* (Bombay: Popular Prakashan, 1986).

[21] For a representation of the complex debate on human rights violations in India, see *Rethinking Human Rights: Challenges for Theory and Action*, ed. Harsh Sethi and Smitu Kothari (New York: New Horizons Press, 1989).

Some Current Debates

Radical Agendas and Reformistic Responses

The activities of most social movements represent a comprehensive critique of prevailing social and economic structures as well as of the growing centralization and authoritarianism of the state apparatus. The state responds either by repression or accommodation (usually partial). The latter would include responding to the demand for a more progressive legislation (as in the case of the *sati* incident in Deorala or in the context of the extensive prevalence of bonded labor or child labor), granting concessions, or strategically attempting to diffuse the critical edge of the movement by agreeing to an endless stream of official consultations, dialogues, and committees. Invariably, progressive demands are met with reformistic responses. This is also evident in the relationship of NGOs with other elements of the formal democratic process.

For instance, while most movements have consciously avoided participation in the electoral process (fearing co-optation and an eventual reform of their politics), others have been compelled to sustain some line of communication with specific officials in government and with other political parties, usually on an issue-to-issue basis. While movements like those in the Narmada Valley have acquired political self-confidence, most groups are still diffident of playing a role in the wider political process in the country, because they feel that they would then be compelled to accept reformistic responses and thus be unable to sustain the radical edge of their work. Other movements think that it is feasible to strike a balance without sacrificing their political mandate.

Idealism and Pragmatism

A majority of initiatives among the groups and movements in the country are premised on a body of ideals. While there may be variations in ideologies and strategies, idealism remains one of the strongest motivating forces of these independent action groups. However, given that the struggle is situated in a contested terrain of power and mediated by a powerful state, radical programs, as outlined above, give way to compromises, creating tremendous frustration and disillusionment. Often the scale and pace of changes imposed from the outside are so relentless that a majority of activists' time is expended in "limiting the damage" and forcing immediate, pragmatic resolutions. The inability to balance ideals and pragmatism, visions and compromise creates significant strain and tension within groups and among group leaders. State repression or the condoning of repression by nonstate actors (for example, landlords intimidating or killing labor organized into a peasant union, as in the case of numerous struggles in states like Bihar) as well as sustained police repression (such as that against tribals in parts of Andhra Pradesh) have also often forced compromise. Such state activity also forces many into further militancy (as in Punjab and Kashmir).

The reverse is also possible. Groups involved primarily in implementing state development programs tend to get frustrated by the slow pace of change and the difficulty of realizing or sustaining gains in the face of entrenched interests. A slow radicalization takes place, often engendering state or private repression. The relentlessness of this tension and conflict often compels these groups to adopt a more reconciliatory relationship with the state and accept a developmentalist agenda again.

Foreign Funding

Funding for social action has been one of the most contentious issues in the nonparty political process. There are five main types of donor sources: multilateral, bilateral, independent (ranging from the conservative to the radical), religious, and U.N. system. While all organizations receiving foreign funds must be registered with the Ministry of Home Affairs, as mentioned earlier, multilateral, bilateral, U.N., and independent donors like the Ford Foundation also require each project to be vetted by the government. Though a lot of the developmental monies help in reducing pressure on a welfare state, they have been criticized for furthering the larger economic imperatives of the industrialized world. The motives of donors as well as their ideological orientations is an issue that remains widely contentious.

Prakash Karat has castigated action groups (particularly those receiving foreign funds), characterizing them as essentially disruptive and as part of an imperialist strategy of penetration of postcolonial societies.[22] Other critics, like Karat, argue that these groups counter and weaken the potential of the Left in India. Also, many of these critics have questioned the morality, integrity, and commitment of activists who are more accountable to the sources of foreign funds than to the society within which they work.

Undoubtedly, funds also create dependency. They make groups more vulnerable, because Home Ministry permission to receive funds

[22] Prakash Karat, "Action Groups/Voluntary Organizations: A Factor in Imperialist Strategy," *Marxist*, no. 2 (April–June 1984). See also Suresh Sharma, "Voluntary Efforts and International Funding," *Lokayan Bulletin*, Vol. 5, no. 2 (1987).

can be withdrawn without so much as a moment's notice. Therefore, in most cases there is a dilution of political perspective and political action.

However, attempts by the government to control the flow of foreign funds are ironic, to say the least, since the government itself has in many different forms and in much larger amounts been seeking foreign funds—not just from institutions like the IMF and the World Bank (institutions that now impose strict conditionalities to the point where they are increasingly directing the country's economy) but also from transnational corporations. A wide range of concessions is granted to the foreign investors, concessions that have a profound negative impact on national sovereignty and on social justice.

In fact, most movements are supported entirely on indigenous funds and are therefore not part of the funders' cycles and politics. Movements like the Narmada struggle are supported by their mass base as well as by contributions from individual supporters in other parts of the country. This makes such movements much more accountable to their constituencies as well as more independent than those that receive foreign funds.

Political Autonomy or Political Party

Political participation is of concern to almost all groups working in the country. Each group differs in the degree of emphasis on participation, what participation consists of, and how it will be realized. One of the most contentious issues has been the relationship with political parties.

One of the better-documented cases that eloquently expresses this is that of Shramik Sangathana, an organization working among tribal and nontribal peasants in Maharashtra.[23] Through the 1970s and early 1980s, the group had successfully struggled to gain control over land and other productive resources. Numerous other social issues were also debated. However, a number of middle-class activists felt that the group had neither the impact nor the political protection that were required to sustain its activity. They felt that these aims could be furthered by their joining the Central Industrial Trade Union, the trade-union wing of the CPM. When the decision to join was finally taken, the group was divided about it, leading to a serious split. Those who did not want the merger argued that not only would there be a dilution of the political autonomy and thrust of the group but also, de-

[23] Amrita Basu, *Two Faces of Protest: Contrasting Modes of Women's Activism in India* (Berkeley: University of California Press, 1992); and Harsh Sethi and Smitu Kothari, *The Non-Party Political Process: Uncertain Alternatives* (Geneva/Delhi: UNRISD/Lokayan, 1987).

spite all assurances to the contrary, the group's priorities would be gradually subsumed by those of the party.

Similar pressures have been experienced by groups all over the country. Often, success in establishing a base in an area motivates representatives of existing political parties to seek the integration of that activity into the party. Refusal to consent to these overtures or those made by the state to become a recipient of state development funds can bring various forms of retribution, ranging from isolation to repression. The case of the Chattisgarh Mines Shramik Sangh (CMSS) is illustrative.[24] A remarkably innovative independent trade union working in the mining areas of southern Madhya Pradesh (Dalli-Rajahara), the union was able to muster significant support, eroding in the process the base of the older, party-based unions in the area. The trade union was able not only to achieve successes in the conventional economistic agenda but also to have a significant impact on the social aspects of the workers' life—health, education, alcoholism, and so on.

As a result of its success, however, resentment grew among the older unions. The CMSS was able gradually to have an impact in the neighboring areas, and in late 1991 one of its main leaders, Shankar Guha Niyogi, was murdered. While this reprehensible act was not the doing of the other trade unions, this case shows the high cost of asserting autonomy from the established structures of society.

Unions and groups like the CMSS have been debating another option: to form a party of their own. Several years ago, over 80 groups began the process of forming a Green Party. Neither of these initiatives has as yet been realized. What is gaining momentum, however, is an even more fundamental debate. Is participation in electoral politics necessary? Is it not possible instead to assert local autonomy and control over the local means of production? On December 1990, more than 150 groups and movements publicly announced a radical program called "Our Rule in Our Villages." While this may be criticized as an isolationist strategy that cannot work, it nevertheless represents the strong sentiment of disillusionment and frustration with the democratic limitations of electoral politics.

This assertion of independence does not mean isolation from the formal political process. In fact, the process of making the formal system (parties and governments) accountable continues. What also con-

[24] There is considerable writing on the CMSS. For a recent article, see Sharat G. Lin, "Shankar Guha Niyogi: Beyond Conventional Trade Unionism in India," *Bulletin of Concerned Asian Scholars*, Vol. 24, no. 3 (July–September 1992), pp. 16–25.

tinues is using the available instruments of democratic institutions, particularly the courts.

From the standpoint of the political parties, there is a growing attempt to recognize independent movements and groups. While the overtures by some of the parties have undoubtedly been perceived as co-optative, the invitations for dialogue have called for a more thorough debate among nonparty groups. A recent statement by George Fernandes, one of India's leading politicians, who has also been a celebrated trade unionist and a minister in two different non-Congress governments at the Center, is indicative of the shifting mood within some parties.

> In the absence of an organized socialist movement, new issues and new challenges have been taken up by radical youth, including women, by setting up action groups and other voluntary organizations. These issues pertain to the rights of women and children and their exploitation; protection of the environment that is being devastated locally and globally by large industry and those who serve its interests; struggles against large dams and other projects that displace hundreds of thousands of people and ravage their lives, even while disturbing the ecological equilibrium. . . . All such groups need to be drawn into the now inevitable struggle against the new economic policies of the government.[25]

Despite such efforts to bridge the gap between parties and the nonparty movements, all indications currently suggest that these relationships will continue to be marked by a blend of dialogue, pressure, and conflict. A dynamic tension continues to prevail between *rajniti* (state power) and *lokniti* (people's power).

Internal Democracy/Accountability

Replicating at times the pathology of trends in society, social action groups and movements are plagued with internal dissensions, secretiveness, lack of democratic functioning, and accountability. Several members of these organizations have been concerned about establishing some mechanism of accountability as well as a more organized forum to represent a collective voice in the face of growing state controls. One of the most controversial steps was initiated by a prominent member of a developmental group who in the late 1980s was a consultant to India's Planning Commission. He proposed the creation of a statutory Code of Conduct for Voluntary Organizations

---

[25] This excerpt is from a meeting held in Hyderabad, March 20–21, 1993.

as well as a National Council that would monitor and recommend "legitimate" groups to the Indian government. Resenting an institutionalized mechanism controlled by the state, groups across the country came together to oppose this move vociferously. They labeled these attempts at official regulation and monitoring as "anti-voluntarism." The move was thus withdrawn. However, the underlying lack of accountability remains a serious internal problem.

The Narmada as Mirror

Most of the dilemmas, challenges, and issues discussed above have faced the movement in the Narmada Valley. As it enters a new phase, the movement is still confronted with the specter of the continuing use by state and central governments of undemocratic means to build the dam. Dam authorities justify this by reiterating that the movement is obstructing the completion of a prestigious developmental project. Since the economic and social benefits and costs are encompassed in the available literature, what is presented below are other Narmada-related issues that reflect the challenges that social movements pose through their efforts to widen the democratic processes in India.[26]

The Narmada Movement

Like many other contemporary movements, the Narmada struggle is part of an important history of resistance. Politically, it shares the legacy of the earlier protests and revolts against the British—particularly in India's tribal areas—as well as of the protracted Jharkhand agitation, in that it represents a sustained response to centralized state control over local economies and to the imposition of "remote" administrative and political processes on local societies. At another level, however, its politics are unique; it is not, for instance, a class movement, nor is it (like the Jharkhand movement) an effort to redraw the internal boundaries of the country to achieve a more politically and culturally autonomous region.

In that respect it articulates the critical legacy of Mahatma Gandhi, of the Chipko and Appiko movements, and of the struggles outlined above that challenge both the growing centralization and authoritarianism of the state and the extractive character of the dominant economic process—a process that erodes and destroys not only the sub-

[26] To cite two recent publications: Special Issue on Dams on the River Narmada, *Lokayan Bulletin*, Vol. 9, no. 3/4 (1991); Claude Alvares and Ramesh Billorey, *Damming the Narmada* (Malaysia: Third World Network/APPEN, 1988).

sistence economies of local populations but also the diversity of their systems of production and their systems of meaning.[27] The invocation of this diversity should not be misunderstood as romanticization of a glorious past that—for those on the margins—never was. It is rather a plea to respect, to understand, and, if one is so inclined, to celebrate the multiple traditions that have evolved in the historical and geographical complexity of the Indian subcontinent. Also, of course, the movement is representative of the growing assertions of marginal populations for greater economic and political control over their lives.

Lack of Elite Response

Across the country there has been significant mobilization for a comprehensive review of the Narmada project. This has involved not just the people to be adversely affected but other political and social groups, lawyers, scientists, and of course the media, as well as leading intellectuals and concerned citizen groups all over the world. The demand for a comprehensive review has now been reiterated in the aftermath of the government's recent decision to relinquish the remaining $170 million due from the World Bank. Increasingly, there is public acknowledgment and support by other groups and movements that have been impressed by the sustained mobilization of the Narmada movement, its tenacity, and its complex strategies and tactics. However, there continues to be, among other concerned sections in the middle classes, the trade unions, and academia, little sustained response. Why?

Some commentators argue that at this time other issues in India are more vital—issues that are straining the political and emotional fabric of individuals and communities. Growing religious chauvinism and fundamentalism, communal strife, escalating lawlessness by both state and nonstate actors, and continuing economic stresses are, they speculate, exhausting the fuel for wider citizen response to situations like that in the Narmada Valley.

It is paradoxical that, although the national press and a significant cross section of the regional press have consistently been favorable to the Narmada movement and have, on numerous occasions, exposed the repressive and apathetic nature of the official response, this has not engendered a wider response among their readership. In fact, even those who routinely respond to other atrocities and injustices are silent. Is this indifference indicative of the social and economic

[27] Chipko and Appiko are forest-based movements in the Tehri-Garhwal region of Uttar Pradesh and in Karnataka, respectively.

gulf between the groups affected and the middle classes and elites? Or is it just that it is simpler to respond to a single event or atrocity that calls for brief intervention than to sustain an ongoing commitment? It is also puzzling that political parties of the Left, whose rhetoric challenges the existing social order and the entrenched power interests, are not openly supportive of the movement.

It is easier to understand the response of parties across the political spectrum. After all, none of them want to threaten their potential electoral base in Gujarat, where, because of a variety of factors, there is perceived to be mass support for the project. Several years of drought have been politically exploited by the ruling elites to sell the Sardar Sarovar Project as a panacea for the vagaries of such calamities. "The SSP will be the lifeline of Gujarat," it has often been officially proclaimed. This, coupled with the expanding requirements of Gujarat's industrial and cash-crop economy, has created wide support for the project as well as a climate in which criticisms of the project are denounced as anti-development and anti-Gujarat. This also, to an extent, explains why most social action groups normally concerned about undemocratic processes in Gujarat do not want to take a public position.

The role of the central government has been no different. Movement representatives have met with successive prime ministers and relevant ministers at the state and central levels, but the response to the basic demand for a dialogue leading toward a review (in the light of the continuing social, economic, and environmental problems) has never been conceded. What is crucial in this process is the recognition that, while the strength of the movement nationally will depend on the extent of local mobilization, such activity represents an important cognitive and organizational shift from the local to the national. Stated differently, the realization that local problems have extralocal origins and legitimation has inspired a widening of the ambit of struggle.

Challenging Economic Development

What probably explains the relative apathy among large sections of intellectuals and other concerned people is the challenge that the Narmada Bachao Andolan and its supporters pose to the dominant model of economic development. The reification of this model as a harbinger of modernization is very deeply inculcated. It continues to shape ideas, images, resources, and people. Any talk of a fundamental alternative is seen as a throwback to a "primitive" past. Dams, to paraphrase Nehru, are "the temples of modern India." They are seen as monuments of progress, as essential elements for achieving self-sufficiency and "national security." The characterization of the Andolan as anti-development, anti-progress, and even anti-national is evidence of the aggressiveness of this worldview.

Social movements are inevitable in a context in which the state legitimizes this model and, in the name of enforcing social harmony, primarily perpetuates the interests of powerful economic and social forces. The strategy, for most social movements, is to resist and restrict the state's exploitative character and seek to transform and democratize it, making it an instrument of social change and a protector of natural resources. This issue gains even more significance in light of the growing understanding of the interconnectedness of these resources not just within a single ecosystem but between ecosystems. These are issues that movements have just begun to grapple with, issues that are central to India's future.

Where does that leave the Narmada movement? Some fear that it will be forced to accept piecemeal reforms. Others feel that it will be compelled to take even more radical steps. Interestingly, both these trends exist in the Andolan, and this tension continues to nurture passionate debates and disagreements, most of which remain inconclusive.

Displacement and Popular Mobilization

Evidence so far suggests that most of those in the submergence area as well as those displaced by other developments around the project will be pushed further to the margins by the project or will experience deep psychological stress if they are involuntarily displaced or scattered in an alien environment surrounded by more powerful social and economic alliances. The challenges that this reality poses are not confined to the dams on the river Narmada. They go to the very heart of the nature of planning, its decision-making processes, and the democratic process itself. Movement leaders argue that what they are advocating is nothing short of a fundamental critique of structures of power and patronage, received categories and ideologies, and representative processes that discriminate against the primary victims of economic development.

Alternatives and Challenges

The cost of irrigation per hectare is approximately six times that of other methods of land and water management. Alternatives are not merely a revival of traditional technologies but involve the whole matrix of democracy, governance, and participation. The issue is not merely one of choosing between small and large technologies but involves deeper questions: What is the water for? How should the water be used? Who decides what kind of agriculture is being practiced?

It is also evident that the diverse systems of production and the diverse knowledge systems in the Narmada Valley will be disrupted, probably irreversibly. Rather than strengthening this diversity, facilitating a comprehensive plan of land reform and land and water management that draws on local capacities and creativity, the planners continue to impose a single homogenizing project. Recent ecological awareness as well as the experiences of dams all over the world suggest that one large project can rarely be appropriate for a complex multiplicity of cultures and ecosystems.

In its very essence, therefore, the movement contests the incorporation of communities, cultures, knowledge systems, and the ecosystems they inhabit and depend on into an instrumental vision of modernization, on terms that are rarely, if ever, set by those who become its eventual victims.

A number of questions can be heard frequently in discussions of movement groups. How, then, do we move forward? If, hypothetically, structural changes in favor of the local communities (with a strategy to address the prevalent economic differentiation and social stratification) are realized, can these communities manage entire ecosystems by themselves? What about the more urgent question of the rights of vulnerable and socially discriminated marginal people? What relationships need to evolve within and between the communities and between them and the "outsider"? What kinds of new institutions need to be created? Who will set the terms for these transformations?

Indian social movements force us to address major domestic and global questions of governance and responsibility. It is true that given the vastness of India and the centrality of party politics, these groups and movements occupy a small proportion of the country's political space. Also, there are few serious and sustained attempts to bring these dispersed struggles together politically. Internal weaknesses and factionalism continue to plague movement activity, and this in turn affects possibilities of achieving a wider political presence.

Furthermore, the overall ideological situation is one of immense flux. In view of the overwhelming realities of growing social violence, the intensive onslaught of discriminatory economic policies, and a homogenizing consumerism that threatens social cohesion and ecological sanity, the spaces that movements occupy and influence need to be considerably expanded.

Of course, there are those who maintain that the diversity of these independent initiatives and their ability to be flexible make for more creativity and innovation. It can also be argued that it is not numbers that are important but strategies and the quality of interventions. A few well-focused and sustained actions can yield far-reaching results.

There is little doubt, however, that movements such as those discussed above have an impact that has been and will remain significant, not just as conscience keepers and agents of empowerment for hitherto subjugated and oppressed communities, but as active articulators of different political visions. Above all, these movements and groups are only a fraction of the wide variety of activities in the various contested sites of power in India. This chapter celebrates this diversity of thinking and action and the numerous ways in which it is transforming the traditional notions of development, democracy, and governance.

6
Cinema and Television

Pradip Krishen

Most visitors to India—academics and journalists included—experience some degree of unease when they come face to face with the sights and sounds of middle-class urban culture. Some years ago, I was host to a British Sanskritist on his first visit to India. I had never known anyone who had read so much about India before setting foot here. Nonetheless, he was restless in New Delhi, so on his third day in India, I took him to the heart of the old city. We walked through the narrow, twisting lanes of Chandni Chowk and I could see that for the first time since his arrival, he was minutely attentive to his surroundings. *This* is what he had imagined India to be, not the geometric skyline of a modern city. After we had been walking for about half an hour, we heard a sudden hum of human voices that seemed to come from every direction. He turned to me for an explanation, his eyes craving the excitement of a real ethnic experience. I told him, not without some enjoyment, I admit, that the radio commentary had just reported an Indian victory over England in a cricket match being played in London. I will never forget the look of abject disappointment in his eyes. India had let him down.

The West meets India on predetermined ground, expecting it to fit the image of static, rural, premodern local cultures. Tourists, after all, come to a land marketed for its exotic oriental traditions, not the strength of its mass media or the size of its cinema hoardings. India colludes in this definition. Guided tours are labeled "Temples and Tigers" or "Peacocks and Palaces" and skirt those aspects of modern, metropolitan India that contradict the Western preconception.

Western scholars and writers are drawn toward those aspects of Indian society that stand out as being peculiarly and authentically Indian, leading to a preponderance of studies of traditional castes and communities and local, rural cultures. Largely responsible for this is the lure of the authentic and the "unspoilt," but so too is an unspoken assumption that the enclaves of Western technology and commerce in India's cities are the provenance of tiny elite groups, who merely replicate the life-style and values of the West. And yet, the products of metropolitan culture in India are *not* replicas of Western popular culture, and the power and burgeoning influence of the mass media in India indicate that they are not relevant to only a minuscule, Westernized Indian elite. Clearly, even though Indian metropolitan culture uses the technology and forms of Western media, it has evolved from specific Indian situations. Far from leading Indian urban society into a sanitized, decultured space where all users of Western technology increasingly tend to resemble each other, the Indian media have fashioned a voice and identity of their own and address a set of uniquely Indian problems and issues.

Only recently have anthropologists begun to investigate the ways in which modern media and market forces have helped to create a vigorous new metropolitan culture in India. Arjun Appadurai and Carol A. Breckenridge use the term "public culture" to refer to a variety of modern, cosmopolitan forms of culture-making. In India, they say, a full-fledged public culture has emerged in the second half of this century:

> It is a conscious product of translocal forces, often located in cities. The institutional bases of this culture production are magazines, cinema, t.v. and advertising. . . . While these productions include matters which are intimate, small-scale and local, they are focused on the values and appeals of public life. [1]

The term "public culture," for Appadurai and Breckenridge, describes a contested arena in which various producers of culture jockey for position and dominance.

> What is at stake in the contest is, of course, no less than the consciousness of the emergent Indian public. The messages of public culture are therefore directed to audiences without regard to the limits of locality or social category. This does not mean that the new images are directed to a homogeneous and universal Indian, but that they are designed to appeal to a diversity of audiences. Their rhetoric is ecumenical, not parochial, and under the present political regime they are intended to create the new citizen.[2]

Under the rubric of public culture, Appadurai and Breckenridge include such phenomena as internal tourism, restaurant culture, sports,

---

[1] Arjun Appadurai and Carol A. Breckenridge, "Public Culture in Late Twentieth Century India," unpublished paper.

[2] Arjun Appadurai and Carol A. Breckenridge, "Why Public Culture?," in *Public Culture*, Fall 1988, Vol. 1, no. 1, p. 7.

and emergent forms of museums and exhibitions, all of which are tied to media and to contemporary forms of taste, display, consumption, and collective identity. In this chapter, I restrict myself to describing the lineaments of the cinema and television in India, which together constitute the most visible and powerful agency in the creation of a national mythology of heroism, and indeed of a modern national identity.

The Evolution of Popular Cinema

India's popular cinema—taken collectively, in all its regional language variants—is undoubtedly the most striking example of Indian public culture in the 20th century. No other entertainment form has enjoyed such spectacular success as a vehicle for expressing and recycling the myths and ideals, the dreams and fantasies of middle-class India. Each year, India makes roughly 800 films that are watched by an average of 10 million people every *day*.[3] This does not include the enormous viewership of films on videocassette and, increasingly, on television. But even these figures do not quite express the extent of the popular cinema's dominance as a channel for the transmission of ideas and information. India's urban environments are cluttered with its billboards, filled with its music. For the casual observer as much as the cultural anthropologist, this is wonderfully fertile terrain, not least because we are getting used to the idea that the cinema does, after all, express something about the society that produces it. And yet, despite its prominence and high visibility, we have only begun to understand how the cinema has been so successful in fashioning its narratives and meanings in a way that often spans regional, class, and, sometimes, rural/urban differences in a vast, polyglot land.

Parsi Theater

It is important to establish at the outset, however, that cinema did *not* invent the stratagems of popular success in India. When Dadasaheb Phalke made India's first silent feature film in 1913, he was operating squarely within the traditions of an established urban entertainment form called "Company" or "Parsi" theater. "Company" referred to the East India Company and to the somewhat disparate mélange of plays, skits, and variety shows that had become a feature of European enclaves in Indian cities in the mid-19th century. Every now and

[3] *Indian Cinema 1992* (Delhi: Directorate of Film Festivals, 1992), p. 3. These figures actually represent a steady decline from a high of 912 films produced in 1985.

again, a professional company of British players would stop over in India, on its way to or from Australia, but for the most part, Victorian theater in India was an expatriate theater—enthusiastic, nostalgic, and usually amateur. Nonetheless, it brought the Victorian melodrama to India in a form friendly and clumsy enough to inspire emulation. In the 1860s, Parsi entrepreneurs pioneered the first Indian dramatic companies, not just in the great capitals of Bombay and Calcutta, but upcountry as well, in Delhi, Lucknow, and Agra. The development of these companies slowly gathered steam as the century progressed.

The Parsis were a small but strikingly successful community of merchants and entrepreneurs who had carved out a special commercial relationship with the British on the western seaboard centered around Bombay. Along with their entrepreneurial spirit, the Parsis had a penchant for adopting European manners. Perhaps their partnership with the British encouraged them to experiment culturally with the abacus of social success in British India. At any rate, it was by no means fortuitous that a small, migrant, entrepreneurial community positioned roughly halfway between traditional society and the British commercial interest in India was responsible for brokering the marriage of a Western dramatic form with the folk traditions of the Indian countryside.

The Parsi theater has attracted surprisingly little attention despite the fact that it offers a revealing glimpse of a translocal, urban entertainment form in an age long before modern communications and mass media.[4] Exhibiting the characteristics of a vigorous, probing public culture, Parsi theater targeted a mix of urban audiences, experimenting and evolving as it attempted to address different sections of the audience and to slide up or down the social scale. Parsi theater also showed great adaptability as it covered different regions and languages, borrowing liberally from local dancing and singing traditions, reworking its image to draw women and children in, and smuggling political messages into mythological dramas. Parsi theater anticipated the aesthetic of inclusion and broad-based appeal, and the mythologization and simplification of the world into easy categories and archetypes, characteristic of today's Hindi cinema. In India, it was Parsi theater that made the first attempt at standardizing a moral universe, and a measure of its success is that the cinema, when it arrived, had little to add to this world view.

The earliest plays in Parsi theater were directly inspired by the tawdry version of Victorian melodrama staged in English settlements in

---

[4] See Lakshmi Narayan Lal, *Parsi Hindi Rangmanch* (New Delhi: Hind Books, 1975); Anuradha Kapur, "The Representation of Gods and Heroes" in *Journal of Arts and Ideas*, nos. 23–24, January 1993.

India. Shakespeare's works, translated into Urdu and milked for every vestige of strong emotion, quickly became one of Parsi theater's staple ingredients. So did a new blend of opera and *tableaux vivants* known as *Indrasabha*, first confected in Wajid Ali Shah's court in the 1850s.[5] "Indrasabha" simply means "the court of Lord Indra"; the name implied that the spectator was being given a privileged view of scenes from a celestial, ethereal world. Not surprisingly, it depicted a heightened, stylized otherworld of verse, music, and dance.

Around the 1870s, Persian romantic epics came into vogue, the most famous being "Laila-Majnoon" and "Shirin-Faryad." A parallel genre of plays set in foreign, exotic locales also gained popularity.[6] All of these plays used a style of flowery Urdu poetry and declamation that established a literary fashion. At about this time, the first commercial companies were established; Pestonjee Framjee started the Bombay Parsi Original Opera Company in 1870; two years later, Khurshedji Baliwallah founded the Victoria Theatrical Company. And Parsi theater as a commercial commodity and a style was well on its way.

It would be fair to assume that early Parsi theater was aimed at the more wealthy classes of urban Indians. It positioned itself alongside other (predominantly male) performance traditions of northern India, such as the *mushaira* and *mujra*. The use of verse and highly Persianized Urdu wove Parsi theater into the fabric of upper-class, Nawabi culture in North India; by this means, it attempted to achieve instant social respectability and acceptance.

There was one important difference, though: Nawabi performance traditions were by now inextricably linked with the bordello, or *kotha*, and Parsi theater seems to have consciously striven to reject any such association. For the next three decades, Parsi theater followed the conventions of folk theater and used male actors to impersonate female characters. This was, perhaps, a way for Parsi theater to claim social respectability on a par with European theater, while simultaneously distancing itself from the opprobrium of decadent Nawabi culture.

But Parsi theater was a strictly commercial enterprise, and the patronage of the Indian elite was not enough to ensure its financial viability. The conventions of literary, courtly Urdu and the esoteric meter of Persian "Bahar" poetry were hardly a recipe for bringing in the au-

---

[5] J. C. Mathur, "Hindi Theatre and Drama in Modern Times," *Sangeet Natak Akademi Bulletin #1*, April 1954.

[6] Some of the favorites were "Yehudi Ki Ladki" (The Jew's Daughter), "Turki Hoor" (Turkish Houri), and "Silver King."

diences in sufficient numbers. Persianized Urdu was therefore gradually jettisoned in favor of a more colloquial style and idiom, which provided the impetus needed for Parsi theaters to spring up in towns across the country. Part of the strategy to gain popularity was the co-opting of the folk traditions of the hinterland, forms of song and dance such as *lavani* from western India, the *yakshagana* from the South, and *rasleela*, *swaang*, and *nautanki* from the North.

During the next two decades, Parsi theater gained a footing in other parts of India and in the smaller towns as well. In the 1880s, Parsi troupes from Bombay visited southern India and spawned imitations in modern-day Andhra Pradesh and Karnataka. One company played at Mysore and impressed the raja so much that he formed a palace repertory.[7] Once formed, these companies had no use for the courtly Urdu poetry used by the Parsi companies from Bombay. Instead, they blended the proscenium style with the devotional dramatic forms from the countryside, but more important, they rendered everything in their own natural idiom, giving birth to the Parsi mythological play.

The Parsi mythological play removed at one stroke the disabilities from which the swashbuckling romantic Parsi operas had suffered. Its appeal was no longer restricted to a thin crust of literati in the big towns. More important, women and children, for whom Parsi theater had not been deemed appropriate fare, were suddenly included too, and in most towns had one show a week reserved for them.

Certain features of the Parsi mythological play are noteworthy. One is the degree to which the stock-in-trade narratives provided an extremely elastic structure that was capable of accommodating all sorts of messages and subtexts. Toward the end of the 19th century, social reform was in the air, and reform-minded playwrights such as Pandit Narayan Prasad Betaab cleverly used the authority of divine tales to push their notions about the evils of the dowry system, or for that matter, the unsuitability of love marriage. Later, as the 20th century progressed, a clear strand of nationalist themes came into being, but in years of political repression and censorship, playwrights found it convenient to take cover behind mythology. Tales of wicked tyrannical rulers lent themselves easily to allegory, and the British authorities found it extremely difficult in practice to impose a ban on what was, on the face of it, merely a traditional Puranic tale such as "Bhakta Prahlad" or "Shravankumar."

The great advantage of co-opting the mythological play was that it allowed reference to a moral universe whose signs and meanings were

[7] A. Rangacharya, *The Indian Theatre* (New Delhi: National Book Trust, 1971).

easily understood and whose codes could be manipulated to address other, newer issues. In the long run, it brought about a standardization of representation within Parsi theater, a new vocabulary of shared stereotypes that the cinema found convenient to accept wholesale. But it is perhaps not entirely coincidental that around 1915, Mohandas K. Gandhi—not yet a mahatma—was beginning to raise a few eyebrows by couching his political speeches in the evocative idiom of Hindu myth and metaphor. For Gandhi this was merely a shorthand way of appealing to the hearts and minds of the peasantry. It was effective. And Parsi theater, if it ever had to defend itself against the charge of introducing religion into entertainment, could have no better defense.

By the turn of the century, many other successful ingredients and conventions that Parsi theater bequeathed to the cinema were evident already. Playwrights of the time stressed the importance of ending each scene with the punch of an Urdu couplet, the *sher*.[8] Half the *sher* would be spoken by an actor, the other half completed by the audience; then while the audience dissolved in raucous clapping and appreciation, the curtain would go down for the scene change. Great store was placed on such special effects.

The most enduring of Parsi theater's innovations was in the field of music, a contribution that has been obscured somewhat by the fact that music is such a staple feature of traditional folk theater in India. Traditional theater uses music in a formulaic way as narrative stylization. Parsi theater, inspired no doubt by its exemplars in Western theater, set out to recover the emotional charge of song from blanket stylization. It achieved this by appropriating the music only for moments of dramatic intensity, in effect shortening the psychological distance between emotionally charged speech and song. In furtherance of this design, Parsi theater invented the roles of the lyricist and the music director, both of whom have lived on in the main credit titles of today's Indian film. The songs became the centerpiece of Parsi theater, and one of the ways of telling whether a new production was a success was to count the number of times the audience cried "Once more!" (in English) after each song. Naturally, the singers *always* obliged. Not until after the introduction of sound in the 1930s did the Indian cinema attain the popularity and commercial success enjoyed much earlier by the Parsi theater.

---

[8] Lakshmi Narayan Lal, "Parsi," cites Agha Hashra Kashmiri, the foremost playwright of his era, who appears to have written a compendium of dos and don'ts for the Parsi stage.

The Bioscope

The silent film era in India was ushered in with *Raja Harishchandra* in 1913, a mythological tale straight out of the repertoire of the Parsi stage. As the production of silent films ground on through the decade and into the 1920s, it became increasingly clear that Indian filmmakers would turn to the mythological story as the stock fare of their cinema. Perhaps this had to do with their sense that without a voice, it was better to rely on familiar tales from the Hindu epics. But equally, it was a way of giving their films a *swadeshi* head start in a market dominated by films from the United States and Europe. After all, fewer than 15 percent of the films released in India in 1926–27 were Indian.

What this reliance on mythology meant in practice was that early Indian cinema turned away from the urban middle-class market and sought its audience in small towns and villages. It was a strategic decision and acknowledged a weakness vis-à-vis the cinema's competitors in the cities. In relation to Parsi theater, the bioscope was, of course, seriously disadvantaged by its silence in an age when music was deemed to be an essential feature of entertainment. And in the competition with American films, Indian filmmakers had not yet found the ingredients of success.[9]

Despite these difficulties, by the mid-1920s Indian silent cinema attempted to address the urban middle classes. In 1925, Chandulal Shah made *Gunsundari* (Why Husbands Go Astray), which portrays a successful Westernized Indian man who has very little in common with his traditional Hindu wife. He spends more and more time away from home in the company of modern (Indian) women, until his wife decides she must win him back by becoming smart and Westernized herself. It is curious that Shah should have implied approval of a modern Hindu wife, because this was not a commonly accepted idea. Shah was not alone in focusing on the ambivalences of East versus West and in opposing Indian tradition to Western modernity, but he was almost certainly alone in approving of Westernization for the traditional wife. The contemporary meaning of the word "fashionable" as applied to women had come to connote everything that was immoral and derogatory. Most films simply equated Westernization with all the ills that beset Indian society—the loss of family values, love, and loyalty, and a surrender to material greed and sexual profligacy. However, Shah seems to have touched a middle-class nerve in dealing with the issue of Westernization per se; he went on to make a

[9] E. Barnouw and S. Krishnaswamy, *Indian Film* (Oxford University Press, 1980). This includes an excellent and detailed account of the history of the silent cinema.

string of successful films with names like *Typist Girl, Educated Wife,* and *Sumari of Sindh.*[10]

One of the biggest problems that the silent cinema faced was the difficulty of finding women to play female roles. Traditional India was strangely ambivalent about the social place of female performers. The "publicness" of their performance militated against Hindu ideals of the devoted, faithful wife, and the tension was managed by invoking a divine calling for women performers on the one hand, but assigning them a place in the social system as courtesans on the other. Because of this stigma attached to public performance in India, persuading "decent" girls to appear on stage or screen was difficult. Folk theater compounded the problem by setting an all-male precedent. Even Parsi theater had resisted the temptation of recruiting girls from the red-light district and instead used male actors to impersonate female characters (and sing in high voices), so the convention was well developed and accepted. For the cinema, however, this was not possible. The close-up rendered the ploy useless, and besides, Indian cinema would suffer terribly in comparison with Western cinema if it were unable to depict female characters. India's silent cinema solved this conundrum by recruiting Anglo-Indian and Christian girls, who did not share the traditional prejudice toward performing in public. The new stars of India's silent cinema had names like Renee Smith, Ruby Myers, Beryl Claessen, Bonnie Bird, and Effie Hippolet. All of them, however, used Hindu stage names to try to perpetuate the charade that they were Hindu girls from "good families." Interestingly, after the "discovery" of these young women, the Parsi theater, not wanting to be left behind, admitted a crop of "real" women as well, and some female stars in the 1920s were well known on both the screen and stage.

Photographs of the time reveal a striking resemblance between the Hollywood look and the appearance of India's female stars of the silent era. Perhaps this had to do with the fact that the Effie Hippolets and Beryl Claessens, because of their backgrounds, were naturally more inclined toward the Western model of fashion and beauty. The recruitment of these Westernized female stars may actually have delayed the moment when Indian women could identify with the women portrayed on the Indian screen. This could well be one of the reasons that the Indian silent cinema failed to carve out a sizable urban middle-class audience.

[10] Shah made three different language versions of *Gunsundari* when the talkies arrived. Cited in "Other Places, Other Pioneers," in *Film India: Looking Back 1896–1960* (New Delhi: Directorate of Film Festivals, 1981).

The Talkie

In March 1931, Imperial Studios of Bombay announced the release of *Alam Ara*: "All Living, Breathing 100% Talking, Peak Drama, Essence of Romance, Brains and Talents unheard of under one banner."[11] India's first talkie featured 10 songs, which seems quite modest by the standard of the films that followed. *Shirin Farhad*, released later the same year, had 42 songs, and *Indrasabha*, the following year, had nearly 70. The bioscope had found its voice and meant to make the most of it.

The talkie required actors who could sing for their supper, and it found most of them on the professional Parsi stage. The ruse of using Christian and Anglo-Indian girls would no longer work, however, because the cinema now required them not just to speak an Indian language with the right accent, but to sing as well, and most of the female stars of the silent era, with the exception of Ruby Myers (a.k.a. Sulochana), quickly faded away. The vacuum was filled by the singing stars, the "Larks and Nightingales," of the Parsi stage.[12]

The arrival of sound made it possible for Indian cinema to appropriate the Parsi theater in every detail, and with the exodus of its personnel, within the decade, the Parsi theater withered to the status of a cheap, degraded theater that played only at mofussil (provincial) towns and village fairs. For the film industry, however, the coming of the talkie film brought several important results. Chiefly, the use of an Indian language offered a natural protection against the foreign film and brought about a phenomenal growth in production.[13] In the first nine years of the Indian talkie, films were made in 17 languages, including Burmese, Arabic, Persian, and even Malay.[14]

The rise of the regional language cinema, in turn, completely altered the structure of the film industry. As the 1930s wore on, the fly-by-night film producers disappeared and production became increasingly concentrated in a few big studios in Calcutta, Bombay, and later Madras, each one with its own language specialization, although the Hindi film retained its preeminence as the all-India film.

---

[11] Handbill of the film, reproduced in *Film India: Looking Back*, p. 37.

[12] Jahanara Kajjan, one of the best-known female singers of the Parsi stage, who later moved into cinema, was known as the "Lark of India."

Master Nissar, the "Nightingale of Calcutta," joined the talkies, but his female impersonations came to an end, and he had to adjust, with some difficulty, to being a man.

[13] In the first year of the talkie, 23 Hindi films were made, but also 3 in Bengali and 1 each in Tamil and Telugu. The next year (1932), Marathi and Gujarati joined the list of languages. By 1933, the number of Hindi talkies had grown to 75, and by 1939, the total number produced was 171. See Barnouw and Krishnaswamy, *Indian Film*, p. 68.

[14] Extrapolated from a chart in Barnouw and Krishnaswamy, *Indian Film*, p. 294.

The 1930s was the era in which Indian cinema turned back to the urban middle classes. In a sense, the bioscope and Parsi theater had coalesced into the talkie. But there were big changes afoot—the swell of nationalism, provincial elections, and the growth of Indian industry after World War I, all of which strengthened the urban middle class and affected the status and acceptability of the cinema. The new respectability of the cinema could be seen in the emergence of the actresses Devika Rani and Durga Khote, both Brahmins, urbane, sophisticated, and Westernized, who, in their separate ways, went on to fashion a completely different image of the Indian screen heroine. It was reflected too in the confidence with which new themes and styles came into being. Each of the big studios, with their stables of actors, came to be associated with particular genres of movies: Imperial Movietone with its version of Arabian Nights fantasies; Bombay Talkies with glamorous, romantic dramas; Wadia Movietone with swashbuckling stunt films à la Douglas Fairbanks; New Theaters with tragic-romantic themes from Bengali literary classics; Ranjit with the "social" film; and so on. For a cinema that had just found its voice, it was a sure-footed start. But then came World War II, and just as it marked the end of social trends and value systems in so many parts of the world, it signaled the decisive end of one phase of the cinema in India.

Postwar Cinema

The end of the war saw huge quantities of speculative finance being funneled into film production. Most of this "black money" had been generated through wartime profiteering in scarce commodities and could not be invested in legal ways. One almost immediate effect of the injection of black money into the cinema was that actors and technicians deserted the studios to work for the highest bidder. This brought about the end of the studio system and the rise of a freebooting, commercial filmmaking culture that came increasingly to resemble the form it has today. The postwar period saw the rise of Bimal Roy and Raj Kapoor as directors; the crystallization of the "formula" film; the extravagant "pageants for peasants" that S. S. Vasan pioneered in Madras; the invention and refinement of playback singing; and, its most conspicuous and lasting contribution, the rise of the movie star. This period also saw the articulation and refinement of the Indian melodrama, with its obsessive interest in the ideal of Indian femininity and its fascination with broad moral themes, narratives of coincidences, and sudden happy endings. The popular film had already, by the 1950s, laid down the ground rules by which the rigid opposition of "good" and "bad" were defined. "Good" invariably meant behavior that stressed respect for family and obligations to kin and friends. Honor, religiosity, and *jigar* (large-heartedness) were important components of "Indianness," which qualified as ideal behavior. "Bad" was defined as the opposite of these values: no respect for family or friends, treachery, greed, and a hankering after Western (material) values. Interestingly, one of the most reliable markers of "good" and "bad" was male headgear, because it allowed an instant iconographic representation of Indianness or the lack of it.[15]

The late 1940s and 1950s were times of enormous change and social upheaval in India. Partition had uprooted millions of people. Industrialization, the search for jobs, and new hopes kindled by independence all led to huge numbers of rural migrants crowding the cities. In towns and in the countryside, the mechanisms of political power and dominance were being tested and reworked afresh. Above all, it was a time of transition, and the contemporary cinema responded with characteristic duality: for all those who wanted easy answers, it proposed a moral arithmetic of traditional values and social types that was as simple as it was specious, and for all others, it offered, as anodyne, the vicarious pleasure of peeping in at a glittering world of wealth and pleasure.

Over and over again, the films of this period portray the city as a frightening landscape of deceit and criminal degeneracy—dangerous, liminal, Western, and located at the opposite pole to all that is natural, moral, Indian, and traditional. The city is rife with bad men who wear suits and hats and sport the efficient but often violent technology of the West—guns and cars. The good men are ingenuous country bumpkins, strangers lost in the city, or peasants, bewildered by the apparatus of Western law and technology. No ambiguity exists about the conflation of "good" with traditional/Indian/rural/simple/weak and "evil" with modern/Western/urban/technological/strong. These associations do not, however, indicate a reflex, conservative rejection of everything Western and modern. Rosie Thomas, a British anthropologist who has published a very handy analysis of the all-time classic Bombay film *Mother India*, has shown how the codings actually conceal a complex working out of the issues of modernity and nationalism. Each film, she says, proposes its own version of dangerous disorder in the moral universe, which it must then resolve "safely."

---

[15] It is ironic that the trilby and derby hats should have come to signify Western/bad at a time when they were much sought after by the Indian upper classes. Apart from signifying Indian or Western, though, hats and other headgear also served to mark religious affiliation, caste, regional identity, and social status.

> The Hindi film audience expects a drama which puts a universe of firmly understood—and difficult to question—rules into crisis and then can resolve this within the moral order. This means that transgressions must either be punished or, more excitingly, made "acceptable," that is be rigorously justified by, for example, an appeal to "humane" justice, a mythological precedent or a perceptible contradiction within the terms of the moral code itself. It appears that pleasure is derived from the image of a dangerously broken taboo erupting within a system that provides the reassuring knowledge that it will be "safely" resolved. Particular pleasure derives from a film-maker proposing new ways of bending the comparatively inflexible system, which means that values and meanings are continually being negotiated on the fringes (and the total system undergoing gradual change so that certain taboos of ten years ago are more acceptable now).[16]

Rosie Thomas's model of Hindi cinema is attractive because it describes a value system capable of adapting to changing conditions. One of the problems with earlier explanations of the moral universe of Indian cinema is that they always described a static, rigidly unchanging schema that would be hard put, for example, to explain the trends toward sex, violence, and revenge in the cinema in the 1980s. Thomas recognizes that even though Hindi cinema uses stable categories and archetypes of good and evil, it is engaged in a process of testing the limits of its own codings.

Typically, this discourse is organized around the archetypal figures of the mother and the villain.

> While a number of factors feed in to construct the terms of this opposition, Hindu mythology is crucial. Mother is frequently identified with (and likened to) figures of the Hindu pantheon, most notably Sita, who circulates in popular "common-sense" currency as the prototype of "traditional" Indian womanhood. Motifs from the Ramayana story of Sita recur throughout the films: the mother with two sons, separation from a husband, threats to mother's chastity, various kinds of penance and, often, a perilous escape from fire. On the other hand, the villainy of Raavan, the monstrous king of the *rakshasas* (demons), who abducted Sita, shows many parallels with that of the film Villain. Moreover, just as the film Villain is repeatedly placed as the "outsider," so was Raavan, a "foreigner," the king of Lanka. The construction of Villainy is however also fed by other current discourses, for example, the fact that *vilayat* is commonly talked of as a place where people are "cold," "un-

[16] Rosie Thomas, "Cinemas on Fire: Negotiating the Mainstream Hindi Film," unpublished paper.

emotional," "like machines" and "without family" (or callously rejecting of kinship bonds and duties) as well as casually profligate."[17]

Ashis Nandy was perhaps the first to point to Indian popular cinema's "ability to act as an interface between the traditions of Indian society and the disturbing—or western—intrusions into it."[18] The Hindi film, he says, gives "cultural meaning to Western structures superimposed on society" while "ritually neutralizing those elements of the modern world which have to be accepted for reasons of survival."[19] Thomas goes a step further:

> The good: evil opposition becomes subtly conflated with another set of ideas: "good" with associations of the "traditional"—that which is "Indian," "bad" with those of the "non-traditional" and the "non-Indian." This means that the "ideal moral universe" becomes integrally bound up with a discourse on traditionalism and nationalism and, in particular, that ideas about kinship and sexuality feed directly into notions about national identity.[20]

Cinema actually inherited this cultural, mediatory role from Parsi theater's preoccupation with assigning moral values to "traditional" and "modern" aspects of Indian life and its use of the framework of the mythological story to underline its points. But the cinema has had a more powerful and far-reaching influence and, despite distinct shifts of style and emphasis over time, has remained remarkably consistent in its attention to the threats to traditional values, externalized and most often expressed in the domain of female chastity.

Why has Indian cinema not moved on from the initial hostility toward Westernization in preindependence India to a more confident assertion of modern Indian values? There are no easy answers. Perhaps "Western/modern" itself is a catchall phrase whose meaning shifts and is constantly reworked to provide a lightning rod for conservative criticism. Or perhaps the answer lies in Anil Saari's description of Indian cinema as "the only communication media [sic] that is willing to reflect the point of view and the perspective of that dominant section of the population which is not part of the ruling elite."[21]

---

[17] Thomas, Ibid., p. 7.

[18] Ashis Nandy, "The Hindi Film: Ideology and First Principles," in *Indian Popular Cinema: Myth, Meaning and Metaphor*, ed. Pradip Krishen, India International Centre Quarterly, Vol. 8, no. 1 (1981).

[19] Nandy, Ibid., p. 85.

[20] Thomas, "Cinemas," p. 5.

[21] Anil Saari, "The Hindi Film: Concepts of Aesthetics and Anti-Aesthetics," in *The Hindi Film: Agent and Re-Agent of Cultural Change*, ed. Beatrix Pfleiderer and Lother Lutze (New Delhi: Manohar, 1985), p. 261.

Popular film, many argue, provides a consistent discourse on traditional values because it reflects the values of culturally and socially deprived sections of society. The values remain constant even as social change and mobility take place, because the "beam" of popular cinema constantly seeks out precisely those sections of society that respond to this rhetoric. Though this is arguable, there is no mistaking the huge emphasis that popular cinema places on affirming traditional values in a changing society.

What then of the "true" mythological film? Has it been edged off of center stage and faded away? We have seen how mythological narratives were co-opted by early Parsi theater, then taken over wholesale by the bioscope companies in the 1920s. The bioscope adopted the mythological material as part of its strategy of defeat, because competing with American silent cinema in the city was too difficult. When the cinema found its voice in the 1930s, the mythological film made a comeback, but only initially and to a limited degree. In the post–World War II era, the mythological film gradually slipped out of contention as a major player. The religious movies made in the 1960s, 1970s, and 1980s were tacky and B-grade at best. Made primarily for rural markets, they were run on special occasions like *melas* (fairs) and religious holidays. On the other hand, the work of Rosie Thomas and others suggests that the mythological genre has actually just changed its clothes and reappeared as secular melodrama, providing simple moral categories and oppositions that inflect and influence the reading of any commercial film.

This tidy picture of Hindi cinema as "mythological in disguise," however, is rudely disturbed by Veena Das's work on a "true" mythological film called *Jai Santoshi Ma*. When it was made in the late 1970s, *Jai Santoshi Ma* seemed to have all the odds stacked against it. It was poorly filmed, with a cast of unknown actors. The special effects were unconvincing when not downright clumsy, but most of all, the film seemed doomed to failure because it told a story about a goddess that no one had heard of. In this respect *Jai Santoshi Ma* violated every rule of commercial success in the world of Hindi cinema. And yet this poorly mounted film became a runaway hit and catapulted a little-known goddess into the center of a new cult in many urban centers in northern India. Veena Das speculated that the film's success was due to the fact that it had somehow sponsored "a myth . . . particularly suited to our times."[22]

[22] Veena Das, "The Mythological Film and Its Framework of Meaning: An Analysis of Jai Santoshi Ma," in *Indian Popular Cinema: Myth, Meaning and Metaphor*, p. 45.

In her pioneering article on *Jai Santoshi Ma*, Veena Das describes the process by which mother goddesses (or their cults) are "born" and the code through which the events in the myth are understood and "make sense." The mother goddess Shitala, for example, rose from a minor deity, who is barely mentioned in the Puranic literature, to occupy an important place in the Bengali pantheon; her cult was closely tied to the spread of smallpox in Bengal in the mid-19th century.

> The myths and rites devoted to Shitala clearly helped to transform the experience of smallpox as an individual calamity to a collective one, and brought it within a framework of meaning for the individual.[23]

The two cults are different in an important way, however. In the Shitala cult, there is a clearly identifiable source of affliction in the demon of (smallpox) fever; Santoshi Ma, by contrast, does not establish herself by annihilating any particular demon of disease or affliction. The sufferings of the protagonist in the film emanate from a variety of diffuse events, so that it seems as though

> . . . the everyday tensions of existence have themselves become shapeless demons against whom the existing gods and goddesses are helpless. The goddess Shitala derives her name in opposition to the heat generated by the fever of smallpox. By analogy, one may argue that Santoshi Ma derives her name in opposition to the diffused feeling of *asantosh*, the absence of peace.[24]

Because of its very simplicity, Das argues that the cult of Santoshi Ma found major acceptance in urban areas "where the demons are shapeless and ubiquitous" and where the knowledge of traditional cults has declined. Just as the development of print technology led to the spread of the Shitala myth and also to its standardization in 19th-century Bengal, the medium of film led to an even greater standardization of the Santoshi Ma myth, making it directly accessible to illiterate people through regular reruns at major Hindu festivals. Unlike the printed versions of a myth, which might still need to be interpreted through the mediation of a priest, film as a medium does away with the necessity of all mediation.

The Parallel Cinema

The art cinema—or the "parallel cinema," as it is more commonly referred to in India—is surprisingly high-profile and influential for a

---

23 Ibid., p. 52.
24 Ibid., p. 54.

genre that has fared poorly at the box office and has rarely been seen outside festival screenings. After two decades of government support for the parallel cinema, the verdict must be that purely in commercial terms, it has been a failure. At the same time, government patronage has ensured not only production funds, but kudos and awards at film festivals as part of a strategy of compensating the parallel cinema for striking out on a lonely path.

On the face of it, it is a little surprising that the government has offered any encouragement at all to a parallel cinema that has sometimes chosen to be radical and stridently anti-establishment. But the truth is that government policy toward the parallel cinema has been less than consistent, reflecting occasional doubts and even hostility toward independent-minded filmmaking.

The government's attitude toward Satyajit Ray's films is a good illustration of this ambivalence. When Ray first appeared on the scene in the mid-1950s, he had to approach the government of West Bengal, hat in hand, for funds to complete *Pather Panchali,* which had already been four years in the making. Ray screened a portion of the incomplete film for the chief minister and a few officers of the state government, one of whom expressed his opinion in an official note:

> My impression is that even when exploited, this picture will not pay as much as is being invested in it. *Pather Panchali* is rather dull and slow-moving. It is a story of a typical Bengali family suffering from privation and family embarrassments. . . . At no stage does it offer a solution or an attempt to better the lot of the people and rebuild the structure of their society.[25]

The note went on to prescribe that the film should contain "a supplementary shot of about 2,500 to 3,000 feet depicting the second part of the story," which would show

> . . . the shape of the village community in the present age, with provision of land reforms, of the Community Development Projects, the National Extension Schemes and an all-round urge in independent India to rebuild the society for better living and through self-help, rather than resigning to one's present condition, to fate, circumstances and certain unknown factors.[26]

To be fair to Ray's official "critics," they had been called upon to evaluate a puzzling, new kind of film. Ray had broken all the rules of

[25] The note was published some years after the event in the *Hindustan Standard*. Cited in Marie Seton, *Satyajit Ray, Portrait of a Director* (London: Dennis Dobson, 1978).

[26] Ibid.

theme and treatment in contemporary Indian cinema. *Pather Panchali,* with its neorealist style, *looked* very much like the pedagogic documentaries that the government produced, but lacked the commentator's "voice of authority." The lack of assertive statement, the absence of a red sun rising over a field of high-yielding wheat, was construed as fatalistic and irresponsible. And if the film was going to be completed with state government funds, the officials felt perfectly justified in "recommending" changes that would make it into what they considered to constitute a good film.

To its credit, the government provided some funding and did not insist on the changes.[27] *Pather Panchali* went on to win unprecedented kudos and a string of awards at film festivals abroad. Ray was instantly promoted to the status of a *sarkari heera,* a jewel that the government was proud to display in its showcase of cultural exhibits. One would have thought that the international plaudits for *Pather Panchali* would have settled the issue in favor of Satyajit Ray and art cinema in no uncertain terms. But neorealism or the "artist as witness" is not a favorite doctrine of officials and bureaucrats. In depicting a decaying feudal order in rural Bengal with felicity and "truth," Ray was an embarrassment to the image of India that the government was trying to project abroad. In 1980 the Bombay film star Nargis, a member of parliament, denounced Ray on the floor of parliament for projecting a negative image of India to the rest of the world.

The notion that "good" art must fall in line with government policy, or at least with the goals of social uplift and development, was a fundamental tenet of official policy. And in one form or the other, government policy toward the parallel cinema has been characterized by an extreme sensitivity to projecting India in "a proper light." In times of political repression, such as the Emergency in the 1970s, the government did not hesitate to call into play its censorship and regulating apparatus, which it had inherited, virtually unchanged, from colonial legislation during World War II.[28] At other times, the government has played the role of a more tolerant, if somewhat erratic, patron, but always with one eye on the mileage that could be gained

[27] The Department of External Publicity, which is a wing of the Ministry of External Affairs, actually banned the film from being shown abroad, and Nehru had to intervene personally to countermand the order.

[28] B. V. Karanth's *Chomana Dudi,* about a poor Harijan's struggle to rent some land, won the President's Gold Medal for Best Film of 1975. The Ministry of Information and Broadcasting, however, insisted that Karanth should insert a caption at the end stating that the condition of Harijans as depicted in the film referred to a period before India's independence, and that the government had since taken steps to lift them out of their poverty.

from a festival of new Indian films on the international circuit. But patrons are prone to demand a certain subservience in return for their benevolence, so the relationship of independent filmmakers with the government has not been easy.

Television

As a genuine mass medium, Indian television is barely a decade old. For the first 20 years of its existence, television was confined to a few metropolitan cities, and remained a stern, didactic medium with audience figures that only flickered to life during showings of musical excerpts from Bombay films. Not until 1982, on the eve of the Asian Games, did the government initiate the expansion of television and the introduction of color broadcasting. Few people had any doubt that Indira Gandhi had one eye on the potential of the medium to boost her image. But it also became clear that the government was determined to retain absolute control over the content and programming of Doordarshan, despite criticism and the constant refrain calling for the establishment of an independent broadcasting authority.

The government defends its monopoly as necessary to ensure a balance between entertainment and education. The commercial world of Bombay cinema, it argues, is too crass, too urban and middle-class, too entertainment-oriented, too opportunistic and consumerist to be able to provide national programming that caters to the needs of the average rural viewer. Only the government, it claims, has the responsibility, altruism, and resources to provide informative and educational programming to combat illiteracy, narrow the gap between rich and poor, and facilitate national integration and development. Its detractors say just the opposite: that television will widen the gap between urban elites and the rural poor, and, as long as it remains a government monopoly, will be misused for political purposes to promote the government in power. Commercial television, the government counters, will erode traditional Indian values through advertisements that promote consumerism and, in the long run, will have the effect of homogenizing local cultures.

In fact, there has been a steady erosion of Doordarshan's stated objective of providing an appropriate mix of education and entertainment. The first earnest attempt to create such a program was in 1984, when Doordarshan commissioned "Hum Log" (We People). Inspired by the success of Mexican "pro-development soaps" aimed at promoting adult literacy, family planning, and sex education, "Hum Log" intended to provide a family-planning message woven into the texture of 156 episodes about the life of a lower-middle-class urban family in northern India. The first few programs elicited a disappointing response, with viewers complaining of too much sermonizing about family planning and of a ponderous story line that did not lead anywhere.[29] After 13 episodes, "Hum Log" was given a mid-course correction: the family-planning theme was diluted and the tone of the entire serial made less didactic.

The results were astonishing. "Hum Log" achieved 65 to 90 percent viewer ratings in northern India, and even in the main cities of South India where Hindi is not universally understood, it received viewer ratings of 20 to 45 percent. In absolute terms, the serial drew an audience of 50 million people, at that time the largest ever to have watched a television program in India, and by its success, launched the era of commercially sponsored programs on Doordarshan.[30] But in the first flush of commercial success, the government lost sight of its educational objectives; "Hum Log" achieved its success by becoming an ordinary, somewhat breathless soap opera, and there was no attempt thereafter to emulate the Mexican strategy of smuggling pro-development messages into the programs. By 1985, Doordarshan had thrown open its doors to private sponsorship. Its most conspicuous success was Ramanand Sagar's "Ramayana," based on the Hindu epic and broadcast on Sunday mornings to a reverent audience of 60 million. Newspapers reported the widespread practice of incense sticks being lit in front of television sets and of people taking purificatory baths before sitting down to watch the "Ramayana." While crowds thinned on Indian streets on Sunday mornings, Doordarshan raked in $20 million in advertising revenues from this single program.[31]

By the end of the 1980s, Doordarshan had all but abandoned its posture of providing a careful balance of education and entertainment. It was making money hand over fist and had virtually allowed the advertising companies to dictate what segments of the market to target. Meanwhile, the network's dreary news and current-affairs programs had lost all semblance of credibility, and there were dark stories of rampant corruption and favoritism within the organization. It is tempting to believe that the government was by now no longer enamored of the intrinsic power of the medium. Two governments in power had lost a general election, and by 1990 there no longer seemed any compelling political reason to preserve the government's monopoly of television. And yet, despite renewed promises of an in-

[29] Arvind Singhal and Everett M. Rogers, "The Hum Log Story," in *India's Information Revolution* (Newbury Park, CA: Sage, 1989), p. 101.

[30] Ibid.

[31] Ibid., p. 70.

dependent broadcasting corporation, endorsed by all the political parties, none materialized.

Today there is a new player, with a new technology that could well change the rules of the game altogether. That player is satellite television, which threatens to shake up the government's complacency as nothing has done before. The phenomenon of satellite viewing was initiated in India by CNN during the Persian Gulf war in January 1991. Three months later Star began transmitting out of Hong Kong. By February 1992, nearly half a million Indian households were hooked up to Star. A year later, the figure soared to 2 million households, which is conservatively estimated to mean over 7 million individual viewers. In the 38-nation (total population 2.7 billion) reach of Asiasat 1, India already has the biggest audience for Star TV. Not surprisingly, a lot of other international competitors are lining up in the sky.[32]

Both the government and other political parties have reacted with alarm, denouncing the satellite as a new form of "cultural imperialism." Early in 1991, the Ministry of Information and Broadcasting seriously proposed jamming foreign TV signals through an earth station in western India. The proposal was ultimately dropped but only because it became clear that it was technically infeasible. The government then considered a legislative ban on dish antennae. Malaysia and Singapore had imposed such bans, and so could India. Once again, the only reason that the government did not go ahead is that it was advised that the Supreme Court would in all probability uphold the citizen's right to receive radio and television signals and strike down any ban on dish antennae as an impingement on individual freedom.

There is no doubt that the government's deep concern about the threat from satellite broadcasting reflects its fears about the end of its monopoly on broadcasting. The government is rapidly losing its position as the gatekeeper of the flow of information. There are more and more alternatives to various government-controlled media, from video news magazine programs such as "Newstrack" to satellite and cable sources, and India is on the verge of a huge explosion of available transponder time for satellite transmission. Doordarshan is already

[32] CNN was, of course, the first. ATN is based in London and its programs are beamed to India via a satellite poised over Russia. CANAL FRANCE began transmitting early in 1993. Malaysia's RTM and TV3, Indonesia's RCTI, the Philippines' ABS-CBN, Japan's NHK, and Hong Kong-Taiwan's Business News Network are all transmitting to India. PTI has recently joined the queue with a transponder leased from Russia. One estimate is that there could be more than 100 competing satellite transmissions to India by the close of 1993.

beginning to react to the competition. One minister of information and broadcasting has been fired, and Doordarshan is now engaged in a series of inept maneuvers to beef up its second (Metro) channel. The saddest aspect of Doordarshan's response to satellite competition is that it has run out of ideas and meets all criticism by scheduling more feature films from Bombay each week.

It will take a technical breakthrough for satellite television to reach the rural viewer in India, and that is perhaps Doordarshan's last bastion of hope. The writing on the wall is that the commercial sponsors at the high end of the market will play the ratings game and desert Doordarshan for the most successful satellite station. Doordarshan knows this, of course, and while it has made a few feeble attempts at improving its performance, it has also connived to ensure that the playing field with the competition is not exactly level. Two recent government directives, for example, are blatant attempts to curb the increasing trend of Indian advertising on Star.[33]

Doordarshan has arrived at a crucial fork in its development as a national television medium. It can try to compete with Star and its proliferating clones on their own terms, and become a purveyor of superficial soap operas and mindless entertainment. If it chooses this course, it may remain solvent, but it will almost certainly lose its raison d'être. Alternatively, it can seize the opportunity to reorient itself by making educational and current-affairs programs with imagination and flair—though Doordarshan will not find this easy. Somehow, it will have to shed the habits of three decades of deadening bureaucracy and political control and discover an idealism and relationship with viewers that has eluded it so far. If Doordarshan can genuinely reorient itself to the rural viewer and make interesting educational and developmental programs, it still has a vital role to play. Otherwise, few might mourn its demise.

At the same time, though it is too early to assess the impact of Star TV on a modernizing society, it is already clear that it has taken a big bite out of the market for films and videocassettes. So far, it is mainly the urban rich who have tuned in to Star. But with new plans for terrestrial broadcasting on the anvil, rural, traditional India needs to brace itself for sights and sounds for which no Hindi film will have prepared it.

---

[33] One directive, issued at the end of May 1993, seeks to prevent Indian companies from using foreign exchange to buy advertising time on satellite if the primary focus of their marketing lies within India. The second directive, issued on June 1, 1993, prohibits Indian companies from advertising on programs that also telecast on Doordarshan, such as international sporting events.

The Hindi film, meanwhile, is facing its first real crisis. Production is dwindling and could drop by as much as 60 percent over the next two years. Television and the video, along with an unscrupulous regime of unchecked piracy, are partly culpable. Middle-class India is getting fatally used to the comforts of being entertained at home. In bidding for attention against the rival claims of television, popular cinema is likely to up the ante by packing in more commercial ingredients: more violence, more sexual innuendo, and more sensationalism. In many big towns in India, cinema-going has become an increasingly male preserve, largely comprising those sections of the working-class population that are migrant and hence without families. Popular cinema is too astute not to know and serve the appetites of its most devoted clientele.

Ironically, it is conceivable that out of the ashes of the all-India Hindi blockbuster, a more modest but vital regional cinema will reassert itself. Hindi cinema and television have tended to be dreadfully insensitive to India's regional languages and cultures. The government-sponsored parallel cinema served as a safety valve for a decade, but with its demise, it is likely that small-budget regional cinema will once again become the focus for energies drawn from a variety of artistic fields. Perhaps decentralization and a close attention to local cultural needs will be the watchwords of a revived Doordarshan as well; it is here that Doordarshan could steal a march on the competition from the satellite channels. But will any Indian government be willing to decentralize Doordarshan and overhaul it radically? Or will nothing short of insolvency convey the urgent need for change?

1992: A Chronology

JANUARY

3 There is mounting pressure within the Karnataka Congress for the removal of the chief minister, S. Bangarappa, for his alleged failure to protect the interests of the state and for creating the new problem of "Kannadigas versus Tamilians."

11 The 15,000-kilometer Kanyakumari-to-Kashmir *ekta yatra* (unity march) led by the BJP chief, Murli Manohar Joshi, enters Uttar Pradesh to a warm welcome from the state's chief minister, Kalyan Singh, of the BJP. The *yatra* will traverse 12 districts including Allahabad and Ayodhya. In an address in Jhansi, Joshi says that the threat to the unity and integrity of the country can only be countered by a strong sense of patriotism and nationalism.

16 The government decontrols iron and steel prices, abolishes the freight equalization scheme, and reduces import duty by 20 percent on certain steel items such as pig iron.

17 The four major factions of the Akali Dal (Badal, Mann, Babbar, and Baba) and two factions of the All-India Sikh Students' Federation (Manjit and Sikh Students' Federation) announce their decision to boycott the February 19 poll in Punjab. In a resolution, these groups charge that in the absence of a concrete and permanent solution to the Punjab and Sikh problems, the elections would be a futile exercise.

JANUARY

19 The Janata Dal national executive expels MPs led by Ajit Singh from the party for six years for "gross indiscipline."

23 Two days after several militant groups, including the Jammu and Kashmir Liberation Front (JKLF) and the outlawed Hizb-ul-Mujahadin, threaten to foil the BJP's plans to hoist the flag on Republic Day in Srinagar, 6 BJP supporters are killed and 40 wounded when militants fire at the buses carrying party members from the *ekta yatra*. Meanwhile, the BJP leader, L. K. Advani, agrees to cut down the size of the *yatra* before it reaches Kashmir. Army and paramilitary forces impose an indefinite curfew in Srinagar.

26 **BJP president Murli Manohar Joshi hoists the national flag at the historic Lal Chowk as gunfire and grenade explosions echo in the curfew-bound city of Srinagar, the final destination of the *ekta yatra*. The event is watched by 70 party members and thousands of heavily armed security personnel.**

28 The Supreme Court begins hearings challenging the constitutional validity of the P. V. Narasimha Rao government's reservation policy for "backward" classes and economically weaker sections. The issues that have come up for the Supreme Court's consideration are whether the limit of 50 percent reservations is correct; whether the "backward" classes can be identified as more or less backward on the basis of economic considerations; whether on purely economic considerations one can create a class without social and educational backwardness under the constitution; whether backwardness can exist purely on the basis of caste; and whether reservations can be done by executive order or only by parliament and state legislatures. The government proposes to convene a conference of chief ministers, governors, and lieutenant governors to discuss

the reservation issue and also to consult leaders of political parties to reach a consensus.

29 The All-India Sikh Students' Federation (Manjit) appeals to the *jathedar* of the Akal Takht, the highest spiritual authority of the Sikhs, to issue a religious decree to the entire Sikh community to boycott the ensuing Lok Sabha and the assembly elections in the state.

India upgrades its diplomatic relations with Israel, allowing for the exchange of ambassadors for the first time.

FEBRUARY

2 Prime Minister Narasimha Rao, participating in the annual World Economic Forum meeting in Davos, Switzerland, and in a gathering of leading European industrialists in Zurich, invites Western entrepreneurs to invest in India's domestic market. Rao outlines changes in India's industrial policies and the measures taken to integrate the Indian economy into the global economy.

9 Pakistani paramilitary forces are deployed about 15 kilometers short of the "line of actual control" in Kashmir to block the passage of JKLF activists who have threatened to cross it on February 11. This move follows the Pakistan government's decision to ban the march.

10 The Punjab government arrests top leaders of six major factions of the Akali Dal and All-India Sikh Students' Federation under the Terrorist and Disruptive Activities (Prevention) Act on the eve of their proposed poll boycott march. The Punjab elections are scheduled for February 19.

12 Pakistani police open fire on militants trying to cross the line of actual control into India and kill three of them.

FEBRUARY

13 Another JKLF attempt to cross the line of actual control into the Kashmir Valley is foiled as Pakistani forces push the activists back and set up road blocks on their march route. JKLF chairman Amanullah Khan calls off the proposed march after a day of bloody clashes with security forces in which at least 13 people are killed and several injured.

In an attempt to stop a poll boycott march, the Punjab government arrests Gurcharan Singh Tohra, president of the Shiromani Gurudwara Prabandhak Committee, and Jagdev Singh Talwandi, a senior Akali leader, and virtually seals off the historic town of Anandpur Sahib from which the march is to begin.

At least 37 people are killed and 5 others seriously injured in the village of Bara near Patna by armed extremists belonging to the Maoist Communist Center. According to reports, 1,000 members belonging to the group converged on the village, set fire to houses there, and killed residents. After the police reach the village, several members of the MCC are killed. The attackers are allegedly taking revenge for another incident in which 10 Harijans were killed on December 23, 1991.

16 In Punjab, 5 election campaigners for Bahujan Samaj Party candidate Om Prakash Sidhwan are killed and 17 others injured when militants open fire near Nawanpind Shokian village in the Jalandhar district. A total of 579 candidates are contesting for the 115 assembly seats and 81 for the 13 Lok Sabha seats.

17 The three chief ministers of the Cauvery basin states, Jayalalitha Jayaram of Tamil Nadu, S. Bangarappa of Karnataka, and K. Karunakaran of Kerala, and V. Vaidyalingam, the chief minister of the Union Territory of Pondicherry, agree to facilitate expeditious completion of all proceedings before the tribunal that is investigating the dispute on the

sharing of river waters. In a joint statement, they attest that in order to ensure systematic and scientific management of the Cauvery waters, effective steps will be taken in the overall interests of the farmers and the people residing in the basin. They also agree to complete the relief and rehabilitation measures for persons affected by the dispute.

V. P. Singh and hundreds of volunteers of the Janata Dal are arrested in Bombay following a rally protesting the government's economic, industrial, and agricultural policies and the "surrender" of the country's economic and political sovereignty to the International Monetary Fund and the World Bank.

19 **The army and paramilitary forces heavily patrol the state of Punjab as its people go to the polls to end five years of President's Rule. Only an estimated 30 percent of the 132 million voters cast their ballots. With the Akali Dal boycotting the poll, Congress scores a record victory, falling just 1 seat short of a three-fourths majority in the Assembly and winning 12 Lok Sabha seats. Its nearest rival, the Bahujan Samaj Party, wins only 9 seats. Punjab's Pradesh (state) Congress Committee chief, Beant Singh, heads the new Congress government in the state.**

22 India and Russia agree to continue with trade denominated in rupees during 1992 as a transitional arrangement, and they sign a trade protocol for the year envisaging a two-way turnover of Rs. 7,500 crore with a technical credit provision of Rs. 850 crore from India. In addition to the trade under the bilateral rupee-clearing arrangement, the protocol also provides for hard-currency trade between business organizations of the two countries. The protocol, which is the first legal document to be signed between India and Russia since the dissolution of the Soviet Union, envisages trade and business cooperation at the enterprise level in the form of barter, buy-back, and counter trade. Under the trade protocol, exports from Russia will include crude

FEBRUARY

petroleum, kerosene, diesel, synthetic rubber, and newsprint. Exports from India will include tea, coffee, soya beans, medicines, and plastics.

23 The left parties reiterate their decision to boycott the president's address to the joint session of parliament and to lead a procession in the capital on March 4 to protest what they see as the "anti-people" economic policies of the central government, the abnormal spurt in prices of essential commodities, the erosion of economic sovereignty, and the abandonment of self-reliance.

25 Presenting the railway budget for 1992–93 in the Lok Sabha, Railway Minister C. K. Jaffer Sharief proposes a 20 percent increase in upper-class passenger fares and a 7.5 percent rise in freight rates in order to mobilize an additional revenue of Rs. 1,366 crore during the year.

27 **The prime minister, Narasimha Rao, is elected unopposed as the Congress Party president. The organizational elections of the Congress have been held after a gap of two decades.**

29 **The union finance minister, Manmohan Singh, announces the 1992–93 budget, which aims to open up India's economy and integrate it into the global economy. The highlights of the budget are partial convertibility of the rupee on the trade account, abolition of import licensing, relaxation of procedures for permission to foreign investors to buy shares in the Indian stock market, and liberalization of gold imports.**

MARCH

1 More than 12 people are injured in Ranchi during the 24-hour Jharkhand strike and the 5-day eco-

nomic blockade called from March 1 by the All-Jharkhand Students' Union and the Jharkhand People's Party. The strike is successful in and around Ranchi but evokes no response in the districts of Dhanbad, Bokaro, and Hazaribagh.

3 President's Rule, imposed in Jammu and Kashmir in September 1990, is extended for another six months.

4 The National Front and the Left Front members of the Lok Sabha petition the Speaker to seek the impeachment and removal of Chief Election Commissioner T. N. Seshan for his allegedly partisan behavior during the conduct of general elections last year and the recent by-elections, especially in Bihar and Tripura.

5 The United States refuses to subsidize the export of 1 million tons of wheat to India because the latter has supplied rice to Cuba. Senior officials in the Indian government see this as a major attack on India's sovereignty in terms of its ability to enter into commercial transactions with a country that is free of any U.N. embargo or other trade sanction.

9 The Narasimha Rao government wins by a margin of 52 votes in the Lok Sabha as the house rejects the first two BJP-sponsored amendments to the motion of thanks to the president's address. The subsequent three amendments tabled by the National Front–Left parties lose by huge margins.

10 India's foreign secretary, J. N. Dixit, tells the U.S. state department that India will neither sign the Nuclear Nonproliferation Treaty (NPT) nor attend a five-nation conference (India, Pakistan, China, Russia, and the United States), proposed by Pakistan in June 1991, to discuss the nuclear issue in South Asia and evolve a regional framework to denuclearize South Asia. India will, however, be willing to continue bilateral talks on nonproliferation.

MARCH

12 The 13-member Telugu Desam parliamentary party in the Lok Sabha splits in two.

16 In Punjab the newly elected Vidhan Sabha (state assembly) meets. A strike called by the Akali Dal parties and militant organizations is widely observed.

20 U.N. Secretary-General Boutros Boutros-Ghali rejects the suggestion that the United Nations intervene unilaterally in the Kashmir issue on the basis of the existing Security Council resolutions.

21 In classified documents that were revealed in the Russian parliament, the Communist Party of India (CPI) is listed as one of the 90 leftist organizations worldwide funded by the former Soviet Union's Communist Party. In 1990 alone, the CPI is shown as having been allocated a payment of $500,000.

22 Bomb explosions, minor clashes, and total disruption of production and dispatch occur in most collieries in tribal Bihar. This marks the beginning of the 13-day economic blockade called by the Jharkhand Mukti Morcha in their demand for a separate Jharkhand state.

The Uttar Pradesh tourism department starts demolishing five temples and shops in the acquired land in the Ram Janmabhoomi–Babri Masjid complex at Ayodhya. The land was acquired by the state tourism department in October 1991. Non-BJP members in parliament strongly protest the land acquisition, demolition, and construction of the boundary wall around the disputed site. Union home minister S. B. Chavan warns the BJP government in Uttar Pradesh that, if the state does not follow the Center's directives, the Center could take over the disputed site in Ayodhya and impose President's Rule, dismissing the U.P. government under Article 356 of the constitution.

25 People in the Manipur Valley stop paying government taxes and electricity and water bills as part of a civil disobedience movement to demand the inclusion of the Manipuri language in the eighth schedule of the constitution. The movement is organized by the All-Manipur Students' Union and the Manipur Language Demand Coordination Committee.

26 India and Bangladesh agree to implement the lease providing the Tin Bigha corridor to Bangladesh, the agreement for which was signed eight years ago. The arrangement will come into effect from June 26, with sovereignty over the leased area continuing to vest in India.

27 It is announced that the Nagaland governor, M. M. Thomas, has dissolved the assembly at the recommendation of the chief minister, Vamuzo, as a result of a "law and order problem." However, later it is revealed that the state was placed under President's Rule under Article 356 of the constitution on an order issued by the president and not on the recommendation of either the chief minister or the governor. On April 11, Governor Thomas is dismissed by President R. Venkataraman.

Punjab chief minister Beant Singh offers a cease-fire beginning on Baisakhi Day (April 13) to militants in a bid to end the continuing violence in the troubled state.

30 The Committee on Jharkhand Matters recommends an autonomous politico-administrative council to be known as the Jharkhand General Council (JGC) for the region. The JGC would have wide-ranging legislative and executive powers. This council model would then become a prototype for replication in West Bengal, Orissa, and Madhya Pradesh, which are part of the tribal belt.

MARCH

31 External Affairs Minister Madhavsinh Solanki resigns, acknowledging responsibility for handing over a document on the Bofors corruption case to his Swiss counterpart, Rene Felber. The source of the document remains in dispute.

APRIL

1 Armed operations against United Liberation Front of Assam (ULFA) militants are resumed in Assam, two and one-half months after they were suspended. Meanwhile, hard-liners within the organization announce their decision to resume armed struggle for an independent Assam. The army is assisted by the Border Security Force, Central Reserve Police Force, and police. The chief minister, Hiteshwar Saikia, says that the ULFA leadership has failed to keep its assurances to abjure violence, lay down arms, and hold peace talks to find a lasting solution to its problem within the constitutional framework.

4 The Cauvery water tribunal's decision not to modify its order from last year directing Karnataka to release 205 billion cubic feet of water annually to Tamil Nadu draws widespread criticism in Karnataka, with the opposition urging the state government to boycott the tribunal and the Karnataka Rajya Ryotha Sangh demanding that the prime minister disband the tribunal.

8 R. K. Dorendra Singh, the Congress Party leader in the Manipur legislature, is sworn in as chief minister, ending three years of President's Rule in the state.

10 The finance minister, Manmohan Singh, announces that India expects about $6 billion of direct foreign investment in the next two to three years, following the opening up of the economy. He further announces that the government is slowly moving to-

ward a regime in which decisions on investment, capital market, and prices of shares will be decided by industrialists and business people influenced by market forces.

12 More than 50 Akali leaders, activists, and leaders of religious organizations are arrested on the eve of the Panthic congregation of various Akali and Sikh organizations to be held at Takht Damdama Sahib.

15 The All-India Congress Committee (AICC), the highest forum of the ruling Congress Party, meets in Tirupati and endorses the government's economic policies promising change with continuity and retention of the Nehruvian model of economy, which envisages achievement of self-reliance through competition.

16 Elections to fill the 10 vacant seats of the 21-member Congress working committee are held after vigorous campaigning. After criticism surfaces about the unrepresentative nature of the successful candidates, on April 20 four resign to make room for Dalits, people from the Scheduled Tribes, and women representatives.

23 Satyajit Ray, the renowned film director, dies at age 70 in Calcutta. A month before, Ray was awarded an honorary Oscar and India's highest honor, the Bharat Ratna, for his long and distinguished career as a filmmaker.

Following an 18-day closure of the stock market in Bombay, the State Bank of India (SBI) officials admit a "systems failure" in the securities market. Harshad Mehta, the "big bull" in the Bombay Stock Exchange, is identified as a major player in the scam.

28 The Bombay Stock Exchange experiences a 570-point fall in its index following a report that SBI has transferred Rs. 622 crore to Harshad Mehta. Two days later, this news prompts an opposition walkout in the Rajya Sabha. Members of both houses demand a probe into the alleged fraud.

APRIL

30 The United States retaliates against India for its allegedly inadequate protection of patents in the pharmaceuticals industry. Indian pharmaceuticals exports to the United States will no longer enjoy duty benefits under the generalized system of preferences. India, along with Taiwan and Thailand, is on a list of countries that will continue to be watched under the provisions of the 1988 Omnibus Trade and Competitiveness Act, Super 301.

MAY

3 Russia categorically says that the transfer of its rocket technology and sale of cryogenic engines to India under a $250 million contract has not been suspended. The contract was signed in 1991 between the Indian Space Research Organization and the Russian space agency, Glavkosmos.

4 India and Russia sign a five-year agreement on trade and economic cooperation, stipulating that all payments be in freely convertible currencies, and agree to find mutually advantageous solutions to outstanding problems, including the supply by Moscow of defense parts and rocket technology. The two countries accord most-favored-nation treatment to each other in trade and commercial cooperation.

10 D. S. Tyagi, chairman of the Commission for Agricultural Costs and Prices, is killed by Sikh militants in Delhi. The Babbar Khalsa International takes responsibility for the killing.

11 The United States imposes a two-year ban on trade and technology transfer to the Indian Space Research Organization as a result of the reaffirmation of the India-Russia agreement transferring cryogenic rocket engine technology.

18 President R. Venkataraman visits China for talks on accelerated cooperation for development. Venkataraman and the Chinese president, Yang Shangkun, emphasize a need to strengthen economic relations by pursuing joint ventures in each other's countries and in other countries.

20 India launches its Augmented Satellite Launch Vehicle and puts into orbit the heaviest scientific satellite launched by India so far.

According to the charge sheet filed by the Special Investigating Team of the Central Bureau of Investigation (CBI), the conspiracy to kill former prime minister Rajiv Gandhi was conceived by the Liberation Tigers of Tamil Eelam (LTTE) as early as July 1987 in Jaffna, soon after the signing of the India-Sri Lanka accord. The LTTE leader, V. Prabhakaran, is charged with conspiracy and murder. Six days earlier, the Indian government banned the LTTE, saying its continued presence in India posed a threat to the country's sovereignty and integrity.

21 The government informs the IMF that by July 31 fertilizer prices will be raised and food subsidies for the middle-income groups will be reduced. These commitments are necessary for the release of the third installment of the IMF loan approved in October 1991, which totals $2.26 billion.

24 A senior Indian diplomat, Rajesh Mittal, is kidnapped outside his residence in Islamabad by Pakistani intelligence men. The Indian High Commission in Pakistan lodges a strong protest with the Pakistani foreign office. India orders the expulsion of two senior Pakistani diplomats in retaliation. India also postpones the foreign secretary–level talks with Pakistan scheduled from June 1 to 3.

27 The beheaded body of M. L. Manchanda, officiating station director of All-India Radio (AIR), Patiala, is found. Manchanda was abducted from Patiala on May 18, 1991, by Babbar Khalsa militants, who de-

MAY

manded, among other things, the relay of only Punjabi radio and television programs in the state. The AIR and Doordarshan [TV] staff of Punjab, Chandigarh, and parts of Himachal Pradesh join in a strike following the killing of Manchanda.

India and Bangladesh agree to set up a home secretary–level joint task force for the repatriation of over 50,000 Chakma refugees from Tripura and the tackling of the transborder insurgency problem involving ULFA activists in Assam.

28 Indian and U.S. warships begin a 24-hour day and night joint exercise off the southwest coast of India. The ships are likely to conduct a wide range of tactical maneuvers in their first joint exercise in over three decades.

29 India approves signing the Montreal pact, which seeks to phase out ozone-depleting chlorofluorocarbons (CFCs). Consequently, India will have to stabilize CFC consumption by 1995, phase out their use, and switch to substitutes by 2010. CFCs are mainly used as cooling agents in refrigerators and air conditioners.

JUNE

4 The Central Bureau of Investigation registers a criminal case against Harshad Mehta, officials of the State Bank of India, and others in the questionable transactions in the securities scam. The deputy managing director of SBI, C. L. Khemani, is arrested by the CBI in connection with the scam. The BJP demands a special session of parliament to discuss the Harshad Mehta case and the setting up of a parliamentary committee to inquire into it.

6 India is the second country after the host country, Brazil, to sign the biodiversity treaty at the two-week-long Earth Summit held in Rio de Janeiro. Kamal Nath, minister of state for environment, is the leader of India's delegation to the summit. Countries of the North and South are deadlocked over the key issue of devising a funding mechanism for purchasing environment-friendly technology to clean the environmental mess created by industrialization.

7 Gujarat chief minister Chimanbhai Patel of the Janata Dal(G), which has merged with the Congress, is elected leader of the legislature Congress Party.

8 Widespread violence, police firing, and alleged booth capturing in Bihar and Andhra Pradesh mar the by-elections to 2 Lok Sabha and 19 assembly seats in the nine states of Andhra Pradesh, Bihar, Karnataka, Kerala, Goa, Madhya Pradesh, Uttar Pradesh, Orissa, and West Bengal and in the Union Territory of Delhi.

15 Former defense minister K. C. Pant is appointed chairman of the 10th Finance Commission, which sets the pattern for the sharing of funds between the Center and the states for the five-year period beginning April 1, 1995.

16 Ten central trade unions demand the scrapping of the new industrial and economic policies and protest the government's plans to privatize the public-sector units and banks; 12.5 million workers join the strike.

18 Congress announces the candidacy of Vice President S. D. Sharma for the upcoming presidential election. A former deputy speaker of the Lok Sabha and a tribal from Meghalaya, G. G. Swell, emerges as the consensus candidate of the opposition parties for the presidential elections on July 13. The BJP, National Front, and CPM support Swell while the CPI supports S. D. Sharma.

JUNE

19 **The independent review commission set up by the World Bank and headed by Bradford Morse, former U.S. congressman and former administrator of the United Nations Development Program, recommends the immediate suspension of further work on the Sardar Sarovar dam on the Narmada River until resettlement and environmental concerns have been met.** However, the current World Bank president, Lewis T. Preston, has reiterated the bank's support for the project while accepting the commission's findings that the policies of both the World Bank and the Indian government have been deficient and need to be rectified.

22 In a major simplification of customs rules, the government introduces a facility for self-assessment of import cargo by importers, a green channel for clearance of cargo, and the rationalization of clearance procedures.

23 Following talks between prime ministers Rao and Miyazawa, Japan announces $850 million in official development assistance (ODA) to India for 1992. The aid amount will be $50 million more than the present ODA of $800 million. Prime Minister Rao also proposes a worldwide dialogue for a review of the Nuclear Nonproliferation Treaty, which is due to lapse in three years. However, Rao rules out India's signing of the NPT, which he claims is discriminatory.

25 Giving a strong signal of support for India's economic reforms, the Aid India Consortium, meeting in Paris, pledges a total of $7.2 billion for 1992–93, an increase of about 7 percent. The fast-disbursing component of this aid will be $3.4 billion, about 45 percent of the total pledges.

26 The Tin Bigha corridor is formally leased out to Bangladesh amid skirmishes between the police and anti-transfer activists.

30 The IMF releases $647 million to India, signifying the approval of the government's macroeconomic stabilization program for 1991–92. It is estimated that during the fiscal year of 1992, India will receive $1.6 billion from the IMF under the arrangement entered into on October 31, 1991, for a total of $2.2 billion to help tide India over the critical balance-of-payments problem.

JULY

1 An indefinite truckers' strike called for by All-India Motor Transport Congress in protest against the *octroi* (tax on goods collected at the municipal limits) and toll tax affects the supplies of essential and perishable commodities throughout the country. The strike is called off unconditionally on July 7.

2 Prime Minister Rao expands his council of ministers with the induction of six new middle-rung ministers and effects a minor reshuffle in portfolios; he also divides the work of the industry ministry and creates the new departments of wasteland development and nonconventional energy.

3 Violence spreads and curfew is imposed in Ahmedabad over the annual *rath yatra* (chariot procession). The VHP calls for a Gujarat strike in protest against the violence in the state.

6 The second interim report of the Reserve Bank of India (RBI) committee headed by the RBI deputy governor, R. Janakiraman, places the total amount involved in the stock market scandal at Rs. 3,542.78 crore.

8 Sikander Bakht of the BJP takes charge as leader of the opposition in the Rajya Sabha following the party's improved strength after the recent biennial elections. Bakht replaces the Janata Dal leader, S.

JULY

Jaipal Reddy. The BJP now leads the opposition in both houses of parliament.

9 **Prime Minister Rao announces a comprehensive inquiry by a joint parliamentary committee (JPC) into the Rs. 3,542.78 crore securities fraud.** Apart from the JPC probe, the inquiry by the CBI and action by the special court is being pursued. The speaker of the Lok Sabha, Shivraj Patil, is entrusted with the formation of the JPC.

The VHP formally begins "renovation" work at the disputed site in Ayodhya, laying the foundation of the Simhadwar (lion's gate). Several thousand *kar sevaks* join the renovation work. The VHP invites *sadhus* and *kar sevaks* from all over the country to Ayodhya in a bid to thwart a possible takeover of the site by the Center. In response, the All-India Babri Masjid Action Committee calls for a strike of all Muslim businesses in the Faizabad district.

The United States reiterates its position on resolving the Kashmir issue. U.S. deputy assistant secretary of state Teresita C. Schaffer says that Kashmir is primarily a bilateral issue between India and Pakistan and that, although the United States would be willing to assist in finding a settlement, it is not responsible for initiating the process.

12 Union home minister S. B. Chavan visits Ayodhya and expresses concern over the security arrangements made by the Kalyan Singh government for the disputed structure. The Center awaits the verdict of the Supreme Court to deal with the case.

15 Prime Minister Rao categorically says in the Lok Sabha that the Babri mosque will never be allowed to be demolished although the government is not averse to the construction of a Ram temple outside the disputed site in Ayodhya.

16 **S. D. Sharma is elected the ninth president of India, defeating the BJP–National Front candidate, G. G. Swell. Sharma is sworn into office on July 25.**

17 **The opposition-sponsored no-confidence vote is defeated by 267 votes to 215. However, support for the Rao government is extended by its allies, including the AIADMK, a faction of the Telugu Desam party, and the Janata Dal splinter group led by Ajit Singh.**

The U.P. government orders the stoppage of construction activities in compliance with the July 15 order of the Allahabad High Court. The VHP and the *kar sevak*s warn the Center that any action to block construction will trigger a countrywide protest with disastrous consequences.

20 Work on the second phase of the concrete platform being constructed by *kar sevak*s begins. A six-foot platform is expected to be ready in a week. The U.P. government disowns all responsibility for the construction.

22 The Supreme Court asks the U.P. government and Chief Minister Kalyan Singh to give unconditional guarantees that no construction will take place near the disputed structure at Ayodhya. On July 23 the Supreme Court gives the U.P. government until July 27 to convince Hindu leaders to stop all construction work at the site unconditionally. The VHP has so far not complied with the court order prohibiting work.

26 The VHP announces that the *kar sevak*s will stop work at 4 p.m. and says that it will leave it to the prime minister to decide within three months whether the disputed shrine is a mosque or a temple. The VHP also announces that the construction of a Lakshman temple will begin on a plot near the disputed site.

JULY

28 Non-BJP members in the Lok Sabha suggest that all parties should abide by the court verdict in the absence of a negotiated settlement of the Ayodhya dispute. However, the VHP claims that the issue is one of faith and therefore cannot be decided by the constitution. The VHP also warns Prime Minister Rao that the *sadhus* will be free to act on their own if the issue is not resolved within three months.

Led by Jaipal Reddy (Janata Dal), many opposition members in the Rajya Sabha demand the resignation of the railway minister, C. K. Jaffer Sharief, claiming that he has improperly awarded the Rs. 630 crore contract for the import of high-tech electric locomotives to the Swedish multinational Asea Brown Boveri.

30 Gurjant Singh Budhsinghwala, chief of the Khalistan Liberation Force, is shot dead in Punjab by security forces.

AUGUST

5 The Supreme Court constitutes a three-member expert panel to ascertain whether the platform constructed on the 2.77-acre plot acquired adjacent to the disputed Ayodhya shrine can support the proposed temple.

6 The minister for parliamentary affairs, Ghulam Nabi Azad, assures the Lok Sabha that the government will extend full cooperation and necessary facilities to the Joint Parliamentary Committee, which will inquire into the multicrore securities fraud. The Lok Sabha unanimously adopts a motion to provide for the constitution of a 30-member JPC, composed of 20 members of the lower house and 10 of the upper house.

10 In a 24-hour period, Sikh militants massacre 48 people, including police personnel and their close relatives, in retaliation for the killing of the founder-leader of the outlawed Babbar Khalsa International, Sukhinder Singh Babbar, by security forces in Ludhiana on August 9.

12 Seventy-two militants, including Gurdeep Singh Sivia, the U.K.-based chief organizer of the overseas units of the militant group Babbar Khalsa International, surrender before Punjab chief minister Beant Singh. Sivia had recently crossed over from Pakistan and was mainly organizing the supply of arms to militants in the state of Punjab.

14 The Lok Sabha speaker, Shivraj Patil, concedes the Ajit Singh group's claim for separate seats by allotting 20 dissident Janata Dal seats outside the party bloc. These members were expelled from the Janata Dal earlier in the week.

15 A general strike is observed in Kashmir on the occasion of Independence Day while militants fire rockets to disrupt the parade at Bakshi Stadium where the governor, Girish Saxena, received the salute. At least 12 people are killed in clashes while 5 others have been shot by the militants in different parts of the valley in the last 24 hours.

16 Pakistan's foreign secretary, Shahryar Khan, on his arrival in New Delhi for a five-day visit, emphasizes that Pakistan for the first time will have discussions with India on the Kashmir issue under the Simla agreement at the sixth round of foreign secretary–level talks beginning the next day. The meeting concludes on August 22 with plans to hold discussions in the future on nuclear nonproliferation in South Asia at the bilateral level.

18 The surface-to-surface missile Prithvi is successfully test launched for the eighth time. The medium-range missile is fired from a mobile launcher at the interim test range at Chandipur-on-sea in Orissa.

AUGUST

The Rajya Sabha approves the extension of President's Rule in Jammu and Kashmir for another six months from September 3.

19 **K. R. Narayanan, an "ex-untouchable" who has been a member of the foreign service and was elected to the Lok Sabha after his retirement, is elected the ninth vice president of India.** He has only token opposition. He succeeds S. D. Sharma, who has become president of India. The vice president is sworn in on August 21 at Rashtrapati Bhavan in New Delhi.

20 Parliament votes to make Konkani, Manipuri, and Nepali "official languages" of India.

26 The three-member Cauvery water disputes tribunal begins its regular hearings on the sharing of the river water between the two contending states of Tamil Nadu and Karnataka.

28 A full settlement and rehabilitation package for those displaced by the Sardar Sarovar Project is agreed on by all states concerned: Rajasthan, Madhya Pradesh, Gujarat, and Maharashtra. The meeting is attended by the four chief ministers, Sunderlal Patwa (MP), Bhairon Singh Shekhawat (Rajasthan), Sudhakarrao Naik (Maharashtra), and Chimanbhai Patel (Gujarat), as well as by the Union finance minister, Manmohan Singh, and the Union environment minister, Kamal Nath, among others.

The Chelliah committee on tax reforms recommends the lowering of corporate tax on domestic companies from 51.7 percent to 45 percent in 1993–94 and to 40 percent in 1994–95, and the taxation of agricultural income of nonfarmers beyond an income of Rs. 25,000.

SEPTEMBER

2 The prime minister, in Jakarta for the 10th nonaligned movement meeting, calls for suspension of nuclear-weapons tests and for negotiations on general and complete disarmament. Rao also holds discussions with Prime Minister Nawaz Sharif of Pakistan on various bilateral issues, including the issue of Kashmir.

7 Russia proposes a comprehensive military cooperation agreement between India and Russia to be signed before or during the visit of the Russian president, Boris Yeltsin, scheduled for January 1993.

15 Bomb explosions and arson are widespread in tribal Bihar areas during the 24-hour Jharkhand strike to demand a separate state comprising the 25 districts of Bihar, West Bengal, Orissa, and Madhya Pradesh.

22 Harshad Mehta, the stock and securities broker at the center of the stock-market scandal in India, is freed after 111 days in custody.

India and Britain sign an extradition treaty and an agreement on the confiscation of extremists' assets. The new legal regime will ensure that the U.K. will no longer shelter anti-Indian extremists operating from British territory. The home minister, S. B. Chavan, and the British home secretary, Kenneth Clarke, sign the agreement.

26 For the first time, India has formally staked its claim to a permanent seat on the U.N. Security Council. Japan, Germany, and Brazil are among the others aspiring to a permanent position on the council, which at present has 15 members.

27 The Union home minister, S. B. Chavan, makes it clear that Amnesty International will not be permitted to tour India to investigate alleged violations of

SEPTEMBER

human rights. Legislation to establish the national Human Rights Commission will probably be introduced in parliament in 1993.

29 Andhra Pradesh chief minister N. Janardhan Reddy submits his resignation. The resignation follows a high-court judgment that invalidated the permission granted by the state government for the establishment of 12 new private medical colleges and 8 dental colleges.

OCTOBER

7 The Union minister for law, Vijaya Bhaskara Reddy, is elected chief minister of Andhra Pradesh.

The Rapid Action Force is formed as part of the Central Reserve Police Force for use in controlling communal riots and similar situations.

10 The killers of former army chief General A. S. Vaidya, Harjinder Singh "Jinda" and Sukhvinder Singh "Sukha," are hung at the Yerawada Central Prison at 4 a.m. General Vaidya was assassinated on August 10, 1986, in Pune. A three-day strike is called in Punjab by the Akali factions and Panthic organizations.

30 A religious parliament (*dharam sansad*) organized by the VHP announces that *kar sewa* to construct the Ram temple at Ayodhya is to resume on December 6. The VHP charges that Prime Minister Rao has failed to resolve the issue, and therefore it is compelled to resume the *kar sewa* that it discontinued in July.

31 An all-party parliamentary delegation that has visited Kashmir recently for an assessment tells Prime Minister Rao that the situation in the state is not conducive to holding elections.

Chandra Shekhar is elected president of the Samajwadi Janata Party (SJP). He succeeds Devi Lal, who was elected chairman of the party's parliamentary board.

NOVEMBER

1 India assures the IMF that it will meet the agreed target of restricting the fiscal deficit in the current year to 5 percent of GDP.

3 A one-day BJP-sponsored *bharat bandh* (all-India shutdown) is called to protest the hike in prices of fertilizers and petroleum products. It is fully observed only in the BJP-controlled states of Madhya Pradesh and Rajasthan.

4 The Supreme Court directs the central government to pay Rs. 200 monthly until 1995 as interim relief to 1.10 lakh additional victims of the Bhopal gas disaster.

9 The Cabinet reviews the sixth round of India-Pakistan talks on the Siachen Glacier. On November 4 the two countries reached a broad agreement on almost all issues including disengagement, redeployment, and creation of a demilitarized zone around the 72-km glacier. However, the settlement falls through as Pakistan does not agree to India's contention of recognizing the present ground positions held by the forces of the two countries.

10 The army is alerted and paramilitary forces are deployed in sensitive areas in Tripura after non-gazetted police personnel, in a virtual revolt against the state government, cease work.

The attorney general, G. Ramaswamy, submits his resignation. The joint parliamentary committee in probing the securities fraud reveals that the Standard Chartered Bank has given Ramaswamy an overdraft of Rs. 15 lakh.

NOVEMBER

11 The Karnataka ministry, led by Chief Minister S. Bangarappa, resigns following the directive of the Congress central leadership. On November 19, Veerappa Moily, a "backward"-class leader, replaces Bangarappa as chief minister.

14 Medha Patkar and 100 activists of the Narmada Bachao Andolan are arrested in Bombay after they stage a sit-in to protest the denial of an audience with Lewis T. Preston, the president of the World Bank.

16 **The Supreme Court upholds the 27-percent reservation of jobs in the central government services for "backward" classes. The Court holds partially valid the V. P. Singh government's decision on a 27-percent job quota for "backward" classes and strikes down the Rao government's order incorporating economic criteria.** The court imposes a 50 percent overall ceiling for job reservations in government, bars reservations in promotions, holding them to be unconstitutional, and enlarges the concept of reservations to extend benefits to the backward among religious minorities.

17 Anti-reservation agitation erupts in northern and eastern parts of India: students burn vehicles and block trains and road traffic to protest the Supreme Court's verdict upholding job quotas for "backward" classes. The worst incidents are reported in Delhi, Meerut, Varanasi, Allahabad, and Sambalpur (Orissa).

23 The National Integration Council meets to discuss the Ayodhya issue and outlines four options to resolve the dispute. The BJP and the VHP boycott the meeting.

Punjab chief minister Beant Singh announces that *panchayat* elections in the state will be held in January 1993.

24 The National Integration Council in a unanimous resolution gives a clear mandate to Prime Minister Rao to take whatever steps he considers essential to uphold the constitution, enforce the rule of law, and implement court orders on the Ramjanmabhoomi–Babri Masjid dispute. Rao announces that the Center will discharge its constitutional responsibility to uphold the law.

30 The dispatch of paramilitary forces (the Rapid Action Force) from Faizabad to Ayodhya without any request from the U.P. government leads to a 25-minute furor in the Lok Sabha.

The Supreme Court waits for a report from its independent observer before making a judgment on the Ayodhya controversy. A division bench comprising Justice M. N. Venkatachallaiah and Justice G. N. Ray observes that in the face of the bona fides and sincerity of the state government, no religious group could succeed in any attempt to start construction work.

DECEMBER

1 **The BJP leader, L. K. Advani, reiterates that *kar sewa* on the disputed land in Ayodhya will commence on December 6 as scheduled and will continue until the temple is completed. He says that the building of the temple is not an issue of the BJP, RSS, VHP, Congress, or Janata Dal but is a national matter that should be honored by all sections of the people, irrespective of caste, creed, or religion. Advani also says that the BJP is committed to constructing the temple at Ayodhya and that the U.P. chief minister, Kalyan Singh, is prepared to "sacrifice" his government to fulfill the "dream of his people."**

The Supreme Court directs the U.P. government and the Center to undertake immediately a joint publicity campaign to "caution" *kar sevaks* against

DECEMBER

gathering on the acquired land in Ayodhya and to warn against violating the Supreme Court restraint on any construction activity.

2 The CBI accuses the highly respected industrial executive V. Krishnamurthy of taking commissions from multinational companies while he was chairman of the public-sector Maruti Udyog Limited and the Steel Authority of India Limited during the 1980s. The commissions, which run into crores of rupees, were allegedly paid into foreign accounts of two companies owned and controlled by Krishnamurthy's sons.

The VHP and some *sadhus* address a large gathering of *kar sevaks* at the disputed site of Ayodhya and declare that the Ram temple will be built there "under any circumstances." However, the U.P. government informs the public that according to the November 28 Supreme Court order, no construction activity can take place on the disputed site. The U.P. chief minister, Kalyan Singh, seeks the cooperation of the chief ministers of all the states in persuading the Center not to deploy its forces in different parts of Uttar Pradesh.

3 The BJP rules out any construction activity in Ayodhya and states that the *kar sewa* to be resumed there will not involve construction. The vice president of the BJP, Sunder Singh Bhandari, says that the disputed structure is absolutely safe under the U.P. government and that the Center should withdraw its paramilitary forces.

The Allahabad High Court announces that it will deliver its verdict on the legality of U.P.'s acquisition of 2.77 acres of land adjacent to the disputed shrine in Ayodhya on December 11.

4 The VHP announces that *kar sewa* at Ayodhya will be performed until December 11, the day the Allahabad High Court will deliver its judgment on the

disputed 2.77 acres of land. The VHP secretary, Onkar Bhave, asks its provincial organizers not to send any more batches of *kar sevaks* to Ayodhya.

The Center decides to release 2,500 members of the Central Reserve Police Force to Uttar Pradesh to be immediately deployed in communally sensitive areas as well as in Ayodhya.

5 H. N. Wanchoo, veteran trade unionist and human rights activist, is shot dead by unidentified gunmen in Kashmir. Wanchoo was a vocal critic of the Union government's handling of the Kashmir situation.

The Supreme Court orders that only symbolic *kar sewa* consisting of *bhajans* and *kirtans* (devotional songs) will be allowed at Ayodhya. It also rules that any construction activity or even moving of building material to the disputed land will be deemed an infringement of its directive.

6 **Shouting slogans, militant *kar sevaks* demolish the Babri mosque. Three domes of the mosque collapse as thousands of frenzied *kar sevaks* storm it, climb atop the domes, and start dismantling the structure with hammers and rods and their bare hands as the state security forces, including the Provincial Armed Constabulary, watch silently. U.P. chief minister Kalyan Singh submits the resignation of his government to the state governor in what is obviously a bid to preempt a dismissal by the Center. The army is sent into Ayodhya along with 50 more companies of paramilitary forces. The Faizabad district is sealed and no movement is allowed across the U.P. border. Curfew is imposed in Allahabad and parts of Varanasi, and security is placed on alert in several states; the army is made ready for deployment in West Bengal.**

The National Front and Left parties demand the resignation of Prime Minister Rao's government for its failure to uphold the constitution. They charge that the demolition of the mosque is the "gravest

DECEMBER

onslaught" on the constitution and secularism by the BJP-VHP-RSS combine and that the Center has failed to discharge its constitutional obligations.

The VHP issues a statement that the damage caused to the mosque was the handiwork of "anti-social elements" who had infiltrated the ranks of the *kar sevaks*. The VHP claims that it is in no way responsible for the incidents as it had made clear its intention that the *kar sevaks* comply with court orders.

7 **Widespread riots rock the entire country in the aftermath of the Babri mosque demolition. Two hundred people are killed and thousands injured in communal violence and riots that leave a trail of destruction across the country. The government pledges to rebuild the mosque. The Supreme Court decides to initiate criminal contempt-of-court proceedings against former U.P. chief minister Kalyan Singh and five senior IAS officers for their involvement.**

8 **VHP and BJP leaders L. K. Advani, M. M. Joshi, Uma Bharati, Ashok Singhal, and Vinay Katiyar, among others, are arrested. The death toll in the riots mounts to 400.** Seventeen thousand personnel drawn from the Central Reserve Police Force and the Rapid Action Force have fenced off the entire disputed area and 85 vantage points in Ayodhya after clearing *kar sevaks* from the site. A commission of inquiry headed by a high-court judge is being set up to probe the events that led to the demolition.

10 Shoot-to-kill orders are given in Calcutta and Kanpur. The countrywide death toll according to official estimates rises to 820. The RSS leaders go underground, fearing that their organization will soon be banned. The Congress Party considers writing to the election commissioner seeking derecognition of the BJP.

The central government announces a ban on five Hindu and Muslim religious fundamentalist organizations under the Unlawful Activities (Prevention) Act of 1967 as the death toll in rioting and clashes with security forces rises to 950. The five banned organizations are the Rashtriya Swayamsevak Sangh, the Vishwa Hindu Parishad, the Bajrang Dal, the Islamic Sevak Sangh, and the Jamat-i-Islami Hind.

11 **The Allahabad High Court holds the acquisition of 2.77 acres of land in Ayodhya by the Kalyan Singh government to be invalid.**

A. R. Antulay, former chief minister of Maharashtra, who was facing charges of corruption, is acquitted by the special judge appointed to hear the case filed against him. The charges related to criminal conspiracy, misuse of office, accepting illegal gratification, and cheating.

12 **After a week of savage sectarian rioting in dozens of cities and towns, the country struggles toward calm. The number of people killed in six days of strife, many as a result of police firing into demonstrations and rioting mobs, is estimated at over 1,200, with more than 5,000 injured.** Several cities and towns lift curfews early this morning, but some cities, including parts of Delhi and Bombay, remain tense.

13 The BJP observes a countrywide "black day" to protest the banning of the RSS, the VHP, and the Bajrang Dal.

14 The five-day-old strike by Indian Airlines pilots disrupts all flight schedules. The government of India requisitions the services of aircraft from Uzbekistan.

17 The BJP apologizes for the demolition of the mosque on December 6 and calls upon the handful of *kar sevak*s involved in it to come forward and face

DECEMBER

legal consequences. A. B. Vajpayee, a leader in the BJP, admits that the BJP and RSS could not fulfill the assurances given by them regarding the protection of the mosque.

BJP chief ministers Shanta Kumar (Himachal Pradesh), Bhairon Singh Shekhawat (Rajasthan), and Sunderlal Patwa (Madhya Pradesh), together with their governments, are dismissed by the Center and those states are placed under President's Rule under Article 356 of the constitution.

The BJP members of parliament demand the resignation of the prime minister and the dissolution of the Lok Sabha. They also submit a memorandum to the president protesting the dismissal of the three BJP state governments and the ban on the RSS, the VHP, and the Bajrang Dal. The MPs, led by Vajpayee, demand a fresh election to the Lok Sabha and claim that the "discredited and irresponsible" Congress government in New Delhi needs to be replaced by a government of the "people's choice." A *Times of India*–MODE survey indicates overwhelming support for Prime Minister Rao. Of the 2,452 respondents, 75 percent believe that there is no need for his resignation and 60 percent disapprove of the demolition of the mosque.

An inquiry committee holds Supreme Court Justice V. Ramaswami guilty of willful and gross misuse of office by using public funds for private purposes when he was chief justice of the Punjab and Haryana High Court from 1987 to 1989. The committee, headed by Justice P. B. Sawant, a Supreme Court judge, states that "continuance in office will be prejudicial to the administration of justice and public interest."

The Supreme Court allows the CBI to resume its probe in the Bofors case and upholds the validity of the First Information Report against the former agent, Win Chadha.

21 **The Lok Sabha rejects a BJP-sponsored no-confidence motion against Prime Minister Rao and his government. The no-confidence motion, put to vote after a four-day debate, is defeated with 334 votes in support of the prime minister and 106 votes against him. Forty-seven members from the National Front abstain from voting.** The prime minister announces that a fund will be set up to rebuild places of worship damaged in the riots in different parts of the country. Rao also suggests a national debate on the role of nonsecular parties and on whether a political party can be allowed to use religious issues as its main plank.

22 The Lok Sabha passes, without opposition, the 72nd and 73rd constitutional amendment bills, which provide for the constitutional entrenchment of elected government at the village level and in cities.

23 The Verma commission of inquiry strongly indicts the Center, the CBI, and the Tamil Nadu police for their failure to provide rigorous security to Rajiv Gandhi, leading to his assassination in Sriperumbudur on May 21, 1991.

25 The Rs. 25 crore relief package to those affected during the November 1984 riots following the assassination of Indira Gandhi is rejected by the Riot Victim Relief Committee.

26 The RSS regroups under a new name, the Ram Sevak Sangh, and plans to launch a new campaign starting January 12, the birth anniversary of Swami Vivekananda. The group plans to meet in Rameswaram in Tamil Nadu next month in order to work out the details. The VHP has also reemerged under a new identity, the Jana Kalyan Samiti. Tamil Nadu is emerging as a safe haven for activists of the outlawed organizations as its chief minister, Jayalalitha Jayaram, has extended support to the RSS and the BJP.

DECEMBER

29 The Lucknow bench of the Allahabad High Court reserves its judgment on the writ petitions that seek to allow worship at the site of the demolished mosque even as the Faizabad district administration refuses to allow worship.

Pakistan asks India to curtail the strength of the staff at its consulate general in Karachi by more than two-thirds. New Delhi in retaliation asks Pakistan to reduce the strength of its staff in India.

Glossary

Some Common Abbreviations
AIADMK: All-India Anna Dravida Munnetra Kazhagam
BJP: Bharatiya Janata Party
BSP: Bahujan Samaj Party
CPI: Communist Party of India
CPM: Communist Party of India–Marxist
DMK: Dravida Munnetra Kazhagam
JKLF: Jammu and Kashmir Liberation Front
LTTE: Liberation Tigers of Tamil Eelam
NRI: Nonresident Indian
RSS: Rashtriya Swayamsevak Sangh
SAARC: South Asian Association for Regional Cooperation
ULFA: United Liberation Front of Assam
VHP: Vishwa Hindu Parishad

Advani, Lal Krishna. Leader of the Bharatiya Janata Party in the Lok Sabha until the Ayodhya crisis. Usually seen as the leader of the "moderate" group within the party.

Akali Dal. The major party of the Sikhs. Governed the state of Punjab until May 1987 when President's Rule was imposed. Its several factions boycotted the February 1992 Punjab elections.

All-India Anna Dravida Munnetra Kazhagam (AIADMK). Ruling party in the state of Tamil Nadu, led by Jayalalitha, one of the most powerful women in Indian politics. Its alliance with the Congress Party collapsed in early 1993.

Ayodhya. Small city in east-central Uttar Pradesh; the city of Ram (or Rama), the god-king who is the hero of the Ramayana, and site of the disputed Ramjanmabhoomi–Babri Masjid shrine, which was demolished on December 6, 1992, provoking widespread rioting and a major political crisis.

Babur. The first Mughal emperor (r. 1526–30).

"Backward" classes. Classes recognized by the Constitution of India as disadvantaged and allowed remedial treatment. In practice, "backward" classes have been defined in terms of caste membership. Composed of Scheduled Castes, Scheduled Tribes, and Other Backward Classes.

Bahujan Samaj Party (BSP). Literally "party of society's majority," which first contested in the 1989 parliamentary election. Led by Kanshi Ram, it attracts support not only from scheduled-caste voters, but also from other "oppressed" groups: Muslims, "backward" classes, and others.

Bajrang Dal. Militant youth organization associated with the RSS.

Bharatiya Janata Party (BJP). Party formed from the Janata Party by elements of the Jana Sangh, with support mainly in northern India. Its governments in Himachal Pradesh, Madhya Pradesh, Rajasthan, and Uttar Pradesh were dismissed after the Ayodhya incident. The largest opposition party in parliament, it favors a Hindu nationalist ideology.

Bhopal. City in Madhya Pradesh, location of the Union Carbide plant that leaked poison gas in the fall of 1984, killing thousands. The multimillion dollar settlement has only recently begun to deliver compensation to the victims.

Bofors. Swedish armaments company that allegedly paid commissions to middlemen connected with the Congress Party and Rajiv Gandhi, in violation of its agreement with the government of India, to secure a Rs. 1.1 billion contract to supply 155 mm howitzer field guns. In the 1989 election particularly, Bofors became a code word for corruption in high places. As late as mid-1993, the investigation had not yet received the names of the holders of the relevant Swiss bank accounts.

Booth capturing. The practice of forcing polling station officials to acquiesce in voting irregularities such as ballot box stuffing.

Chandra Shekhar. Prime minister of India from November 1990 until the May 1991 elections.

Chief minister. The equivalent of the prime minister in the government of Indian states.

Communal. Refers to ethnic communities, most commonly Hindu and Muslim; a "communalist" is what opponents call those whose political identity is bound up with their ethnic or religious identity and who allegedly put their community "above" the nation.

Communist Party of India (CPI). The less influential of the two major Communist parties.

Communist Party of India–Marxist (CPM). The stronger segment of the Communist Party of India after the split of 1964. The CPM has run the government of the state of West Bengal since 1977 and competes with the Congress Party for power in Kerala.

Congress Party. The dominant Indian national party since independence, it formed the government after the 1991 elections. Led by Prime Minister P. V. Narasimha Rao, who is also party president, it governs in the states of Gujarat, Maharashtra, Andhra Pradesh, and Karnataka. Also known as the Congress(I), the name of the faction created by a party split in 1977 and initially led by Indira Gandhi (the "I" stands for Indira).

Crore. Ten million (10,000,000).

Dalit. Literally "oppressed" or "ground down." The term for Scheduled Caste persons preferred by militant and educated Untouchables and by many of those who sympathize with their aspirations.

Dharma. A core concept of Hindu philosophy with a wide range of meanings, including "the right way." It can be used to mean "religion."

Dharmashastra. The body of centrally important religious texts of Hinduism.

Doordarshan. The monopoly television network owned and run by the government.

Dravida Munnetra Kazhagam (DMK). Tamil nationalist party, led by M. Karunanidhi. The major opposition party in Tamil Nadu.

Emergency. Declared by the Indira Gandhi government in June 1975, it lasted 21 months; opposition leaders were jailed, press censorship imposed, and the constitution amended to restrict the judiciary. Ended with the defeat of Indira Gandhi in the 1977 election.

Five Year Plans. Formulated by the Planning Commission and approved by parliament, these analyze the economic situation of the country and set out broad goals and specific guidelines for investment and other economic policy, for both public and private sectors. The first plan covered the 1951–56 period. The current plan is the eighth, covering 1991–96.

Gandhi, Indira. Daughter of Jawaharlal Nehru and prime minister from 1966 to 1977 and from 1980 to 1984, when she was assassinated by her own Sikh bodyguards.

Gandhi, Mohandas K. The preeminent leader of India's fight against British colonial rule from 1919 until independence. He was assassinated in January 1948 by a Hindu nationalist fanatic. Also known as Mahatma Gandhi. The respectful title "Mahatma" literally means "great soul."

Gandhi, Rajiv. Son of Indira Gandhi and prime minister from 1984 to 1989 when the Congress(I) lost the parliamentary election. Assassinated on May 21, 1991, while campaigning in Tamil Nadu.

Harijan. Literally, "people of God." The name Mohandas K. Gandhi coined for the Scheduled Castes. See also *Dalit*.

Hindi Heartland. The belt of states in which Hindi is the major language spoken: from west to east, Rajasthan, Haryana, Madhya Pradesh, Delhi, Uttar Pradesh, and Bihar.

Hindutva. Literally, "Hindu-ness." Used as the title of a book written in 1922 by Hindu nationalist leader V. D. Savarkar to argue that Hindus were a nation. It is now used as the equivalent of "Hindu nationalism."

Jammu and Kashmir Liberation Front (JKLF). Militant group fighting for the independence of Kashmir.

Jana Sangh. Hindu-chauvinist party formed in 1951 with strength mainly in North India. It merged with the Janata Party in 1977 and reemerged as the Bharatiya Janata Party after 1980. Much of its political cadre was drawn from the Rashtriya Swayamsevak Sangh.

Janata Dal. Party formed from the Jan Morcha, the Janata Party, factions of the Lok Dal, and a Congress Party splinter group known as the Congress(S). It had 141 of the 144 seats held by the National Front in the Lok Sabha elected in 1989. Led by V. P. Singh, the party split in November 1990, with Chandra Shekhar leading a new Janata Dal (Socialist). It split again in January 1992, creating a new party, led by Ajit Singh.

Janata Dal(A). Party formed after a split in the Janata Dal. Led by Ajit Singh, it has supported the Congress Party government.

Janata Dal(S). Party formed by defectors from the Janata Dal in November 1990 and led by Chandra Shekhar. It formed a government with the support of the Congress(I) that lasted until March 1991.

Janata Party. Created from a wide variety of opposition parties to fight the 1977 election. It formed the government in 1977–79. Merged with the Jan Morcha and other parties to form the Janata Dal.

Jati. Caste or subcaste that defines acceptable interactions in marriage, dining, and other caste-related practices.

Jharkhand. The region of east-central India (covering parts of the states of Madhya Pradesh, Andhra Pradesh, Orissa, and West Bengal, but mainly the southern segment of Bihar) in which various tribal people live. Name given to the state or autonomous region sought by those people.

Kar sevak. Literally, "one who does service through work." In the Ramjanmabhoomi–Babri Masjid agitation, a volunteer dedicated to demolishing the mosque and building Ram's temple.

Kashmir Valley. Also the Vale of Kashmir. The spectacularly beautiful valley of the river Jhelum, a part of the Indian state of Jammu and Kashmir (the other major regions being Buddhist-dominated Ladakh and Hindu-dominated Jammu, with other regions claimed by India now controlled by Pakistan and China). Populated almost entirely by Muslims, it is the political heartland of the state.

Khalistan. Name given to the sovereign state demanded by Sikh militants in Punjab.

Lakh. One hundred thousand (100,000).

Left Front. Electoral coalition of the Communist Party of India, the Communist Party of India–Marxist, and several small leftist parties.

Liberation Tigers of Tamil Eelam (LTTE). Leading Sri Lankan Tamil militant group, which seeks a separate state for Sri Lankan Tamils in the north and east sections of the island. Banned in India because of its apparent responsibility for the assassination of Rajiv Gandhi.

Lok Sabha. Lower house of India's bicameral parliament. Equivalent to the British House of Commons, it has 545 members, who are directly elected from district constituencies for a five-year maximum term.

Mahabharata. One of two major epics of India. Describes the internecine warfare that results from a feud of succession involving descendants of the legendary king Bharata.

Mandal Commission. The common name—from its chairman, B. P. Mandal—of the Backward Classes Commission, which in its report (published in 1980) proposed far-reaching governmental regulations to increase the employment of "backward" classes.

Naxalite. A revolutionary or radical activist ready to adopt violent means. The name comes from participants in a rebellion in Naxalbari, West Bengal, in 1967.

Nehru, Jawaharlal. Nationalist leader who served as prime minister from 1947 until his death in 1964.

Nonresident Indians (NRIs). Persons of Indian origin living abroad, including those holding citizenship elsewhere. Allowed certain privileges denied to other foreigners with respect to owning real property, investment, and travel, among other things, in an effort to keep them attached to India and to attract their foreign exchange.

Other Backward Classes. "Backward" classes other than the Scheduled Castes and Scheduled Tribes. Typically defined in caste terms to mean the nonelite, non-Untouchable jatis.

Panchayati raj. Literally, a council of five. A village or jati council. Panchayati raj is the system of rural local government introduced in 1959 and changed significantly since, with variations from state to state. A constitutional amendment to standardize the system and give greater powers to both panchayat and central government (thus weakening the role of state governments) was passed by the Congress government in late 1992.

Planning Commission. Government body that prepares Five Year Plans, which provide a broad framework for public and private economic goals.

President. In India, the equivalent of a constitutional monarch, who gives formal assent to bills but whose powers are severely restricted. Elected by members of parliament and the state legislatures for a five-year term. Currently the president is S. D. Sharma, a veteran Congress leader, elected unopposed in July 1992. The vice president, elected in August 1992, is K. R. Narayanan, the first "Harijan" to hold either office, who had a distinguished career in the foreign service and then entered politics as a member of the Congress Party.

President's Rule. Suspension for six months of a state's assembly and direct rule of the state by the central government through the centrally appointed governor, typically when the state government loses its majority or is deemed unable to govern due to a "disturbed" political situation. The states ruled by the BJP at the time of Ayodhya were placed under President's Rule, and a second six-month term has been approved by parliament.

Rajya Sabha. Upper house of India's bicameral parliament. All but six of its 256 members are elected by the legislatures of the states for staggered six-year terms. Roughly equivalent in power to Britain's House of Lords.

Ram temple/Babri mosque (Ramjanmabhoomi–Babri Masjid). Literally, "Birthground of Ram–Mosque of Babur." Ram (or Rama), an avatar of the god Vishnu and the hero of the Ramayana, one of the two great epics of Hinduism, is believed to have been born in Ayodhya on a particular spot of ground, on which a mosque was believed to have been built by the Mughal emperor Babur. The mosque was demolished on December 6, 1992, and a shrine to Ram was re-installed on the site.

Ramayana. One of two major epics of India, it describes the adventures of Ram, a warrior-king and the incarnation of the god Vishnu.

Rashtriya Swayamsevak Sangh (RSS). Militant Hindu organization founded in 1925 and associated with the Bharatiya Janata Party, the Vishwa Hindu Parishad, and the Bajrang Dal—the members of the "Sangh parivar (RSS family)." The RSS draws its membership mainly from urban and lower-middle classes and seeks the consolidation of a Hindu nation.

Reservation. The provision for quotas in legislative bodies, civil services, educational institutions, and other public institutions, typically in proportion to the percentage in the population, for qualified members of Scheduled Castes and Scheduled Tribes, and, in some places, for Other Backward Classes.

Sabha. Literally an "assembly," it also is extended to mean "association."

Samiti. Literally a "committee," it usually refers to an organization, typically a voluntary organization.

Sati. A widow who immolates herself on the funeral pyre of her husband; by extension, the practice. Outlawed since the 19th century, there are still, very rarely, cases of *sati*.

Satyagraha. Literally, "truth-force." A term coined by Mohandas K. Gandhi for civil disobedience, especially courting arrest.

Scheduled Castes and Scheduled Tribes. List of Untouchable, or Harijan, castes and tribes drawn up under the 1935 Government of India Act and subsequently revised. Legislative seats as well as government posts and places in educational institutions are reserved for members of these castes and tribes.

Shari'a. The central body of law of Islam, centered on the Qu'ran and the sayings and traditions of the Prophet Mohammad.

Shastra. Hindu religious text (generic).

Sharma, Shankar Dayal. President of India, succeeding R. Venkataraman. Elected to a five-year term in July 1992.

Shekhar, Chandra. See Chandra Shekhar.

Shiv Sena. Militant nativist communal organization based largely in the towns of northern India. It was founded in Bombay in 1966 to agitate against South Indian immigrants to the state of Maharashtra. In the 1989 and 1991 parliamentary elections, it formed an alliance with the Bharatiya Janata Party. Led by Bal Thackeray, it played a major role in the terrible Bombay riots of January 1993.

Sikh, Sikhism. The religion of Sikhism was founded in the 16th century by the first guru, Nanak, drawing on Hindu devotionalism and Islam. Persecuted by the later Mughal emperors, Sikhs developed into a martial community, led by the 10th and last guru, Gobind Singh; a Sikh kingdom in central Punjab was defeated by the British in the mid-19th century.

Simla Agreement. Peace pact signed in 1972 by India and Pakistan, formally ending their 1971 war over Bangladesh and affirming the line of control between India and Pakistan in Kashmir.

Singh, V. P. Prime minister of India from November 1989 to November 1990 and leader of the Janata Dal. Former finance and defense minister under Rajiv Gandhi.

South Asian Association for Regional Cooperation (SAARC). Organization formed in 1985 to enhance regional cooperation in social, economic, and cultural development. The SAARC members are Bangladesh, Bhutan, India, the Maldives, Nepal, Pakistan, and Sri Lanka. Postponed after the Ayodhya incident, the seventh SAARC summit was held in Bangladesh in April 1993.

Sri Lanka Accord. Signed by Indian prime minister Rajiv Gandhi and Sri Lankan president J. R. Jayewardene on July 28, 1987, in Colombo, the accord provided for the ending of the guerrilla war by

Indian armed forces, which were to disarm the Liberation Tigers of Tamil Eelam and other Tamil extremists, and for the holding of elections to newly empowered provincial assemblies in which Tamils would gain significant autonomy.

"Super 301" provision. Section 301 of the 1988 U.S. Omnibus Trade and Competitiveness Act designed to discourage unfair trading. Countries found to be trading unfairly or discriminating against American goods may have preferences for their goods canceled and restrictions such as special duties imposed by way of retaliation.

United Liberation Front of Assam (ULFA). A protest movement advocating autonomy for the state of Assam.

Vishwa Hindu Parishad (VHP). A movement seeking to reinvigorate Hinduism; leader of Hindu sentiment and organizer of actions regarding the Ramjanmabhoomi–Babri Masjid controversy, although precisely what its responsibility was for the demolition of the mosque is not clear.

Suggestions for Further Reading

Battling the Past, Forging a Future? Ayodhya and Beyond

Andersen, Walter, and Shridhar Damle. *The Brotherhood in Saffron* (Boulder: Westview Press, 1987).

Gopal, S., ed. *Anatomy of a Confrontation* (New Delhi: Viking, 1991).

Nehru, Jawaharlal. *The Discovery of India* (New Delhi: Oxford University Press, 1991).

Savarkar, V. D. *Hindutva* (New Delhi: Bharti Sahitya Sadan, 1989).

Varshney, Ashutosh. "Three Compromised Nationalisms: Why Kashmir Has Been a Problem." In *Perspectives on Kashmir*, ed. Raju Thomas (Boulder: Westview Press, 1992).

Weiner, Myron. *The Indian Paradox* (Newbury Park, CA: Sage, 1989).

Foreign Policy in 1992: Building Credibility

Bradnock, Robert. *India's Foreign Policy since 1971* (New York: Council on Foreign Relations Press, 1990).

Damodaran, A. K., and U. S. Bajpai. *Indian Foreign Policy: The Indira Gandhi Years* (New Delhi: Radiant Press, 1990).

Gould, Harold A., and Sumit Ganguly. *The Hope and the Reality: U.S.-Indian Relations from Roosevelt to Reagan* (Boulder: Westview Press, 1990).

Limaye, Satu. *U.S.-Indian Relations: The Pursuit of Accommodation* (Boulder: Westview Press, 1993).

Percy, Charles H. "South Asia's Takeoff," *Foreign Affairs*, Winter 1992.

Thakur, Ramesh. "India after Nonalignment," *Foreign Affairs*, Spring 1992.

Economic Reforms: Birth of an "Asian Tiger"

Bhagwati, Jagdish. *Indian Economy: The Shackled Giant* (Oxford: Clarendon, 1993).

Jalan, Bimal. *India's Economic Crisis: The Way Ahead* (New York: Oxford University Press, 1991).

The Constitution, Society, and Law

Baxi, Upendra. *The Crisis of the Indian Legal System* (New Delhi: Vikas Publishing House, 1982).

Galanter, Marc. *Law and Society in Modern India* (New Delhi: Oxford University Press, 1989).

Keith, Arthur Berriedale. *A Constitutional History of India, 1600–1935,* (Allahabad, India: Central Book Depot, 1961).

Social Movements and the Redefinition of Democracy

Desai, A. R., ed. *Peasant Struggles in India,* Vol. II (Delhi: Oxford University Press, 1985).

Kothari, Rajni. "The Non-Party Political Process," *Economic and Political Weekly,* Vol. 19, no. 5.

Sethi, H., "Groups in a New Politics of Transformation," *Economic and Political Weekly,* Vol. 19, no. 7.

Sheth, D. L. "Grassroots Initiative in India," *Economic and Political Weekly,* Vol. 19, no. 6.

Singh, K. S., ed. *Tribal Movements in India,* Vols. I and II (Delhi: Manohar, 1985).

Cinema and Television

Krishen, Pradip. "Knocking at the Doors of Public Culture: India's Parallel Cinema," *Public Culture,* ed. Carol A. Breckenridge, Fall 1991.

Krishen, Pradip, ed. "Indian Popular Cinema: Myth, Meaning and Metaphor," *India International Center Quarterly,* Vol. 8, no. 1 (March 1981).

Ray, Satyajit. *Our Films, Their Films* (New Delhi: Orient Longmans, 1976).

Seton, Marie. *Satyajit Ray: Portrait of a Director* (London: Dennis Dobson, 1978).

Singhal, Arvind, and Everett M. Rogers. *India's Information Revolution* (Newbury Park, CA: Sage, 1989).

About the Contributors

Granville Austin holds a Ph.D. in modern Indian history from Oxford. While working in India, he was a fellow of the Institute of Current World Affairs, the Ford Foundation, the American Institute of Indian Affairs, and the Woodrow Wilson International Center for Scholars. He has also served in the U.S. Information Service and Department of State. The author of *The Indian Constitution: Cornerstone of a Nation* (1966), Dr. Austin is currently researching and writing a book about constitutional development in India from 1950 to 1985.

Jay Dehejia is President of Cambridge Group International, which advises North American and European clients on the development of business in South Asia and with members of ASEAN. He has been involved in directing new investments in emerging markets of Asia for more than 25 years and has lived and worked in Australia, Hong Kong, the United States, Belgium, and India. Mr. Dehejia received his M.A. from Cambridge University and M.S. from the University of California at Berkeley. In 1969 he was adjunct associate professor at the University of New South Wales.

Smitu Kothari is among the founders of Lokayan (Dialogue of the People), a center promoting active exchange between nonparty political formations and concerned citizens from India and the rest of the world. He is editor of the *Lokayan Bulletin* and was recently a guest lecturer at Cornell University. He has edited (with H. Sethi) *Rethinking Human Rights: Challenges for Theory and Action* (1989), and *The Non-Party Political Process: Uncertain Alternatives* (1987). Mr. Kothari is currently writing a book on the Narmada River and editing *Ecological Justice: Nature, Culture and Democracy in India*.

Paul Kreisberg is Senior Research Fellow at the East-West Center in Honolulu. He was in the U.S. Foreign Service from 1953 to 1981, serving in the Consulate General in Bombay and the Embassies in Karachi and New Delhi, and was Director of Studies for the Council on Foreign Relations (1981–87) and Senior Associate at the Carnegie Endowment for International Peace. He has traveled widely in Asia and and written extensively for newspapers and magazines on developments in U.S. policy toward India, China, and other areas in Asia. Mr. Kreisberg is currently writing a book on India at the beginning of the 21st century, based on extensive interviews with Indians throughout the country.

Pradip Krishen is a film director living in New Delhi. He has directed *Massey Sahib* (1986), *In Which Annie Gives It to Those Ones* (1988), and *Electric Moon* (1991). Mr. Krishen has written several articles on the cinema and is now working on his next feature film.

Philip Oldenburg is an independent scholar who teaches at Columbia University. He is the author of various publications on India, the most recent of which is the article "Sex Ratio, Son Preference, and Violence in India: A Research Note." Dr. Oldenburg is currently conducting research on grass-roots governance in India.

Ashutosh Varshney is Associate Professor of Government at Harvard University. He holds a Ph.D. from the Massachusetts Insititute of Technology. His teaching and research are in comparative nationalism and ethnic conflict, political economy of development, and government and politics of South Asia. He is completing his first book, *Democracy, Development and the Countryside: Urban-Rural Struggles in India,* and is the editor of *Beyond Urban Bias* (forthcoming). His articles have appeared in *Daedalus, Journal of Development Studies, Comparative Politics,* and *Economic and Political Weekly*. Dr. Varshney is currently working on a project entitled "One Image, Multiple Realities: Islam, Nationalism, and Politics in India."

About the Book

A common theme in the India Briefing series has been India's resilience in the face of turmoil and tragedy. This year's volume demonstrates that India is under greater stress than ever before. In the country's severest test, India's secular foundations were shaken by the storming and destruction of the Barbi mosque in Ayodhya. This act of violence brought to a head the ideological and communal tensions that have continued to wrench the country since partition in 1948. *India Briefing, 1993* offers a long-term perspective on the eruption in Ayodhya, showing its connection to the perennial question of Indian national identity.

The volume also assesses India's foreign policy and its economic reforms, which were disrupted but not derailed by the events at Ayodhya. In the wake of the loss of the Soviet Union as an ally and trading partner, the foreign policy chapter points to increased cooperation between India and China and Indian efforts to improve economic relations with East and Southeast Asia, the European Community, and the United States. The economic chapter explores the growing momentum of economic reform, despite the Bombay stock market scandal and the riots and bombings of early 1993.

Legal reform takes its place next to economic reform as a vehicle for improving the quality of life of India's 885 million people. A subsequent chapter discusses the Indian Constitution, how the rule of law in India has worked to better the lot of minorities and underprivileged social groups, and the need to protect civil liberties better and increase access to the judicial system. Showing that democracy is exercised not only in the courts but at the grass roots, another chapter chronicles the growth of citizen-based groups fighting for social and economic justice. The book concludes by exploring the evolution of contemporary popular culture and the dilemma of state-controlled television in a democratic society.

The events of late 1992 and early 1993 constitute a critical test of India's extraordinary resilience as the country grapples with unprecedented change in all aspects of its national life. The contributors to *India Briefing, 1993* aim to increase readers' understanding of this vibrant evolutionary process.

Index